ADVANCE PRAISE FOR
TALENT CHOOSES YOU

Provocative. Straightforward. Engaging. I would go as far as to say that every employer branding specialist who does not read this book, will really miss out on valuable learnings. But this book is not only for branding specialists. **James has written a must-read business book for the modern recruitment professional.** And not only for those. A must-read for all people in all facets of hiring as C-business/hiring managers.

This book isn't just about how to create a more successful employer brand. It's ultimately an answer to the question of how can we learn more about what works and discard what doesn't. It gives you directions. It teaches you new perspectives and different ways of achieving your goal.

Whether you are a startup or corporate, there are important lessons here for you on your quest towards building a business. And we all know that's not happening without hiring and attracting the right talent. If you really want better talent, it's time to stop with recruitment methods that don't work. Thanks to this book you will understand why employer branding is the best way to achieve your hiring goals.

Talent Chooses You **is the roadmap for the next hiring revolution.** This book will help you to reinvent your hiring. The title literally speaks for itself. I believe it's about time to start listening!
– Eva Baluchova, Wearebridge.io

James Ellis is a unique and necessary voice in our industry. His debut book - Talent Chooses You - lands as you would expect a James Ellis product to land - passionate, fearless, idiosyncratic, funny and true. **Essential reading for any employer brand specialist**, it's value extends to cover all those who care about fixing our broken recruiting experience. Your Space Cat has to be protected, and you best start by reading this book.
    – Hung Lee, Recruiting Brainfood

In a sea of self help and how-to books on the market, rarely do you come across one that inspires you philosophically and motivationally. James addresses the broken nature of hiring in a modern age while simultaneously providing insight into what's possible when humanity meets aspiration. **Talent Chooses You is the new bible for the employer branding practitioner and the novice alike** and is a must read for any HR professional seeking to improve the quality of their candidates.
    – John Graham, Amgen

James Ellis has been bringing his own brand of magic pixie dust to the employer brand space for years, and this book is that sparkling powder in written form. The reckoning is here. Ellis does a masterful job of breaking down the simple and glaring fact that times have changed and it's not enough for a brand to just 'build it' and expect for talent to come. Brands need to build, massage, evolve and demonstrate purpose to thrive. Talent chooses you – and you should choose James as your shepherd to shift your mindset and do the hard work to actualize what's best for your business."
    – Holland McCue, Delta Air Lines

Talent Chooses You takes recruiting on a wild ride that elevates employer branding as the critical component in our competition for the next generation's best and brightest. **When James Ellis challenged the reader to go 'above the funnel where the game rules are set', he had me for the duration.** Weaving his interviews of highly successful practitioners, consultants and thought leaders chapter by chapter added depth to his story and brought to life the principles to Hire Better with Employer Branding.
    – Gerry Crispin, CareerXroads

TALENT CHOOSES YOU

Hiring Better with Employer Branding

James Ellis

Saltlab

ISBN: 9798640916393

First Printing, 2020

Printed by Amazon, United States

Saltlab
Attn: James Ellis
421 W Melrose
Chicago, IL 60657

saltlab.com

Cover and book design by: James Ellis

There is one voice I listen to in this space above all others and that is James Ellis. **His take is fresh, honest and actionable**, all three things you need to take a good idea and make it work.
– Allyn Bailey, Intel

In many ways, this book is the practical, concrete wake-up call the employer brand industry's always needed. It's sharp and honest. It cuts through the fluff that so often conspires against "brand." And it provides a clear roadmap for creating a magnet that attracts the people who align with your mission, vision, and values – while also politely repelling the ones who don't. At the end of the day, branding isn't about appealing to everyone. It's about knowing who you are and who you want to be, and relentlessly focusing on doing things that help you live that vision. James gets that. **And his book can help employer brand professionals build a more compelling case for doubling down on the efforts that create real, tangible business value.**
– Josh Zywien, Paradox

James has always brought a unique, entertaining, and insightful communication style into the world of employer brand, and this book is a perfect reference to all the great work he has done. Equal parts informative and entertaining, **you will learn how to position employer brand strategically into an organization**, especially when communicating to key stakeholders.
– Alykhan Rehmatullah, Altru

Reading this book felt like spending 1:1 time with a wise employer branding shaman. What you're about to read is a **doctorate-level course in employer brand**, packed to the brim with tactical advice to empower you to get meaningful EB work done at your organization. This book is a surge of fresh air, blowing dust off decades-old beliefs and practices that do not work in our modern world of work. It is a playbook for employer branders, and a trail guide for those looking to enter this fantastic field. I'm not exaggerating when I say that **you will be changed after reading this generous outpouring of wisdom** that we need right now.
– Allison Kruse, KForce

True to form, James keeps it on the nose and pulls no punches to make sure that he is doing his part to ensure that high quality Employer Branding is hitting the market. **A great guidebook to help you deliver your own testimony for your brand**.
– Elizabeth Lembke, Transforming Talent

Excellent advice on creating your employer brand, and optimizing your business results from it.
– Coby Schneider, Intel

James has written a much needed "mirror" for the recruitment industry and is showing us what isn't working. Without pandering or punishing, we're finally being given an opportunity to learn from our collective mistakes and acquire actionable tactics for attracting the right talent by understanding our own DNA. Regardless of whether you're in a leadership role, an in-house recruiter, or work for a third party agency, **"Talent Chooses You" is the road map to understanding the importance of employer branding and how to build value for everyone involved.**
– Chris Murdock, IQTalent Partners

Very few people create as much content as James Ellis, for the benefit of so many. Ever since he was on The Employer Branding Podcast discussing how he 'protects space cats' at Groupon, I've known he is one seriously original thinker in this space. **This steller resource of a book lets you plug into his brain, and methodically covers everything employer brand professionals ought to know.**
– Jörgen Sundberg, The Employer Branding Podcast

James Ellis

Talent Chooses You

CONTENTS

"Birds born in a cage think flying is an illness."
- Alejandro Jodorowsky

"Too many people believe the future
is something that happens
and just rolls them over in its wake."
-Cindy Gallop

"Inspiration is for amateurs;
the rest of us just show up
and get to work."
- Chuck Close

ANTE

WHO IS THIS BOOK FOR AND WHAT ARE WE TRYING TO ACCOMPLISH?

Recruiting is a mess.

If you disagree with that simple statement, please turn around and ask for your money back. Because if you think recruiting is done well and effectively in companies, we're not going to have a lot to talk about.

What worked ten, twenty, and fifty years ago is still being practiced as "current state of the profession." Collecting resumes by the dozens and hundreds, waiting weeks to contact candidates, mass "thanks but no thanks" letters months later (assuming you don't just ghost them), zero feedback after coming in for interviews, searching in vain for purple squirrels that never existed, and all the rest of recruiting's bad habits that kind of and sort of worked generations ago just aren't cutting it anymore.

And if you needed me to tell you that, you have not been paying attention. Welcome to the modern era! Grab a phone and a helmet, because it's gonna get crazy.

Competition for talent is growing. The business is screaming (and usually at you). Leadership demands results. No one believes your data (assuming your vendors can provide any that can pass any kind of test). But rather than look for brand new solutions, recruiters think only in terms of recruiting. They look to add bodies and tools to do what they've always done just a little bit faster or with slightly fewer clicks. But making something that isn't particularly effective work a little faster isn't an answer. If you spend your energy trying to build a slightly better landline in a world of smartphones, you're missing the point entirely.

The reckoning is here. What worked before no longer will. The writing is on the wall (and the ATS, and the job board, and the resume warehouse, ad infinitum): Change or you will be crushed.

In the face of such dire horizons, there is a solution you can use to create the necessary change within your organization to keep from getting crushed. Depending on how much you embrace it, it might even help you hire better talent faster and retain them longer. Employer brand as a way of looking at your hiring issues is going to be the engine that fuels change in recruiting, recruitment marketing, HR, and leadership for the next decade. Businesses that embrace it will absolutely be able to fill their talent needs faster and cheaper and will start gobbling up the market share from those still applying horse-and-buggy thinking to a Tesla world.

The choice is yours.

More than anything, this book is a philosophy book, which might seem strange. You might have hoped to pick up a self-help, follow-the-check-boxes, paint-by-numbers plan on how to slap some of this "employer brand stuff" on your company and then go about your day. Sorry to disappoint, but that's not this book. Besides the fact that tactics generally have the half-life of your average internet meme, you don't need me to tell you about tactics. You're smart enough to come up with those on your own. In fact, you're probably already using some really good ones. But without a sound strategy, those tactics are all action without intention. You've got the gas pedal floored, the wheels are spinning, but you have no sense of direction or destination.

What you need is a change in mindset, a change in perspective to see a bigger picture than just recruiting or even talent acquisition. You need a new philosophy. With this new outlook, you'll be able to see new value is everything you already have in the tactics you're already using. You'll have better conversations about how and when to use them and a whole framework to help

3

you evaluate their potential.

Which is another way of saying you need to think things through on your own, but this book will help.

I wrote this book as an employer brand professional, a practitioner in the dark arts of using branding as a means of changing other people's minds. I want to change the world, and I want you to, too. I am a firm believer that pretty much anyone smart enough to try and read this is smart enough to make massive impacts within their business. You just need a different way of seeing what's right in front of you.

So let's go on a journey of change. The company you save may be your own.

THE FEAR WALL

Have you ever done karaoke? Of course you have. We all have. You get all excited to make an idiot out of yourself or show off your special talent, so you flip through an epic binder and pick a song you'd like to sing. Maybe it's an old favorite, something from deep in the catalog, or maybe you just pick a new song to keep everyone from thinking you're out of touch. You write the song number on a slip of paper and hand it to the karaoke DJ with a dollar bill.

And then you wait for them to load your song and call your name. And that is when things take a turn.

All your (possibly alcohol-inspired) excitement and anticipation turn to fear. What if instead of looking a little silly, you really do make a fool of yourself? What if everyone watches you fail? What if you don't remember any of the words or can't find the key or miss the beat so badly that the song becomes almost unrecognizable? Having heard all your friends (or worse, coworkers) chant your name as you stepped up to the mic to wow everyone, what if it turns out you can't really sing?

This is the fear of putting yourself out there, and it is the worst.

I bring this up, not to kick the barely hanging-on karaoke industry, but to tell you what it's like to write a book. You see, there was a weird six-week period where I had nothing to do (don't get jealous;

as an independent consultant, those are fear-filled weeks), so I needed to distract myself from the steady stream of "you'll never work again" voices in my head.

Every week, I publish an employer brand-focused podcast called The Talent Cast. I start with an idea or just a topic—usually sparked by a conversation, a book, or podcast, or even what I'm working on at the time—and just explore it in front of the mic. It is almost 100% extemporaneous, this monologue I record in one take. I really love doing it, and I have a nice-sized audience who seems to get something out of it. As Seth Godin has said, "There's something magical about starting something, putting your name on it, and putting it out into the world." But let us be clear: I invite criticism, mockery, and humiliation every single time I turn on my microphone or push an episode out into the world. Even when I know the topic I'm going to talk about backwards and forwards, there's a chance I misspeak, that I have proverbial spinach in my teeth, and end up looking like a fool. It is a dance between my desire to express and teach and the fear that comes from being that open.

But that magic has continued, and I have been putting the podcast out every week for more than three years, leading other people to find me. Putting your content into the world is like a beacon to those who need it, who likely need more of what you are giving, creating strange communities and pockets of people. As Momus once said, "Warhol said we'd all be famous for fifteen minutes, but on the internet, we'll all be famous to fifteen people." The more I published, the more I found my tribe. I found my fifteen people.

But during those six weeks between projects, I needed something bigger to distract myself, so I started writing. And writing. And writing.

At the beginning, this was just going to be a long-ish blog post to "prove" the value of employer branding. Then it hit 3,000 words. And as I realized I needed to define employer brand in order to prove it, I realized I wasn't going to be able to capture it in 8,000 words. Or 12,000. What was this thing? And when was it ever going to end? And there was a point where I asked myself, would anyone ever want to read something that long? I had started pulling on a thread of a very big sweater and couldn't stop.

At that point, I made the mistake of telling a few friends what I was doing, and they asked to see it. As it hit twenty and forty thousand words, they made notes in the margins and encouraged me to finish it as a book.

Then I hit the fear wall.

Here were my peers, my betters and those who were trying to learn, cheering me on as I stepped up to the mic. The first draft took six weeks. The second took more than a year.

The fear is real, people. Would this book make any sense? Would anyone care? Had I missed the optimum time to put it out? And was I fooling myself?

So here I am, at the moment of truth. My song has started playing. And while I may be dredging up every last bit of confidence and self-possession to make it look like I know what I'm doing, I assure you I'm absolutely petrified as I step up to the microphone to sing.

ABOUT THE INTERVIEWS

A few years ago, I asked my then-two-year-old daughter what she thought daddy's job was. I really didn't think she'd even given it a thought, but I was curious. At the time, I was global head of employer brand for a large public company, whose unofficial internal mascot, carried over from its scrappy start-up days, was "Space Cat," a cat that lived on a spaceship. My daughter hardly paused before she looked at me and said, "You protect Space Cat." Which, if you think about it long enough, was exactly what I was doing.

Sometimes it pays to get other perspectives of what's right in front of you.

At last count, I've written about 83,000 words on employer branding for this book, and frankly, even I'm sick of hearing my voice as I write. I can't imagine what it would be like for you. So I wanted to break things up here and there.

But beyond that, while writing a book is like unfurling a flag, claiming some level of expertise on the subject of talent attraction, there are no true experts on the subject. We're all building the road in front of us as we go, so I wanted to include perspectives from some of the amazing people I've gotten to know in the last six or seven years.

Their perspectives come from their own experiences, both as

candidates and as recruitment and hiring practitioners. Some are agency folks, helping client companies solve employer brand problems. Some own their company's brand, managing it from the inside. I brought in product people, builders, writers, curmudgeons, speakers, thinkers, bomb-throwers, and goofs.

The one thing they all share is an understanding that there is a better way to hire and to think about talent (maybe even thinking about them as human beings every once in a while). But, most importantly, their perspectives often differ from my own. And you know what? They're just as right as I am. And I am so glad I got the chance to include them.

Some interviews were on video and some were written, but they all have valuable things to add. And while they gave me their time and consideration, all I can offer in return is my sincerest thanks. I appreciate the help, and I appreciate them.

A NOTE TO BRITISH READERS

Yes, I know that employer branding was invented by Simon Burrows in London more than 25 years ago and that the "textbooks" for the subject were written by Richard Mosley, a fellow Brit. Where in the US we focused on recruitment marketing, the UK really spent the time perfecting the concept and process of managing an employer brand, making huge strides in this very new idea.

So on some level, employer branding is a very UK and European subject (and no, I'm not conflating the two areas).

Of course, the reality is that I am not British. I'm sure my parents would like me to suggest that my year living in London in the 1970s as a baby had some impact, but I can't really say that for certain. I'm a Yank with a marketing-heavy background, and there might be some speaking the Queen's English who might suggest that I am an interloper in the employer brand space. And on some level they are right. Americans have only recently picked up on the power of employer branding, and much like Guinness, parliamentary process, and The Great British Bake Off, things change somewhat when they cross the pond.

I would like to say for the record that I have deep respect for my brothers and sisters from the other side of the pond who came before me (and note the number of British voices I've included here), as I try to push the concept of employer branding forward one more step. No disrespect is intended. I just think we can all think harder, be more creative, and do better work. So let's keep pushing together.

ACKNOWLEDGMENTS

If this book is rubbish, it's my own fault. But if it is a success, I have a LOT of people to thank.

First, if it weren't for conversations with Lindsay Parks, this thing probably would have died two or three times. The level of self-doubt that goes into something like this is staggering. I was revealing pretty much all my thinking around my profession and would have nothing to hide behind if I was off base? But Lindsay took a crack at very early drafts and told me to keep going when I needed to hear it. So she gets the first credit after mine. She also helped me figure out the title, so thank you, Lindsay. (Now it's your turn, dork!)

Second, there's the one and only Elena Valentine, my own personal mastermind group. When this whole project fell apart, she was the one who helped me see how to put it back together again. Elena, I can't wait to eat tacos with you again.

A massive thank you to all the people who gave their time and attention to me in the form of interviews. They are all scholars, rogues, saints and mensches. You'll see who they are soon enough.

Then there's my own personal board of inspirations and aspirations. Nancy Goldstein, Tracey Parsons, Marrit Ingman, Abby Cheesman, Torin Ellis, Audra Knight, Ben Gledhill, Iain Hamilton, Charu Malhotra, Andrea Hurtado, Hung Lee, Holland McCue, Dina

Medeiros, Zakiya Nashid, Derek Murphy-Johnson, Angie Verros, Shane Gray, Bryan Chaney, Katrina Kibben, Eva Baluchova, Joel Cheesman, Chad Sowash, Jess Von Bank, Katrina Collier, Kirsten Davidson, Beth Carter, Tiffany Lee, Madison Butler, Brad Farris, Jill Salzman, Sehare Hemani, Melinda Benoit, Jason Kent Crowell, Andrew Gadomski, Lex Kramer, Stacey Kraft, Rob LaMorte, Gabriel Hitt, Maria Paris, Henry Eschricht, Katarzyna Do, Sean O'Grady, Kortney Kutsop, anyone who's ever contacted me through The Talent Cast, and all the people I probably managed to forget to write down here. Thank you all for…well, just being you.

This book was edited by Diana Ceres of Blue Dragon Consulting. Yeah, I let someone copy edit me. You're all welcome. (If you could see her comments, she LOL'd at that.)

And since you're some crazy person who reads prefaces to books like this, do yourself a favor and go read everything you can get your hands on from people like Richard Mosley, Bryan Adams & Charlotte Marshall, Blair Enns, Cindy Gallop, David C. Baker, Seth Godin, Tom Peters, William Gibson, and Adam Morgan. They are all geniuses, and I highly recommend reading them all as much as you can.

Finally, unending thanks and love to my lovely wife, Becki, who remains my biggest supporter and toughest gut check. As the kids say, get yourself a partner who can do both.

James "Employer Brand Nerd" Ellis
Chicago, IL, May 2020

Talent Chooses You

14

PART ONE: REINVENT YOUR HIRING

I remain stunned by the number of people who need it explained to them just how bad hiring has become. Neither the recruiter, the hiring manager, and certainly not the candidate enjoy any part of it. We all hold our noses and see it as an evil best avoided or gamed.

This broken system is how we expect to bring in the people who make our company go. It's almost a wonder anyone ever gets a job ever.

But until you pop the hood and see how badly mangled the engine is, you can't hope to fix it. And fixing it is the ultimate goal here.

To those offended, because they see themselves and how they further this broken system, I have only a modicum of empathy.

One recruiter or one human resources business partner can't be expected to change the industry on their own. But they can be expected to stop living in the past and be willing to try something (anything) new.

Dive right in and see how messy it gets. I promise there's a better world on the other side.

CHAPTER ONE:
THE MODERN WORLD OF
HIRING IS BROKEN

THE POWER OF TALENT:
DO YOU REALLY WANT BETTER TALENT?

This statement is terrifying (mostly to HR) but completely true. Not every business needs talented people to grow and thrive. But the kind of level of talent your business really needs will determine 80% of your talent strategy, of which employer brand is the most obvious element.

You can define talent any number of ways, but at its most root level, talent is where you value one person (their experience, skill set, education, attitude, aptitude, personality, certifications, network, etc.) over another. You can see that person A is likely 20% more valuable than person B, and thus you desire to hire A more than B. In fact, you might even be willing to pay A-level talent more than B for the same role.

If your world is one where "talent" is a euphemism for commoditized people who fill seats and do as they are told, such talent may be hard to discern and may not be work valuing (thus, once meeting base requirements, you would be comfortable picking whoever accepts the standard offer for this role). This is the kind of business for whom the haystack model is designed. For you, you should focus on the volume of applicants and invest in recruitment marketing and advertising. Someone else will help you with that. As the delta between "great" and "good enough" has no value, your company will not value doing the hard work of attracting great talent.

But talent isn't binary. You don't have or not have talent. Talent occurs across a spectrum and has a variety of facets. For the purpose of this conversation, we'll keep things simple.

Top-Tier Talent

First, you have the *A players*. These are the best of the best—the people who will help you not just do the job, but also expand the role, helping to reinvent it to create opportunities for the business that weren't available before. They are the ones who are willing to push boundaries, take risks, and try new things (often beyond what others are comfortable with). They are the game changers. These people are the most talented and most desirable. All things being equal, you would rather hire an A player than a B or a C player, simply because they expand your business's options for growth.

Second-Tier Talent

There's nothing wrong with *B players*. They are pretty darn good at their job. They work to expand their skill sets, to identify more efficient ways of working, and to adopt new ideas into the job as they are introduced. They are engaged with the work and willing to go deeper, provided they don't have to invent the path forward. Frankly, most of your best people are B players: They're doing great work, but not trying to turn you into the next Google, Netflix, or Tesla. They want better, but they don't push and upset the apple cart to make magic happen. Each one of them is useful and valuable, and you would hate to see them go. But more than that, you value these employees far more than C players.

Commoditized Talent

C players can do the job. However, they won't be engaged, and they won't change the game. Frankly, they won't even blow your socks off. To them, the job is a job that they take just enough pride in to not be bad at, but they aren't staying extra hours without the bribe of a reward or threat of punishment. Their intrinsic motivation isn't something you can tap into. All companies have a lot of these people. Maybe they were once B players who just disengaged or knew how to ace the interview and cover up deficiencies. Maybe you have programs (formal or not) in place to help them get with the program or get out. These are the people you can't outright fire because they are doing the job as given to them. All things considered, you only keep them on the payroll, because you can't afford to be short a body.

We won't go beyond C players, because I'll assume you'd either have already fired them or would be smart enough not to hire them in the first place.

Why am I bothering to define the concept of talent? Because you have to understand that A players either know that they are A players, or they have a sense of their value to a company. The days of expecting a diamond in the rough, someone who simply doesn't know how to properly value themselves, to just apply out of the blue and be hired far below their value, are gone. Sure, every third blue moon you get lucky, and someone comes in asking for an entry-level gig when you can plainly see they should be making twice what that role normally offers. But it's so rare, and it's not something to build a strategy on. It's a plan based on hopes and wishes.

If you want someone great, they know they have something valuable to offer. And if you value them, so will someone else. If you want and can use better talent, you need to shift strategies so you aren't trying to engage just anyone. You want someone specific. Someone skilled and experienced. Someone who is going to be selective. Your post-and-pray approach of casting wide nets will simply not resonate with someone who hears those bland messages from recruiters all the time.

THEY AREN'T YOUR EMPLOYEES; THEY'RE SALARIED VOLUNTEERS

No one works a job anymore. When there are more open roles than people to fill them, when there is little to no stigma in job hopping, when it is common knowledge that better pay raises happen when someone moves from one company to another rather than being loyal, we have to rethink how we see the people who come to work every day.

It used to be having a job opening was power: Managers and recruiters could demand compliance and loyalty from total strangers, dictating all the terms of engagement, including how candidates should format their resumes and what constituted "appropriate attire" to wear to an interview, while keeping the candidate the dark at all times, expecting them to wait quietly for someone to let them know if they were getting a job offer or not.

We've built and installed massive enterprise systems to attract, select, and collect talent based on the idea that the hiring manager is smart, wise, and good, but the candidate is always hiding something. Every line of a resume or CV is questioned like an Agatha Christie screenplay, looking for a murder weapon and motive. Interview rooms should just install bare light bulbs dangling from the ceiling and be done with it.

The entire process is adversarial. But then, when the hiring manager selects the candidate, we're all supposed to let bygones be bygones. What started with unvarnished dubiousness and incredulity is supposed to magically evolve into trust and a commitment to teamwork? That should sound crazy, but look around: That's how almost every company in every country does it.

But today's demand for talent, far outpacing the supply, puts talented candidates and prospects in the driver's seat.

Well, we all say stuff like that, but all too often we say that under the assumption that this power shift is an aberration, a storm to be weathered until things get "back to normal." That's not what is going on here. This is the way the world works now, And the fastest way to shift your thinking is to stop thinking of these people as candidates or employees, but as volunteers.

Why think of them as volunteers? Well, every morning, they volunteer to show up. Throughout the day, they volunteer to give their effort and attention to you. Every moment when working, they volunteer to show up and care about the task in front of them. And as they go about their workday surrounded by other job options, they are faced more choices. The goal is that they choose to work for you and they make that choice every single day. Treating them like they are somehow beholden to you for a paycheck, insurance, or sense of themselves is asking for heartbreak every day.

Seeing them as volunteers forces recruiters and managers to flip the entire recruiting script from having the best bait that draws people to you into a strategy in which you have to communicate why they should choose to volunteer for you.

People don't volunteer at places they don't care about. Ask anyone volunteering at a school, animal shelter, soup kitchen, donation center, or standing on a corner asking people for a minute of their time. Every single person has a fairly well-articulated reason for being there. They chose to show up and take this task on. Paid or not, the work or goal means something to them. They made the choice to do this.

No one wants to work at a place they loathe. No one wakes up and thinks of ways to make their job suck more. And yet the stats are crystal clear: Most people aren't engaged at work. If they didn't wake up that way, whose fault is it? Yes, I just accused you of

22

creating the problem of employee engagement. Go ahead. Tell me I'm wrong.

If you don't adopt this mindset of treating staff and candidates as volunteers, you'll never be able to attract and retain talent, because there will always be a choice in front of them and eventually they'll choose someone else.

INTERVIEW:
ZAKIYA "ZA" NASHID

I've known Za for a few years, and the best way to describe her is "consummate professional." She owns the North America employer brand of one of the world's best-known consumer product companies, but she'll tell you she's just an "employer brand practitioner." As the owner of such a large brand, it is easy to get pulled in a million directions and even more agendas, managing agencies, partners, vendors, stakeholders, and the like. But her superpower is in seeing the direction forward and applying the will to make it happen. She really is a pro and makes it look really easy in the process (which we'll both tell you, it's not).

How Do You define "employer brand?"

In its simplest form, employer brand is the reputation of an organization as an employer. An employer brand describes the employer value proposition and is built from the perspectives of the organization, internal employees, and external individuals. It is also the process of defining and positioning who you are as an employer and sometimes includes who you aspire to become.

What do most people get wrong about employer branding?

Two things stand out to me instantly. One is authenticity and transparency when building employer brand messaging. When you build an employer brand manifesto, messaging, look and feel, etc., it should be authentic to who the organization is. I see some organizations use very generic messaging that is very disconnected from the brand and doesn't truly provide any insight to how the organization is unique and different from others. Some organizations lean too far into aspirational messaging that doesn't reflect the current state of the organization. Even if there is some aspiration, you should be transparent about the journey you are on. I feel this is a miss sometimes, and it reflects when employees/candidates showcase their disconnect in online reviews or by word of mouth.

Second, I think a huge miss is when activating an employer brand organizations put a lot of effort into external channels and miss internal opportunities to engage and educate employees. Employees are the strongest advocates of the brand, and, if done right, when building the employer brand, employee voices should have been included. It is important to create a strategy that includes internal communication, employee engagement, and advocacy. Make sure your office and internal channels reflect EB messaging, host events, create content for employees to share, showcase employee stories internally, educate employees during onboarding, etc. This can have a huge impact on retention, internal mobility, advocacy, and referrals.

What advice would you give?

Build strong internal relationships with key stakeholders and employees. For example:
- Ensure you are lockstep with communications and marketing when it comes to the connection between the corporate brad and employer brand strategy.
- Get to know your employees. If there are any employee resource groups, this is a great way to identify key employee stories for ongoing content.
- Build ways of working with the Talent Acquisition and HR community. You should be speaking the same language to the business. Also, educate the HR team on EB/RM (Recruitment Marketing) and how it fits within the HR/business strategy.
- Measure everything! Identify what is important to the business and design EB metrics that showcase impact.

What is one surprising thing you've seen or done that worked?

It's the smallest thing, but coaching individuals on how to leverage LinkedIn to become a talent advocate. I guess it is not that surprising, because there is a benefit for the employee with this action, but I didn't expect it to be so popular. A lot of the time it is my entry point to discuss the broader Employer Brand strategy with leaders and teams. I sat with each member of the C-suite to update their profile with EB content and branding and discussed how we could build more dynamic stories and leverage employees as advocates with their support and encouragement.

What is employer branding's biggest challenge?

Employer brand is slowly developing. Organizations are trying to figure out how to leverage our skills and how to embed the function into the organization. You will see employer brand practitioners at different organizations sit in many different functions within an organization depending on the goals and work on very different things at times. The biggest challenge I see is managing expectations with very limited resources in both headcount and budget. We are asked to do a lot with a little which makes it very difficult to reach the level of impact we ultimately want to reach and is expected at times.

HIRING IS A GAME OF QUALITY, NOT QUANTITY

L et's pretend you are selling tacos. Or donuts. Or toothbrushes. It really doesn't matter. These things are cheap items, maybe costing a dollar each. So you set up a stand or cart and hawk your wares. Anyone who walks up with a dollar in their pocket is a viable customer, and your job is to convince them that your item is worth the dollar to them. Perhaps it will give them more than a dollar's feeling of satisfaction to eat that taco. Or it will crave that sweet tooth in a way they'd be willing to spend two dollars. Or that brushing will keep them from needing costly dental work down the road. Either way, your item has value, and they'd be a fool to reject it. The conversation is about value conversion.

Which is fine. This is typical commerce: I have a good or service to sell, and I will sell it to whomever can pay for it. You have a dollar. I have a taco. Let's make some magic happen! Your goal in this space is to replicate this transaction as many times as possible. Having sold the taco, you look to sell another. You are rewarded for selling lots of tacos. Becoming the best taco salesperson is a game of quantity and nothing more.

In this process, do you ask your buyer if they have a college degree? Did you confirm that they have a reliable mode of transportation? As you are both in the same place, you don't wonder if they live close enough to you. But are they certified to eat a donut? Do they have at least five years' donut-eating experience? Can they provide names and contact information for three people who can confirm they know their way around a donut? How many different varieties of donut can they discuss with confidence? Hmm...I see a gap of three months in which you were not eating donuts. Can you explain that gap?

Have you ever heard of someone saying they only had one donut and were going to sell it to the "best" customer? The one who was a cultural fit to the mission of your donut?

Of course not. That would be insane. Again, you have a donut and they have a dollar. To quote comedian Mitch Hedberg, why do we even need a receipt? This transaction is completed. It doesn't matter if they don't have a work visa, a degree, or can pass a drug test.

Dollar. Donut. Done.

But when we are hiring, we aren't selling donuts or tacos. We're looking for a specific person to do a specific job. We wonder what school they went to, what other jobs they've had, and what the outcomes of their work was. We immediately reject them if they don't have enough experience. We reject them because they don't "fit." We reject them because they were arrested and tried for fraud. We reject them because someone was just a little bit better.

Hiring isn't a game of quantity, because we're generally filling one role and we want the best possible person to take that job. We want one person, so we seek the best person.

This seems prima facie obvious, but it is the difference that underlies all hiring and differentiates it from almost any other kind of profession. It is foundational to everything and what differentiates employer branding from every other kind of marketing and branding in the world. The rest of the world is looking to bill more hours, sell more time, build more widgets, train more people, take more cases, fix more pipes, and take on more clients. We live in a world driven by quantity, and blindly applying marketing and sales techniques designed for quantity to a model designed for quality is a disaster waiting to happen.

If you are selling tacos and you sell a million tacos, you're getting a raise. You're getting a bonus. They'll put your picture on a wall above the words "Salesperson of the Year."

But if you're "selling" jobs and you get a million people to apply, you're getting fired.

Applying great, clever, or even genius-level marketing thinking won't solve recruiting and hiring, because they are so different. Tennis, golf, and billiards are all played with round balls, but you can't switch one ball for another and pretend it's the same game.

This difference isn't academic. It is an industry built on a very different foundation to almost everything else we know and do. But embracing this difference is the beginning to solving your hiring problems.

ENTROPY KILLS THE SYSTEM: RECRUITING'S 99% PROBLEM

Perhaps you were thrown by the suggestion that recruiters are still doing some things they did 50 years ago and that the advent of technology hasn't made huge sweeping changes in the process of attracting, sorting, and selecting talent. Like rehabbing an old house, the walls and paint may be new and there might be wiring for sound systems all built into it and now there's a huge steam shower, but all of it sits on a foundation that predates the war. The foundation creates the shape of whatever sits about it, so no matter how new the house, it is constrained by decisions made decades ago.

The same is true in recruiting. Sure, there are versions of AI that can pull a potential needle out of the haystack of applications in the blink of an eye, but recruiting is still based on a model of building lots and lots of haystacks as a means of finding needles. When there's a problem finding someone great to fill a role, the foundational thinking starts with "we need bigger and better haystacks, because with a big enough haystack, we'll always have the talent we need." Like Archimedes with a lever, a recruiter thinks that with enough applications, they'll be able to hire whomever they want to. This makes recruiting a quantity game, which we already decided it isn't. Some companies have so many applications on file, they look like a stand-alone white-labeled LinkedIn.

And they collect more every minute.

Look at the core tech stack of any company. They have an Applicant Tracking System (ATS) to manage the process of opening jobs and holding applications as the foundation to recruitment thinking. It forces the recruiter to focus on spreading a job opening to all relevant job boards, making their core purpose to ensure the maximum number of job seekers can see the opening. Then recruiters share that job on social media. Then internally, they ask people on the team to share the job (and the referral) with their networks. They might buy ads on websites to ensure passive candidates can see the opening. They might hold recruiting events to pitch it in person. They might hold sourcing sprints to ensure people who might be a good fit know about the role. They build outreach messaging to go find more potential fits and beg them to consider applying. They build the haystack, because that's how they are resourced and it's what we've asked of them.

The strategy is purely one of scale: Get the most possible people to apply, and later the recruiter will winnow the list down into something manageable. Every element in this process is designed to create the most applications. It is a dragnet, cast as wide as possible and trolling the seafloor to collect prized fish indiscriminately with rocks, dead animals, and anything else that happens to be in the ocean. While sourcers will focus on the potential quality of a candidate, the ad won't. The job board posting won't. The social posting won't. These tools are quite literally paid to scale: The more eyeballs that see it, the more they can bill. Consequently, a given requisition is littered with plenty of candidates who can't do the role and will never be given serious consideration.

This is the definition of wasted effort.
Depending on the role and location, a recruiter could see dozens to hundreds of applications for the posted role. I've seen openings closed early, because there were already 350 applications, more than a single recruiter (without some help) could review in a reasonable amount of time. But for the sake of discussion, let's say that you get 100 applicants in each open role.

First off, congratulations. Getting 100 people to apply is no easy feat. That's why companies pay good money for tools that push open roles onto hundreds of job boards and promote them to be at the top of given searches. Getting 100 applicants means that you're "recruiting effectively" (please note the heavy use of sarcasm in those quote marks). To anyone outside of recruiting, however, that doesn't sound effective at all.

In this haystack of 100, because this is a game of quality rather than quantity, a recruiter's job is to sort out the people who just aren't capable of doing the job. When you see the statistics that a recruiter reviews a resume for an average of 30 seconds, you might wonder how anyone without superhuman powers can review a resume in 30 seconds. They can't. But at this stage of the process, the recruiter isn't looking to understand the candidate. They are only focused on filtering people out. Don't have the right education? Out. Not enough experience in a given skill set? Out. Gaps in the resume? Out (though, this is less of an issue these days, but I still know plenty of hiring managers who reject people with time gaps without hesitation). Lots of jobs with short tenures? Out. Their last title was too elevated? Out. Their last title was too low? Out.

In the haystack model, the recruiter is removing hay, piece by piece, and ensuring it isn't a needle. It doesn't take long at all to see if something is obviously hay. Even if you find a piece of gray hay or a heavy piece of hay, the process turns a haystack into a pile of potential needles, something far easier to evaluate. So the recruiter goes from 100 applications to 20 candidates who can't be eliminated out of hand.

This pile of 20 is given more consideration. Does the cover letter suggest the right attributes? Are there success stories and positive outcomes in the resume? Do they have all the skills or just some? The recruiter begins to sort-rank these 20 to identify the 10 or so candidates who could potentially do the job. Those people get a phone screen.

In the phone screen, the recruiter is looking to eliminate people again. Do they sound like they have two heads? Out. Do they have the wrong temperament/attitude? Out. Does the recruiter get the sense that the applicant is puffing up their experience and abilities? Out. The pile stands at the final five, who are brought to the hiring manager.

The hiring manager might toss some of these lucky few back, but the goal is to pick from these candidates. An interview pool is formed and dates are set, and over the course of a few days, some candidates are rejected and the remaining ones are ranked in terms of preference. The number-one candidate gets an offer, and if they accept, all others are dispositioned, which is the euphemistic way of saying they are rejected.

This doesn't even enter into the all-too-distinct possibility that the hiring manager doesn't like any of the candidates presented and asks the recruiter to start again and post a revised job on the ATS, beginning the cycle anew.

This is how most companies go about hiring, and it looks the same today as it did decades ago when applications would come in via an ad in the Sunday papers rather than an internet job board. In its quest to fulfill the business need that a new hire solves, the company will interact directly with 100 applicants (ignoring those who see the ad or posting and decide to not apply, the people who get fed up with the ATS and give up halfway through the application process, the employees who refer applicants, and all the other potential touchpoints).

Think of it: Interact with 100-plus people to get one (potential) hire (who has only a 50/50 chance of being seen as a successful hire and staying a year or more). Have you ever seen how saffron is harvested? A human has to use a pair of tweezers to extract a single hair-like tendril from an orchid that only blooms a few days a year. Think of all the soil, water, sun, fertilizer, and human energy it takes to get enough strands to flavor a single dish and you're in the realm of how hard it is to hire. Because of all that work, saffron is more valuable by weight than gold. Recruiting, however, isn't seen that way.

But what about the 99 people who didn't get hired? If we look back at the recruiter's journey, let's see what happened to all those people who pinned some level of hope on getting the job and didn't.

The 80 who were rejected out of hand, because they didn't

33

obviously seem like a fit or could do the job in the 10- to 30-second resume review process? Well, at best they will get a form letter. This form letter will be the same for every single role, be it an intern, team leader, or director. Sure, there might be some code to insert someone's name and role applied for into the letter to "personalize" it, but the content will have all the warmth of a roll of tin foil. The letter may say that it is sorry that the process will not continue, but no one will feel any emotional connection to a letter borrowed by legal from a third-party worksheet with HR's oversight.

Let us be very clear. The goal of the form letter is not to create goodwill. The goal of the form letter is not to actually thank someone for their application. The goal of the form letter is not to express sorrow that they will not be considered for this role. The actual goal is to tell the applicant that the process is over and that there is no need to contact the recruiter about this role. The purpose is to spare the recruiter the task of having to talk to the applicant, because they are no longer valuable to the recruiter.

And that assumes the applicant is sent anything. Data on what percentage of companies actually bother to send a form letter at all is hard to come by, mostly because most companies think they are sending those letters, since their ATS is automated so the letters go out on their own and recruiters and HRIS don't have to worry about it. But my informal surveying (US-based) suggests that as many as 50% of all companies let applications fall into a black hole and applicants never hear a single thing. This "black hole" effect is getting better, but remember we're measuring "better" by who gets a form letter. The bar, as you can see, is quite low.

Recruiters will say (and I know this, because this is how they comment on my posts on LinkedIn) that these people don't deserve anything more, because they simply didn't meet the base criteria and should never have applied in the first place. To these recruiters I ask: How well-written are your job posts? Are they or are they not designed to attract the maximum number of applicants? When I look at the bullets and it says "must have an intermediate level of experience with Excel" what does "intermediate level" mean? Is there a standard set of levels to base that off of? Does this job require VLOOKUP and pivot table experience, or an understanding of how to read formulas? Those things (and all the other elements in 95% of all job postings) are not well-described or defined, asking the candidate to make those up on their own, resulting in people who interpreted the poorly written posting incorrectly and are now bearing the indifference of the world's recruiters.

We've built massive systems to attract as many applicants as possible and begrudge candidates for doing so.
Yikes.

And the 10 who survived the first pass of potentially meeting criteria but are getting rejected for smaller and more subtle reasons? They get the same form letter. These are people who are not prima facie unqualified, but the system will treat them the same as the "riffraff" who cluttered up the ATS. So here are people that have some skill and talent and they get the tin foil.

Let's look at these 80 people as a group for a moment. Are these evil people? Of course not. They had the ambition or gumption to complete an application process, so they aren't necessarily lazy. They have some skills, just not the ones required to do this particular job. Unless your company is tiny, could there be other roles these people could thrive in? That is to say, these people are potentially valuable in the future, either as candidates, as connections to candidates, or as consumers.

And the candidates who were rejected after a phone screen, what do they get? Each one of them spent 30 minutes of their time talking to the recruiter. They literally gave their time to the company and got nothing back. Well, they got a form letter, and we know how well that works.

Finally, what about the handful of people who came in for an interview and didn't get the job? These are people who gave a lot of time, who may have taken vacation time off work to get dressed up and print some resumes only to be rejected. There's a good chance these people won't get the form letter. They will likely get a quick call from the recruiter, but this is hardly much of a step above the form letter. Most companies are terrified to give candidates any useful or actionable reasons for not getting the job or feedback they can use to improve their performances at other interviews.

And I know some companies who've set up their ATSs such that after getting the rejection call rejection, they also get the rejection letter, almost as a way to nail the casket shut and ensure no possible, positive brand association would be left standing.

This is the 99% problem. The standard recruiting system doesn't fit our modern expectations, and recruiters are going around creating negative brand associations in 99+ people for every person they help hire. What other business could see that kind of burn rate and feel comfortable about the future?

Most recruiters are forced to behave like goldfish, approaching each requisition as if it were their last. Their mantra is, "Once I fill this role, I'm done." Then new requisitions come in, and they are almost surprised, starting the process from square one every single time. Their worlds are overrun with requisitions and candidates, so it's almost impossible to remember a rejected candidate from the last opening who might be amazing for this new one.

But recruiters, slaves to the ATS and recruiting machinery, are still sending form letters. They are rejecting candidates without feedback. They are taking people's time and giving nothing back to 99% of them. What are the odds that these people, having (sometimes) gotten that "warm" form letter, would jump at the chance to apply again? If you asked someone out and they rejected you, how likely would you be to ask again? Especially when there are countless other opportunities to consider?

Even though job boards show hundreds and thousands of other open roles for candidates to consider, recruiting assumes that the company, the holder of the open role, has all the power and that not only are there unlimited people in the world they could talk to, there will also always be more. And all these people will willingly jump through hoops for the chance to potentially get the job. Does that sound like the modern talent playing field? It doesn't to me. So when recruiters lament how hard it is to find great talent, it's not true. There is plenty of great talent out there. They just don't want to talk to the recruiter. That could be because they are so blissfully happy in their current role, or because they had a negative experience with that recruiter and have chosen to not engage with them again.

The recruiter was born into a world where burning an applicant or candidate rarely, if ever, had negative consequences. But in this interconnected world, in a place with long memories and searchable email systems, the callousness is coming back to haunt recruiters. People remember and will refuse to be treated that way again.

RECRUITING DOESN'T HAVE TO FEEL LIKE
A CORMAC MCCARTHY NOVEL

Why paint such a bleak (albeit accurate) picture of the current state of modern recruiting? As proof that employer brand is necessary. The machine recruiters have been running for so long isn't working any more. Process has created so much negative emotion towards recruiting and the company, that every recruiting engagement becomes adversarial, where recruiters lie to lying recruiters who are covering for lying hiring managers.

It is necessary to look at this situation and see it for what it is: unmaintainable. The machine creates 99 angry and frustrated prospects for every one it might extend an offer to. Those 99 people tell their friends and post their discontent on social media, making the job of a recruiter and the company that much harder every day.

But when you only have a hammer, every problem will get the same solution. Recruiters only know how to recruit. They only have those tools to do that. They have no spare time to try something new. Their key performance indicators (KPIs) are focused on making and clearing the haystacks that make their lives tougher. They can't be blamed for it, but that also means they can't solve the problem they created.

Employer brand is that solution. Not a tool. Not a platform. Not a website or course. Employer brand is a way of seeing the world more clearly, from a systematic perspective, so you can change the machine. It's more philosophy in action than anything. But seeing it as such allows you to solve more of the important talent problems in your company, which is problematic, because we haven't even defined what employer brand is yet.

CHAPTER TWO:
LET'S DO IT BETTER
THIS TIME

WHY EMPLOYER BRANDING IS THE BEST WAY TO REINVENT YOUR HIRING

Why did you get out of bed this morning? Why did you wear that outfit? Why did you show up to that job? Why that kind of coffee or type of lunch are you having today? Why did you decide to go home when you did (instead of five minutes earlier or later)? Why did you watch that show before you went to bed?

"Why" is the question of our age. It determines how we see ourselves, what we do, and how we do it. We live in a world with abundant resources, choices, and options, a world filled with technology that your parents all but think is magic, where any fact, song, show or movie, article, book, or idea can be at our beck and call within seconds. If you can do anything, what you choose to do isn't based on basic constraints, but on why you want to do something.

So why do we do anything? Understanding and tapping into the why is the secret to connecting with great talent and getting them to work for you.

You've heard the old story about two stone masons. Ask the first what he's doing, and he'll tell you he's building a wall. Ask the second one what he's doing, and he'll say he's building a cathedral. One of them is doing a job and the other is creating something sacred and holy. Which one is going to do better work? Which one will stick around to clean up their work space and do the extra little bit of effort to make sure everything is "just right?" Which one

41

is going to be more professionally satisfied? Which one will lead a happier life? The one who has a stronger "why" associated with the job. Why break your back doing such hard work? For the paycheck or for the satisfaction of creating something that will live on and provide spiritual sanctuary?

It's not some old parable, but a reminder that the why drives so much of what we do. And yet, we forget its power when it comes to bringing in the best talent to help us grow a business. We spend time, energy, and money attracting people to the role, training them, and measuring their performance, but we assume they show up for the paycheck. When great talent says they want more, we don't ask them what would make them happier. We just throw money at them. We might talk a good game about providing support, of being a "family," of wanting to move mountains together, but when the chips are down, we longingly look at the compensation and benefits team to squeeze more cash out of the coffers.

The days of working to collect a paycheck are gone. Anyone who is talented can choose where they want to be, and anyone who can't choose won't make a meaningful difference in our bottom line.

Which is why we need to start asking "why?" We need to ask our employees why they work here. We need to ask the leadership why the business exists. We need to ask managers why they hire who they hire. We need to ask candidates why they did or didn't apply.

Because once you start to dig up the whys, once you understand people's motivations, what intrinsically makes them more productive and happier, what motivations you support and reward, you are going to have a very different understanding of what kind of people you should hire and what you can say that will thrill them.

Employer brand helps you get past decades-old recruiting processes and HR structures to realize that business success starts with the why, that it gives you the power to change entire cultures and businesses, and that it allows you to compete and win against any other business.

Yes, that sounds like a lot. But it is something you can do starting right now.

CHANGE YOUR PERSPECTIVE

The fundamental shift being brought about by employer brand thinking isn't that we get to use marketing tools to attract applicants. It isn't about making cool ads and using sexy terms like "brand architecture" or "experience marketing." The real change is that it shifts our perspective on how we see the process of hiring.

Today, who is in charge of hiring? Who's responsible for bringing new talent in the door? Recruiting, of course. But think back on any great hire you've ever made. Did the recruiter scope the job? Did they determine the title or level? Chances are, they didn't even write the job posting or decide how to market the job. When candidates came into the ATS, how much flexibility and leeway were they given to spot and present interesting prospects who weren't exactly a match but had the promise to perhaps be more? Can the recruiter stop an executive scandal from getting out? Did the recruiter control who was on the interview loop to ensure, for example, that a female candidate would have at least one woman interviewing her? Did the recruiter sit in every part of the interview and make sure the hiring manager wasn't distracted by their phone and engaged with the candidate? And even when they facilitate the negotiation, do recruiters have any real negotiating power? Every single thing on this list creates, shapes, and determines how successful the recruiter will be hiring, but the recruiter has no power over them.

Flipping the script, is the Human Resources Business Partner

(HRBP) responsible for the number of applicants? Is the Comp team ever evaluated by time to fill? Is the hiring manager ever shown a dashboard to see that their quality of hire scores are lower than standard? Of course not. Recruiting has a huge part of hiring, but we can't lean on them when hiring isn't going well, because they can't fix it, certainly not by themselves.

Instead of seeing recruiting as the driver of hiring, employer brand gives us a chance to step back and see hiring as something that the entire company is responsible for. Every part of the company has some impact on hiring, but if we keep pushing the "Recruiter" button when we have a talent need, we will never solve the problem. It's like blaming the waiter that your food is too salty. They may be your contact point, but they didn't season the dish.

As director Alejandro Jodorowsky once said, "To a bird born in a cage, flying is an illness." Recruiters, born and raised in cages that made sense decades ago, stopped seeing the bars long ago. They need to see employer branding not as an illness, but as a means to freedom.

Singers are going to sing and dancers are going to dance. Thus, recruiters are going to do what recruiters do. As we measure them by how many roles they fill and time to fill, they are incentivized to look at the problems of hiring the same old way. Ask a recruiter to fix their hiring problem without asking them to shift their perspective first, and the answer will be to hire more recruiters or increase the salary. The problems that keep you from hiring better talent faster aren't too few recruiters or bad tools. A great company that really leverages employer brand thinking can hire great people without an army of recruiters. They solve the problem by seeing the situation differently: They see things from a bigger perspective.

INTERVIEW: BEN GLEDHILL

B en is a deep breath of fresh air in an industry that is as likely as not to eat its own tail. The head of resourcing transformation at Thames Water, Ben will be the first guy to say to your face, "that's pretty dumb, mate," and chances are, he's absolutely right. Ben is smart, creative, and willing to say the emperor has no clothes, which is why I'm such a fan. Ben doesn't get sidetracked by fads and trends. He fearlessly comes up with solutions that seem too simple to work, yet always do. He might be best known for the "Recruitment Marketing Toolbox on $115 a month" guide that he regularly updates, proving that you don't need to spend big to succeed, so long as you're willing to get your hands dirty.

How do you define "employer brand?"

Your Employer Brand is what people on the shop floor or on the job boards say about you. You don't own it, however, you can influence it either positively or negatively. Your EVP, or as I prefer to call it "People Proposition" is your people deal, your give and get.

What do most people get wrong about employer branding?

I think the sheer size and impact of it. It is not just your Glassdoor, your careers website, or even how many awards you win. It is the entire ecosystem linked with people, from awareness all the way to offboarding. Don't think funnel, think loop.

45

What advice would you give?

Do your own digging, first. Ask what, where, why, and who. Understand your own ecosystem, its touchpoints, and take it from there.

What is one surprising thing have you seen or done that worked?

Proving your commercial worth first. That means building relationships with key stakeholders to illustrate the strategic impact of what you do through solid and measurable metrics before launching big campaigns. How do you know when things are "working?" Look at your key metrics throughout the life cycle to verify that each element is working as it should be. You might look at clickthrough rates, conversion from initial awareness, quality of hire, EVP review scores, internal mobility, even up to NPS for people leaving. No one metric is better than another, but if you understand and illustrate how each element links to the next, you're in the driver's seat.

What is employer branding's biggest challenge?

Two things. One, organizations need to realize that their employer brand and the ingredients that make it up are just as important, if not more so, as their overall corporate brand. Second, let's really empower people across the company and enable them to tell their story.

STOP THINKING ABOUT THE RECRUITING FUNNEL AND FOCUS ON THE TALENT FUNNEL

For the last ten years, it's been hammered into recruiting's heads: You folks aren't as smart as marketers, so go use the tools and methodologies that marketers use to get smarter. Ten years ago, recruiters didn't think in click-through rates, conversion rates, impressions, or reach. They simply hadn't been taught or embraced the sales funnel.

I should know, because I was one of those people touting the magical power of a good funnel. Embracing the funnel made a lot of sense at the time, because it was based on the idea that the decision to take action was a process, a journey if you will. At the time, recruiting was still reeling from a sea change in the industry as it moved from classified ads to the internet.

When the model of recruiting was to put ads in the paper on Sunday and wait for resumes to show up Wednesday, there really wasn't much of a journey. If there was, it was measured in seconds, as the reader scanned the paper, looked for relevant openings, and sent the resume to the listed address. The reader went from "I know nothing about this company" to "here is all my professional information" in the time it takes to circle an ad with a pen. The candidate either immediately saw the opening as something they could or couldn't apply for and moved on to the next ad. Given the space limitations and cost for posting a job (did you know that the Sunday want ads usually drove the most revenue for a newspaper in the 1990s?), there wasn't much room to "sell" an opportunity, just enough to define the title or company a little. There wasn't room for a 500-word job posting describing the culture or company mission, so no one thought about looking for it. At best, you got a logo or some black clip art to attract the eye.

The internet changed things when the space for an ad became effectively infinite. You didn't have to stop at 75 words to list the job, you could write a small book that showed up on web-based job boards. And with jobs from around the world available to anyone with a modem instead of being limited to the region of the newspaper, they could see bigger ads from more places. The project manager in Tampa would see amazing opportunities from Toledo, but the ad looked like the ads from the local gig in Tampa. So the ads evolved by adding more information, a company boilerplate, and some stuff about equal opportunity, with a cursory listing of benefits.

Now, a candidate had more information to work with and could make a slightly more informed decision. But more information means more consideration and more time. They could look at company web pages and learn what the company did or even what it stood for. They could see if news stories about the company turned up in search engines. Suddenly, the journey from "I don't know this company" to "here's my professional history" could take days and weeks. There was no immediate feedback anymore as to how effective the job posting was. In the newspaper days, if a posting failed, you could tell by Thursday's mail delivery and make a change in time for the next Sunday paper. The new model made everything far more fluid.

Hence the sales funnel, now relabeled and repurposed as the recruiting funnel:

In a model where the journey takes multiple stages, the funnel is a great way to help you see where problems exist. An ad that promises the moon might attract a lot of attention, but lose that interest

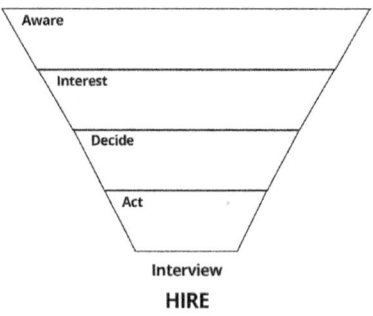

when a simple Google search uncovers multiple lawsuits against the company for fraud. Without the funnel, you might think the ad was bad and rewrite it, not realizing that the ad was effective in attracting the attention it needed. The model focuses on where the problem existed, instead of blindly trying to increase awareness or change sentiment.

The power of the funnel grows as the journey becomes more convoluted, because it simplifies the complex. I can imagine the recruiters on the day they realized that their candidates were all going to Glassdoor directly from the job posting to see the public ratings and reviews of the company. Without the recruiting funnel as a model, you can see how recruiters would have seen it as a threat and attempted to stifle it instead of seeing it as a valid new step within the journey and learning how to leverage it. In fact, that's exactly what happened, as recruitment leaders either ignored the channel or attempted (poorly) to game it.

Seen through the lens of the funnel, it is just another step in the journey, a place where clever recruiters could reinforce their story, both by asking employees to leave reviews and by responding to the negative reviews by reframing them. That also explains why Glassdoor's own play to turn its platform into a job board didn't play out: It had established itself as a necessary step, deep within the journey for people looking to screen companies and validate interest, not a place to start the journey. Meanwhile, a large job board like Indeed had planted its flag at the top of the funnel as a place to find jobs. But since that position demanded its business model be based in advertising, it didn't have the credibility for its reviews to make an impact. Thus, one company bought them both, likely to create a hybrid one-stop job-shopping platform. The future will reveal the value of that strategy.

At each stage of the funnel, people need different things. At the top of the funnel, they need to know what the company is and what the opportunity is. It's just basic information, but necessary to take the next step. What's the value of spending scarce time researching random companies when you could spend that time learning about companies with an open role? Once you have the prospect's attention, they will begin to look for information with which to make a decision. But what information exactly?

Think of the information someone needs to decide to apply as a hierarchy much like Maslow's Hierarchy of Needs. First, they need to learn about the company. What does it do, how big is it, how stable is it, does it align with my worldview? Once the opportunity makes sense from a company standpoint, they want to know where the opportunity is. Studies show one of the major factors that allows a prospect to reject an opportunity is how easy the new commute will be. Some people don't have access to cars and need to know how close to public transit it might be. In some cities, it will need to be bikeable or walkable. Location also helps a prospect begin to envision themselves in the new role, because they start to think about things like, where will I get my coffee in the morning, is it close to my day care or a new day care facility, or what will I have to do for lunch?

After the broader context of company and location, the candidate will think about the specifics of the job. What are the tasks being performed and what is the level or title of the role? Can the prospect do, or stretch into, this role? Good talent knows there's no value of applying for a role or level they can't do or aren't prepared to tackle and will move on.

If the talent knows they could do the job, they'll ask themselves what the work experience might be like. Is this a 9-5 gig or something they'll expect to put 12 hours days towards? Could they work from home? Are the teams competitive or collaborative? Will they have a nice chair, computer, and desk, or is it an open bullpen with hand-me-down machines? No answer is wrong or right, but each answer will feel more like a potential home than another to a given prospect.

The problem is that most companies do a horrible job understanding their own culture and do an even worse job communicating it in a credible or findable way. How many companies say they are like a family? How many companies just stop at saying they have a "great culture" without giving any sense of what that means? This lack of information creates a vacuum that the best prospects need filled, thus allowing rating and blind gossip sites to flourish.

But the big question at the top of the hierarchy is the hardest to answer: Can the prospect see how this job might lead to a feeling of personal or professional satisfaction? Unlike the other levels of the hierarchy, there's no concrete information to portray here. You can't state "yes, you will find professional satisfaction here" like you can list an office address or the team remote work policy. The answer not only relies on a deep lack of information, but also in the prospects knowing themselves enough to see how and why they might be happy. For example, sick of the bureaucracy and politics that come with working at a big firm, someone amazing might seek a small company, not realizing that even small companies have their own flavor of politics and processes to navigate. At this level, the prospect either knows they are trying something new and are prepared to make the experiment with imperfect information, or think they have a crystal ball. Either way, being right on this question, both by the candidate and the company seeing a potential fit, is a coin flip.

Much in the way a recruiter screens candidates by looking for reasons to reject that person as a means of speeding up the process, many prospects are looking for reasons to weed employers out of the consideration set. A consideration set of three or five is much more manageable for picky A- and B-grade talent than a set of twenty or fifty (as opposed to C-grade players who have yet to see an Apply button they don't like).

To put it simply, for ten years, the recruiting funnel enabled a huge leap in recruiting thinking by giving recruitment marketing a framework that made a basic kind of sense. It wasn't perfect, but it was a better framework than "I posted the job and nothing happened!" The job wasn't to pump and dump ads or content everywhere, but to understand where the prospects were in the journey, what channels they leveraged, and what messages they might be interested in hearing at that stage. For years, the recruiting funnel was simply how a recruitment marketer saw the world.

If we worked in a world in which we took raw inputs and processed them into outputs, the recruiting funnel would be enough. It would be all we would need to understand how successful we were being in attracting, finding, and hiring talent.

51

But the world continues to evolve and the funnel needs to evolve with it.

I'M GETTING HUNGRY. LET'S EAT!

In a recruiting funnel model, a recruiter or sourcer's job is to find talent. Think of them as hunters, stalking prey through the forest. They find the tell-tale signs that someone valuable is around (articles, conference write-ups, comments on other people's posts, mentions by other professionals, etc.) and track it down. A smart recruiter even knows when to hunt in packs, to leverage the hiring manager or network connections of the talent to talk the brand up and suggest they consider the company or the role. They flood the prey's social channels with positive mentions of the brand, invitations to coffee or events, articles about similar people at the company, helping the prospect build a nest of brand perception that drives application and hire.

There was a time when we hunted for food this way, too. We stalked game across the plains or in the forests, with each successful kill providing great meat for the tribe. And while meat is delicious, deriving a majority of your nutrients and calories this way is a tough way to live. You exist in a feast and famine model, where you have more than you can eat one day and not enough the next, depending on your ability to hunt and the availability of animals around you.

Recruiters know that even if they stumble across a pod of great talent, say a cluster of great sales managers or consultants, they can only hire one. There's literally too much talent one day, but they all disappear in time for the next requisition, requiring the hunter/

recruiter to start from square one each time.

As a business, it is hard to commit to growth, new clients, deliverables, locations, competencies, and products if you can't rely on the talent who make them all happen. Recruiting is the team designed to ensure there's enough talent to meet business demand, but they alone can't predict feasts or famines.

Which is why humans eventually stopped hunting for most of their food and learned to farm the land. Rather than hunting and hoping to chance upon talent, they planted it and cultivated it. We developed systems that supported its effective and efficient growth. We designated the area of our land where only farming occurred. We domesticated animals not for food, but to help us cultivate that land. Sure, if animals were available, we still hunted, but the availability of food we raised ensured that famines were far less common and we could count on that food when we needed it.

The top of the recruiting funnel suggests that "food" just shows up. As a sheep or a bison wanders by, you grab it and eat it. The animal simply appears, is suddenly in the area, and you decide to hunt it. You become opportunistic, taking advantage of good opportunities, never actually thinking about where those opportunities come from, why they happen, or what you can do to create more opportunities. At best, you can pack up your tribe and try to follow the herd of food, but really, it simply exists and you react. You don't need to feed the bison. You don't need to teach sheep to breed and grow. You simply take what you can find and process it.

That means that the recruiting funnel moves in one direction: Things come into the top. You process them down. The world spins, things happen, and eventually you reap the outputs. In a space where talent is abundant, there's no need to do anything more than pluck it from the land. This is how recruiters worked for decades before you: posting ads and waiting for the applications to arrive. It wasn't hard to hunt when herds of deer or caribou covered the landscape. The real test happened when they game was much less plentiful.

Think about what it must have been like when the abundant

herds simply disappeared, where the hunting immediately became scarce, and where the drought made fruit wither. What did they do first? Much like recruiters today, they worked very hard to maximize the limited resources they had. They built tools to help them hunt faster to take advantage of when food did appear. They used more of the animal, leaving less and less for scraps. They built systems that allowed some people to do nothing but track the animal and signal food to the hunters who passed the animal back to camp for processing. They were focused on optimizing what they could, because they didn't see a way to change their own context. They couldn't demand more food show up, so they made more of what they had.

This should sound like most recruiters' lives. Relying on old-school thinking and building processes on top of them to extract more value from a diminishing supply, they don't think they have the time, resources, or agency to look up and consider a different way to live.

FUNNEL THINKING: FIND PEOPLE TO BRING TO THE TOP OF THE FUNNEL

Like those primitive hunters, it is time to start to develop farming techniques, first to mitigate the feast or famine cycle we find ourselves in, but ultimately to actually set up a system that produces more tomorrow than we could use today, to ensure that we can meet the business's demand for talent.

The way you do that is to expand your horizons and see beyond the limitations of the recruiting funnel.

The goal of the recruiting funnel is to fill the top of the funnel, not caring where people come from that fill it. That's reactive hunter thinking. A farmer thinks about what needs to be done to encourage more to happen. They are proactive, making the outcome more likely with each step.

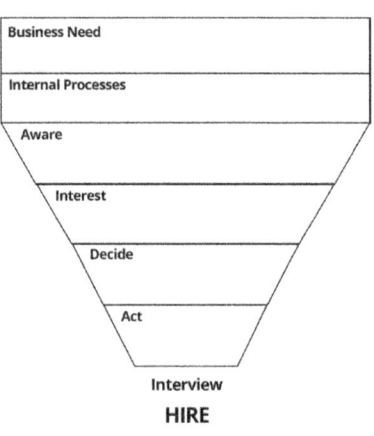

So where does talent come from?

The obvious answer is from people looking for jobs. This is a deeply transactional model: I have a job, and you need a job? Bam. Done.

But let's remember that better grades of talent aren't trolling job boards looking for these transactions. This is where more meager talent lives, because they are effectively commoditizing themselves. (If they were great, someone would have poached them well before they came on the market.) Again, if this was all you needed, you really wouldn't be having these problems.

What if we looked above the funnel?

To most recruiters this is like staring into the sun. "Above the funnel? That's not my job. That's not something I control. The job descriptions and requisition approvals appear as if by magic, and I process them to the best of my abilities."

But above the funnel is where the game rules get set, so we need to spend some time thinking about where they come from, because they are a huge function of recruiting success. Let's start by saying that this conversation occurs independently of the team and process your company has built in order to create approved requisitions. In some companies they come from the head of HR, from others they come from the HRBP or even the hiring manager directly. It might even involve executive approvals or information from your compensation and benefits team. Let's take your process and call it the process, regardless of how many people and steps it takes and move forward (I'm trying to help you hire, not reinvent HR as a process, thank you).

So what happens when a requisition comes through that says "We need an amazing nurse, and we're willing to pay 70% of the standard wage for that person."? Or, "We need an electrician who has an MBA."? Or even, "We need to hire ten experienced salespeople in Topeka in the next 60 days, despite the fact that no one in Topeka has any idea who we are."? Depending on your process, none of these things are surprising. But where do these requests come from? They come from a business need.

There's a saying in marketing: When someone comes in asking for a ½ inch drill bit, they don't actually want a drill bit. What they really want is a ½ inch hole. Take it a step further. What they really want to do is hang a painting or mirror. Seth Godin goes as far to say they don't want to hang a mirror, they want the feeling of having completed a project, or want to get someone off their back, but for this conversation, we can focus on what the purpose of the hire is.

So when someone says they want one of these impossible hires, what they are doing is reacting to a business need. When they ask for a cheap nurse, they are reacting to imperfect information about the nursing labor market, perhaps because they haven't had to hire a nurse in ten years and somehow think what they paid then is still the going rate. Perhaps they need an electrician who understands a P&L statement, because that person will be managing a line of business and assume you need a full MBA to do it. Maybe the business sees an opportunity in Topeka to sell their products and worry that not moving fast means the window on that opportunity will close. Perhaps one or two sales people immediately will help sate their appetite as you spend longer filling out the rest of the team.

The business has a business need and demands the talent to fill that need. The recruiter can take the request and work to fill it, but that makes them an order-taker, someone who does what they are told. Are you an order-taker? Do you want to be surrounded by order-taking recruiters? Of course not. That kind of position says you don't have much skill or experience beyond knowing how to write an InMail or navigating the ATS. Maybe that's true as an entry-level recruiter, but I would suspect that a pro like you brings a lot of information to the table that this process doesn't leverage.

For example, you know what wage you need to pay a nurse to get anyone who can spell RN in the door. You know there are probably ten electrician MBA people in the country and have a good sense of what it would take (salary, title, bonus, opportunity package, etc.) to woo them over, or even what it might look like if you found an electrician who had managed a business before, or an MBA candidate who has spent time in an electrical components company in the past. You might suggest a single immediate hire in Topeka to extend the timeline to something reasonable, or suggest what kind of signing bonus it would take to make ten salespeople accept your offers that quickly.

You're an expert, a consultant. You understand the talent market better than they do, more than likely. You need to find a way to inject your expertise into the business need process as it comes together. That's how you begin to reject the frame of "order-taker" and showcase your ability as a consultant to make a far greater impact.

But the business need is only one of the things that makes the requisition happen. There are a lot of HR processes that get brought to bear before the approved req lands in your lap. Yes, compensation and benefits are a part of it, but you need to think bigger. Where is this job going to live (organizationally and geographically)? What's the title and level? What are the experiences, skills, and certifications that will be required, and which will simply be "nice to haves" that will determine the size and quality of the potential talent pool?

All of these decisions have a clear and direct impact on a recruiter's ability to fill the role. Every single one of them directly impacts how many people will see, consider, and apply for the role. Every. Single. One.

Give the requisition an insanely complex and "understandable only to people who work inside the company" title, and no one will look at it. Defining the role as being based in a given city or forcing someone to come into the office every day is a very different talent search than one with work-from-home or remote work options. Hiring someone at a manager level or director level has clear implications when trying to attract someone who has experience in larger organizations. The very text of the job posting can double or halve the number of people who respond to it.

A good recruiter can't let other people make all those decisions in a vacuum, not when the recruiter has expertise. You need a means to influence and shape the role and how it is positioned and communicated to the world to have any chance of success.

Full disclosure, accepting this new view of the world, means that a good recruiter is now accepting more responsibility and work in the hiring process. At least, initially. But that's the investment you need to be willing to make to make your world better. Prepping the soil and planting seeds in the sun is back-breaking work, but it yields long-term benefits.

The goal isn't to ask recruiters to do all the work. The goal is to start to shift from seeing a recruiter's job as recruiting to seeing it as playing a vital role in hiring, a process that every element of the company needs to support.

Yes, the recruiter asking to be a part of the framing and approval process for the requisition is using time they probably don't have. No, most recruiters are not trained copywriters who can turn any job posting into poetry. The shift, much like the hunters becoming farmers, will feel awkward and unnecessary at first, as you begin to develop skills and use your resources in places you aren't used to. But it won't take long before a recruiter's influence will support their work farther downstream. By eliminating more and more of the "crazy" requests, less time is being spent hunting for the impossible. By helping shape and frame roles before they go like on job boards, recruiters are ensuring that people are more likely to listen and consider the opportunity. Smart work above the funnel makes less work closer to the bottom.

Less work doesn't mean more time at the foosball table, but it does mean focusing less on the work of moving candidates through the ATS or facilitating them through the interview process and more on building relationships with people who haven't even entered the funnel.

As we discussed, great talent doesn't want to apply. It wants to build relationships with companies (and the people within those companies) to begin to understand what the brand offers. That process, from the candidate side, takes a lot of time. No one wants to feel rushed as they make a life-changing decision. Recruiters, positioned to understand the brand as a whole and particular roles in the specific, will become the perfect connection between the prospect and the brand. Recruiters can share stories, articles, videos, facilitate informational or informal interviews, and remind prospects of events and other educational opportunities, giving great talent a chance to make a decision based on the most amount of information and a timeline they drive.

In sales, this might be called account management. Sales people may be measured on their output, but they know that sparking and nurturing relationships is how real sales get done. Recruiters can follow suit. And I'm about to show you how.

BUT FIRST: WHAT IS A JOB?

There's no doubt that asking, "What is a job?" seems like a strange question. But as the core unit of measurement, coin of the realm as it were, we should at least define it. Not as in, "the thing you do to make money" but as a recruiting concept. In your own role, you are expected to find someone who can be hired to fill a job, to get someone to come in and do "the job," but what exactly is that?

There was a time not long ago when most jobs were well defined. Everyone knew what the accountant did. Everyone knew what the assembler did. Everyone knew what the tool and die guy did. Everyone knew what the janitor did. Each person had an assigned role, and they did that role. There were government entities who, with the help of HR leaders around the country, defined every job: This is what a nurse does. This is what a computer programmer does. This is what an office manager does.

When I was in high school (late 1980s), as part of finishing 10th grade, they made us look at a book of career definitions and said, "It's time to start thinking about your future, so pick two interesting jobs and write essays on why you would want to do that job." The book itself was years old at the time, suggesting that jobs just… were. The assumption was that having picked one, you would pick a school that would qualify you for that job and put you on the path to your adult life.

I'm not talking about "the days before people had goofy job

titles," but a time in which you could look at any company's org chart, pick a box at random, and have a solid understanding what they did and accomplished all day, because everyone shared a common understanding of what a machinist, salesperson, and truck driver (and pretty much everything else) was.

These days, that feels outlandish to the point of being laughable. Someone defined a job? And that definition existing long enough to exist in a book, one a high school could have on hand and still have presumed validity? Tell me another one!

We live in a time when our roles change on a very regular basis. We're expected to learn new skills, expand our ability to make an impact, and rethink our role every year, every quarter, and sometimes every week. How you described what a "data scientist" or "marketer" or "office manager" did on a daily basis two years ago would get them fired today for lacking the ability to create value.

But that book I paged through in high school was built on descriptions of jobs that HR could use to request applications. They could build a library of jobs to be tapped as new roles opened. And recruiters were expected to leverage these descriptions when finding appropriate candidates. It was a way of making sure they were comparing apples to apples, not apples to fine art students, with a background in film and a penchant for telling blue-collar stories, who wanted to crack into marketing.

Job descriptions, the legal and HR-driven descriptions of what the job is, exist to protect the company against lawsuits from people who didn't get the job or were fired. They say things like "must be able to carry 25 pounds" to allow themselves the ability to reject or hire people with physical disabilities.

As the world becomes more (and more) fluid, our ability to develop and think about job descriptions hasn't budged, which would explain why 98% of all job postings are atrocious. The job description is trying to describe a future state despite the fact that its current state is barely understood, and it will certainly change every day. It's like trying to chart the shape of a wave from the beach: We're at the wrong perspective to see it clearly, it is moving too much to really understand it, and the medium we chose isn't really suited for this type of thing.

We're trying to advertise for a position that will soon be changing using a medium that doesn't change. The math will simply never add up.

The job descriptions are no more designed to attract candidates as a manual is designed to get you to buy a television, so we build job postings, which don't have the same kind of legal concern as a description. But that's really hard when, at best, we end up describing the job how we think our parents would have seen it from a distance. (Try reading most job postings as if your elderly mom was trying to sound like she knew what any of the words meant, and suddenly it makes a lot more sense why these postings are so bad.)

The obvious end result of trying to build useful, effective, and attractive job postings based on these horrible descriptions is that no one wants to tackle an impossible task, and when they are forced to do so, they use the least amount of effort (and honestly, who can blame them?) As the most important tool in attracting talent, it's no wonder recruiters have such a hard time finding applicants. On almost every level, they are building talent strategies on a foundation of sand.

The "average" talent process (business need to hire) takes about three months. A lot can happen in three months. For example, how much did the business need change between the day the hiring manager asked their HR person to open a requisition and the new hire started? How much did the industry expectations change in that time? How much did the job change? Think about the job of a warehouse worker, a job we assumed would always be needed, and how introducing a few robots onto the floor to help move materials around changed this belief. Before the robot, people moved stuff. After the robot, they needed to be more precise to accommodate the robot. Before the robot, their job was based on how many orders they could fill in a day. After the robot, they get a raise for thinking of process changes that allowed the robot and person to work together more smoothly. The job is almost completely different in the space of weeks and months, so the person you thought you were looking for when the business need appeared isn't at all the person you hired.

The concept of a job isn't "pilot" or "mechanic" or "sales rep." All jobs should have the same root job description: create value for the company. How they create value will evolve as the needs change. The ability for the mechanic to replace a broken belt on a motor may be what the job was on day one, but by day 90 the job might be focused on implementing tools that predict when the belt is worn and needs replacing before it fails on the job site. It might be about training crews on how to maintain equipment to make failures less common. It might be about inventory control systems and fuel usage and building relationships with vendors to get the best pricing. The mechanic is still driving value for the company leveraging mechanical knowledge, but he or she isn't replacing as many broken belts. The value of the question is bigger than belt quotas, and it expects the employee to see more ways to add value.

So when you're hiring a mechanic, are you asking for the fastest changer of broken belts? Is that what the job is today? And more importantly, is that what the job will be tomorrow? The job doesn't change because of circumstances beyond our control. It also evolves because the people who are doing the job change. I've met people in every walk of life who can lament that their job is too rigid and unwilling to embrace new thinking. Maids, DMV employees, sales reps, and HRBPs (yes, even them) see how they can grow their job to better support the organization. They want access to better tools that extend their ability to create value, to streamline or reinvent outdated processes that increase their productivity, to automate busywork-like tasks to free people up to do deeper work. People's innate and intrinsic drive to do better and more will certainly be slowed by your outdated job descriptions, but never truly contained. So stop trying.

A job is a fluid concept. What you think it is today is not what it will be tomorrow. We should approach how we hire accordingly.

And even as the job morphs, we should evolve our concept of a "successful hire." How do you or your company define a "successful hire?" For example, is it someone who accepts the offer? Someone who shows up for their first day? Someone who makes it to day 90? Someone who gets a positive evaluation after a year? If people are truly intrinsically motivated to do more and better, could we define a successful hire as someone who is promoted? Or someone who is potentially promotable?

Think about it from an economic perspective. Every single person you hire wants a raise. Heck, most of them expect it. But if they just do their job as you defined it at the initial business need level, do they deserve one? If they do the job as you define it and don't push things forward, and if they don't create efficiencies or increase productivity, why would you give them more?

So if everyone wants a raise and it's not fair to pay people more for the same amount of work (cost of living adjustments not withstanding), everyone is now driven to push for improvements and promotions. This shouldn't be an outlier, this should be the expectation. You and your business should endeavor to never hire anyone they can't see as being promotable in the future.

This is exactly how leadership sees talent, not as cogs in a machine but as bets that have the potential to pay out at a huge rate. Maybe not every middle manager got this message, and they are trying to optimize a perfectly smooth system. Management is often motivated less by growth and more around not getting yelled at by their bosses, staff, or clients. And it's likely that most recruiters don't see things like this, which is where the friction lives.

When you hire for a role, the role is temporary, both because the role evolves and because the person doing the job will push to do the things that increase their rewards. So I ask again, how are you defining a "job?"

FUNNEL THINKING:
LEVERAGING PEOPLE TO HELP YOU
FILL THE TOP OF THE FUNNEL

Having looked above the funnel, it is now time to look down, down past the focal point of most recruiting funnels: the hire.

This is rarified air for most recruiting professionals. Their role, as has always been described to them since time immemorial, effectively stopped the moment the new hire showed up on their first day. Some recruiters show up on day one to say hello and wish the new hires well, and others may even check in on them a few days or weeks after the start date. However, even that little bit is fairly uncommon.

But below the hire is…well, the entire business. Rather think of this part of the funnel as "the stuff that happens after the hire and has nothing to do with me." Think of this as the resources and channels every recruiter could (and should) use to shortcut the typical recruiting funnel.

The people below the line have been hired. They know the

company at a deeper level than any candidate. They show up every day, suggesting some level of engagement because (or despite) they've seen the good and the bad and internalized their own reason for it. They aren't wondering how much the marketing sizzle reel reflects reality. They already know.

These are amazing untapped resources because they exist below the hiring line, a place recruiting has been encouraged to ignore, (Unless you've been invited to a lot of business strategy meetings lately. Exactly).

But all that ignorance ends now. Yay!

Internal Candidates/Developed Candidates
If we can break free from "what the book says" concept of job descriptions and embrace the idea that a job is a deeply fluid thing, the perspective of the business, HR, and recruiter must evolve as well. This means taking the development of your people seriously. Too many companies (in my experience, almost all) pay lip service to the idea that their people are their greatest asset, but they don't support their growth. The expectation is that employees must figure out their own growth path, find time to grow, and use their own money to pay for that growth. How many of you, for example, have had some sort of company policy in place to help develop your skills, but your boss wouldn't give you the time to do it?

This leads to a company demanding growth of its people, but not supporting that development. Look around. Do you even have a talent development team? If you do, is it supporting the growth an employee wants, or is it simply teaching the employee how to "manage" people (read: how to not put the company in legal jeopardy) if they get promoted. This isn't skill or personal development, it is rule socialization. It is establishing and embedding into each employee what the company (actually, HR) wants them to learn about not breaking rules.

Sounds like a "dynamic and fun work environment," doesn't it?

Take it a different way. If you needed to learn a skill, perhaps you wanted to experiment with building a chatbot that helped you screen and schedule a phone screen. There is an easy case to be made that this would save you and all the other recruiters a good deal of time every week, and the cost would not be very much. Would your company give you any time to work on it? Would they pay for an online class about how to build simple bots? Would they buy a simple software package that made the bots work? Or is it more likely that if you killed a few weeks and built it and proved its value, the company would implement it for all recruiters and thank you for it? Would the expectation be that some kind of reward (likely less than your time and resources to build and test it) would come at year end? This is a company that doesn't support growth and development, but one that takes advantage when presented with it.

There's nothing wrong with that model, per se. Great talent is naturally motivated to create that growth. But as your company isn't investing or fostering it, you've simply given that great talent a reason to leave to a place that will hire a recruiter who now knows how to build bots. The irony of that is that if you left the company, and they had to go out and replace you with a recruiter who builds bots, they'd be spending a lot more money on outside talent than if they had supported the talent to begin with. That's because the external talent will always be more expensive than the internal talent that you likely take for granted.

Talent development is labeled a "cost center" by so many organizations (assuming they even have such a team), which in itself is a pretty sad commentary on the state of most company's approaches to retaining talent. If you want talent to stay, they should give them a place to grow to. They won't want to stay in this role as you've defined it for long. So not adjusting your thinking (and policies) to suit the changing role is an invitation to leave.

Okay, okay. Enough doom and gloom. Within all this is a huge opportunity for you. If you invest and support growth, reward it appropriately, people will stay. The fastest way to make that happen is to ask recruiters to start all new requisitions with a quick search of internal talent. Where the talent development's team is always begging people to please show up and engage and grow, the recruiter has the best bait in the world: a better and more rewarding job.

The cost of hiring exceptional talent from the outside is far more than the cost of promoting from within. Yes, these people already know the team and management and politics and culture, making the path from start to profit far faster, the recruiters get to spend their time hiring more junior roles. This adjustment in focus allows your organization to hire a higher percentage of your people at entry level, allowing you to build systems (cheaper and faster on a per unit basis) that bulk hire. You can hire three entry-level folks for the cost of one seasoned employee. You can attract the best level of entry-level candidates, because you are now investing in promotion from within, giving those entry-level candidates a path to work towards, driving longer tenures at a lower level of investment.

Hiring internally and internal mobility are often hampered from within. Hiring managers see the known quantity of the internal candidate as less attractive than the potential (and usually) mythical unicorn outside the company walls. I think of the movie High Fidelity where John Cusack's character has that realization that the "new relationship" is more attractive because it's fake, because you don't really know them as well as the existing relationship. The existing relationship is imperfect: You know their flaws and have seen them at their worst. Compared to the sexy resume or LinkedIn profile, internal candidates can't compete on a head-to-head basis. That external candidate has built a profile designed to hide imperfections and show off successes. It is a kind of Kabuki theater, where they are only showing off what they want you to see and hoping you don't look too hard around the glossy picture.

Hiring managers have to ascribe proper value on the in-house talent that already knows the brand, has already been successful within the company, and seems willing to extend their tenure and spread tribal knowledge to other parts of the company. Compare that to the candidate who might be a fit and who has the potential to one day drive value, maybe. Hopefully. It's a bird-in-the-hand situation that is usually considered on the individual and transactional level, but must be supported by the company, the culture, and the strategy. The company must reward managers who hire from within.

The other hurdle are managers unwilling to let great talent go, even if it is within the company. That manager has invested in more raw talent, grown them, and is looking to reap the rewards. When some recruiter or manager comes knocking, asking them to give it up, the request isn't for the person, it is to exchange lost productivity for the team for enhanced productivity for the organization as a whole. When recognition and rewards are localized like this, fiefdoms dominate, talent isn't shared, and the cost per hire rises. The manager has to know that the second the recruiter solves a problem by filling a role from within, they will set themselves to solving the new problem of filling this junior role as fast as humanly possible. A support system that rewards based on company success and processes that help replace talent as they are moved up the chain is the only way to get manager buy-in.

Training and development can be expensive, especially without a strategic plan that supports what the company is actually doing. Instead of teaching everyone to "manage" their staff (worst case: calling it "leadership training," which is hilarious) or getting tiny incremental improvements by force-feeding them task-based skills, they should shift the entire organization towards adopting an internal-first mentality. Development of internal staff for their next job is far cheaper than having to always hire externally to replace the talent you couldn't retain.

Second-Place Finishers

Nobody likes leftovers. Not me, not my four year old, and not your hiring managers. I don't know why, but for some reason, I'd be happier to cook myself something from scratch than just reheat whatever I had last night, even if starting from scratch is more work for a meal I can't be sure I'll like.

It must feel the same for recruiters: You've got a great candidate you've already talked to, who has already been pre-sold on the brand. They know a bit about the company, and maybe even came in for an interview. Many of the people on the interview loop really liked them and were inclined to hire, but they got edged out by someone slightly stronger. The recruiter spent almost an hour on the resume review, the phone screen, and scheduling the interview. The hiring manager brought together two to four other people to talk to that person for 30–60 minutes each. Then there's the time to complete feedback and debrief. By calculating those people's

71

salary with the amount of time spent, you can quickly see that you may have already spent hundreds of dollars educating a candidate you would have been happy to hire if it weren't for that slightly stronger candidate.

But the fact that they were passed over makes them tainted goods to so many hiring managers. This is one of the few places where the fallacy of the sunk cost gets reversed: We are thrilled to toss out the other candidates, despite how much time the company has invested in them. I don't know anyone who feels a second's remorse about the time, energy, and money put into these people before we send them that worthless "thanks but no thanks" email and resign them to the circular file. And this is unique to recruiting and indicative of how we can, and should, be changing. Any business that takes that same approach of tossing out leads and buyers wouldn't be in business for very long at all.

Recruiting has long labored under the "there's always more fish in the sea" assumption. Don't worry that everyone who applies wonders if you even got their applications, because it just feels like a black hole to them. It's not a big deal to ask candidates to take time off of work and come to your office, meet people, and then take weeks to get back to them. It's fine to ask people to invest time and effort in your brand and give them nothing, no feedback or meaningful or useful information about how the candidate could have done better in return. Go take a look at job hunting forums and look at the horror stories from candidates who are ignored, ghosted, and generally treated like grist for the mill.

At the same time recruiters complain about how no one will respond to their InMails and emails. They can't understand why the industry is often held in such low regard. I wonder: Could this sentiment be the result of the recruiting industry's practice of treating each requisition as a "winner take all" situation, where the selected candidate gets an offer, negotiation, and communication while everyone else gets a form letter? It doesn't matter if you keep calling the process "dispositioned," these candidates don't feel dispositioned, they feel rejected. Would you expect those rejected candidates to say nice things about you to their networks? If you're hiring a mechanical engineer, who has more credibility: the recruiter, or another mechanical engineer? And what happens when you dispositioned their fellow engineers poorly before? How much harder does that make an already hard job for a recruiter?

If you shift gears from "disposition people however you want, there's always more people to talk to" to "talent exists in an ecosystem, so let's support and nurture that ecosystem to help me succeed" you increase your overall odds of success simply by not antagonizing people you might need to recruit in the future.

But more immediately, second-place finishers are an amazing source of talent, provided you treat them right, especially when you have to give them the news that they aren't getting the offer.

Referrals and Advocacy
I have yet to meet a company who thinks they do referrals wrong. Sure, if you look at their referral metrics, they only get 5-10% of new hires through referrals, but that's not their fault.

Other companies might know their referral program isn't working and that it isn't driving the volume of candidates they expected, but they have no idea why.

That's willful blindness. They are pretending that building a referral program the way everyone else does it will work. Spoiler: Most companies are doing it wrong, because their thinking is still stuck in the old school "I have an open role, so they should be desperate to join me" ideology instead of a "how do I get people to want to volunteer to help us here?" mentality.

Referrals are the gold standard of hiring. You know the statistics showing that referrals tend to be better hires who don't ghost you, who stay longer, who drive more value over longer tenures, and who are generally more engaged (to say nothing of how engaged a referring employee is).

Referrals are seeds that sprout in the right dirt. Build a culture in which staff don't feel like their professional needs are being met, and it's like salting the earth and wondering why the crops won't grow. But if you have a culture that reinforces a reason people should work there, if you reward people who align to that reason, and if you remind people that if they like the why, their networks might, too, then you have the beginnings of a successful referral program.

Referral program failure has two root causes: no one wants to or no one remembers to.

In a company with sagging morale and a growing culture of disengagement, no referral tool in the world will create referrals if no one is willing to suggest them. Drowning people won't grab an anvil, no matter how easy you make it for them to hold. If they are looking for the exits, they won't be suggesting that their friends and connections join in. A poor-performing referral program is a fairly obvious sign that those less-than-stellar employee engagement surveys might be right. In that case, the problem isn't your referral program, but something deeper you need to solve before you can expect anyone to send you new referrals.

If your company's culture isn't toxic and has generally positive engagement scores, the problem isn't the tool that keeps people from referring. It's the timing. Have you already announced your referral program? Did you do something semi-lavish or splashy, like your CEO making a fool of themselves in front of staff to show how committed to the program leadership is? Maybe you put posters up and sent an all-staff email. Don't tell me that all you did was build a page on the company intranet and assumed people would find it there.

That's crazy. If it's July 4 and I told you the secret to staying warm, what are the chances you'd remember that in the height of summer heat? Almost none. But if you tell a chilly person how to stay warm, they will remember and act. We launch and announce referral programs on HR's schedule, not on the staff's schedule, which is why they usually fail. This leads to the common refrain of, "I'm not sure why we're not getting referrals, so let's increase the bonuses." The effect is the same.

Alternatively, the company can invest in an expensive piece of software that no one remembers to use and becomes a budget line without value. Just because there's technology involved, it doesn't change the rules: Don't announce a generalized recruiting campaign or tool, ask a manager to ask their team (who know the team and the role) to refer someone for the specific open role as the role opens. That's how you get people to act.

And at this stage, we need to get clear about something. A referral program isn't a salary-support program. It can't be seen as a transactional way to collect bonuses. Because the bonus isn't actually why people make the referral. (If you want proof, double your bonuses and announce it the way you announced the initial program: Your referral rate won't be any higher a month later.) The bonus is a thank you, a tip or gratuity to recognize the effort. What you need to focus your messaging on is how bringing in talent helps the team, helps the company, and supports the culture around that team member. People make referrals to great companies to bring people they like into great companies. A big referral feels nice, but it creates a tension in the referrer's mind: "I get a mediocre salary increase for doing a great job, but if I bring people in, I could see thousands of bucks all at once? Shouldn't I be valued for the work I do and the work I do?" Suddenly, a great reward undermines the intention.

So don't assume the dollar figure drives action. All the messaging should be "we" focused (in the "you and us" kind of way, not in an "all of us in charge" kind of way) to pull the right emotional triggers, which you do at the right time.

Employees who refer people to you are also the ones who advocate for you. They are the ones leaving great reviews, the ones talking about how great it is working for you on LinkedIn and Blind. They like your content on social media and share it. They stoke the fire that increases brand awareness and reach. They talk to people who would normally ignore you. They help you fill the top of your funnel.

You might want that advocacy to happen organically, to be the result of such love and passion for your company that people all but break into song to tell the world. I'll be gentle and call that "unrealistic." People might be aligned to your mission, they might feel a connection to their boss and to leadership, and they might feel like they have the agency to speak up. But it is still a business, right? They might say the wrong thing and get in trouble or even fired. What might feel like a harmless little joke might be the next reason your company is in the news. The upside of sharing can get overwhelmed by massive downside, making it a lousy risk to make. People don't talk about work unless they know the rules. So make it clear where the boundaries are.

Have you looked at your onboarding process? At companies of size, there's always that one part of the process in which a lawyer shows up and all but turns into Freddy Kruger to scare the new hires. That person makes clear all the horrible things that will happen if the employee, on purpose or inadvertently, discloses something they shouldn't. Words like "fired for cause" and "lawsuit" are bandied about, giving the new hire, that eager new spirit, the clear impression that the smart play is to never speak or write anything in public ever again.

This is not how advocacy starts. That's not to say that you should ignore the lawyers and ask people to say whatever they want. You should create rules that satisfy the regulatory, legal, and communications concerns that also allow the employee to be that positive voice in the world about your brand.

Alumni and Boomerangs

Don't blame millennials for normalizing "job hopping." Blame companies who were comfortable paying external talent higher wages than internal talent for the same job. Blame those companies that would happily increase salaries to meet industry standards for incoming talent but play the "3% raise for people already succeeding in the role" game. In an effort to speed up the process of attracting new talent, these companies incentivized job hopping and made it clear that the best way to make more money was to leave.

HR wrung its hands about this publicly for years, attempting to shame people into "being loyal" without paying for that loyalty. It didn't work. Now, companies are calling job hopping "the new normal" and adjusting their talent strategies accordingly.

Twenty-plus years ago, people leaving were given the cold shoulder, told not to let the door hit them as they left, and felt like they were now dead to the company. These days, hearing stories like that paints management as defensive, petty, and unenlightened, certainly the sort of things companies try to hide on Glassdoor reviews. These are emotional reactions, certainly. The hiring manager depends on the employee to generate value and revenue and isn't always able to see discontent and dissatisfaction brewing. In a world where a better salary and a chance at deeper job satisfaction is only a job hop away, when each day is a choice, employees are reacting to bad management by walking away. Punish them for making that choice, and they'll burn you on review boards and gossip sites as they pack their personal belongings. Make them feel less than for choosing their own path to success, and they'll immediately begin crafting pithy put-downs to say to people who ask, "You used to work there? What's it really like?" (As an aside, you do realize that helping them succeed is how you keep them, right? That's become obvious? Good. Just checking.)

But it doesn't have to be that way. If people changing jobs is the new normal (see also: gig economy, freelancer nation, professional nomads), you can change how you respond to them. As you wish them well with sincerity, as you offer to give them a glowing recommendation on LinkedIn, as you suggest to grab coffee in a few weeks to hear how things are going, you are making great deposits into the goodwill karma bank.

Leaving is the litmus test for employees: This is the moment when they are going to disappoint you, and you have no clear incentive to be nice anymore. They expect you to give them shock and anger. Instead, give them excitement in their new journey and wistful regret that you couldn't keep them longer.

In return, they will repay you in multiple ways. First, this is when you should be asking for a positive review on review sites. They expected anger and you gave them cheer. That pleasant surprise turns a three-star review into a four or five almost every time. Your ability to eliminate negative reviews before they happen is the difference between a mediocre 3.4 and a stellar 4.2 over at Glassdoor.

And that positive sentiment doesn't end at the review. Your reaction will positively color their entire experience, applying some slightly rosier lenses to how they see their tenure, which will result in them saying positive things about you to their networks. Your job is to build an army of ex-employees who remember their time with you as positive, as a means of growth, as a great step in their own career. They, in turn, become your ambassadors, spreading your message to people you'd never normally reach.

Think of it this way. Your recruiter has found an amazing candidate for your role. That shiny new candidate is connected to someone who just left. You have to know that the next thing the candidate does after the recruiter outreach is to ping their colleague who will either sing your praises or pour poison in their ear.

Better yet, knowing that you left things on a positive note allows your recruiter to send a very different outreach message. Instead of a generic "I have an open role you'd be amazing at..." message, they can say, "I see that you know [ex-employee]. Ask them what working here was like. If you like what you hear, I'd love to have a conversation about how you could make a deeper impact here." Aside from having a far higher response rate, you are setting the entire recruiting process up for success by treating them as peers instead of begging them to engage.

The final positive impact is that supporting alumni positively is that you are creating the opportunity for boomerangs. Boomerangs are people who left and then come back, perhaps years later. They are the ultimate testament to what your company is like to work for, as they have no illusions about who you are or what you're like. At some point, they made a choice to grow their career somewhere else, but now they want seconds from you.

Boomerangs are worth their weight in gold. First, they know your company and how things work, so their onboarding will be a snap. They will be in a position to drive value in a fraction of the time of a standard employee. They already know your processes and people. They already know how to get things done. In fact, they might even know the hiring manager, lowering uncertainty on both sides and speeding up the hire.

Second, you don't bring boomerangs back at the same or lower level: They come back higher up. Recruiters know that the higher up the totem pole, the longer the candidate search. Anything that shortens the time to fill for more senior roles means lowering their time-to-fill rate and getting more time to do other work.

Finally, boomerangs are great, because they bring back with them experience to help expand your company's perspective. Imagine an entry-level sales rep you trained and developed. They leave after two years for another sales role. When they come back, they are bringing experience seen through your own lens: They don't just bring random experience. Those new ideas are pre-filtered through your company's own way of doing things. We've all seen new leaders without much previous internal experience or tribal knowledge start demanding that everyone do things the way they are used to. They are grafting new thinking onto an existing organization, and it will likely get rejected. Because a boomerang already knows you and has learned through you, what they bring should align and elevate, not throw things in disarray.

But if you don't invest positive feelings into your alumni, you can't make boomerangs. With so much choice out there, why would anyone come back to a place that treated them so shabbily? And if you really need them, you'll end up paying a steep premium in terms of salary and bonuses to make them forget.

INTERVIEW: TRACEY PARSONS

Tracey spent time at some of the biggest agencies in recruiting before becoming a product person for a little thing called SmashFly. There, while she spent a lot of time trying to figure out how to help employer brand and recruitment marketing managers like me do their job better, she was the unofficial evangelist for the revolution in recruiting we're living in today. Since then, she's started Parsons Strategic Consulting, going deep on candidate persona and candidate experience. And while I remain a smidge skeptical on over-indexing on candidate experience, Tracey always makes me think and often changes my mind. (It helps that she always makes me laugh.) An unassuming expert and an absolute gem of a human, she's one of my favorite speakers, clearing away the clouds of our industry to show what should have been obvious all along.

How do you define "employer brand?"

The honest expression of what it means to work at your company. It's the intersection of your company's aspirations, internal realities, and external perceptions.

What do most people get wrong about employer branding?

They rarely focus on external perceptions. Many companies fail to ask the audience they are trying to attract to their company what they believe is true, or what they feel is unique about the organization. Instead they over-rely on their own aspirations. Consequently, many employer brands gloss over the fact that work is hard. So hard that we have to pay people to come do it. Working at a company is not all sunshine and roses, but many employer brands I review and audit sure paint it that way. It's a miss because no one believes it's true.

What advice would you give?

Talk. To. Your. Audience. Do not go over-aspirational. Be honest and tell people the truth. If you can ground yourself in what's not only unique to you, you have to go the extra step to tell that story through the eyes of the employee. Your employees will be the reason you're successful and believable. If you tell people the great thing about working here is <pick any common core value>, you have to tell them what that specific core value means to you and how your team executes against that value, or it's just another word like anyone else has.

What is one surprising thing you've seen or done that worked?

For a number of customers, I've interviewed silver medalists in one-on-one settings. When I did this, I learned that what the customer thought was cool about their brand didn't matter to the audience. What the audience thought was cool about the brand, the brand didn't realize that really was their unique differentiator.

What is employer branding's biggest challenge?

Getting the C-suite to give a hoot. I think we are struggling with how to really prepare and share a value proposition on employer brand and what you can gain from a well-executed employer brand expression. I fear we have too many people sitting in leadership who still believe people are lucky to have a job at their company. We really need to start understanding and espousing that we need candidates as much as they need us. It should be more of a dance, less of a fight.

WRAP-UP

Since that was a lot of "look how everything you think you thought you knew about recruiting is wrong," it might serve if we could regroup.

It's true that modern hiring has tried very hard to not deviate in any meaningful way since the start of the industrial revolution. Why would it want to? That's when the company exerted maximum power and control over the process and outcome of the talent process, so I can understand why it would be averse to reinventing itself to reflect modern contexts.

But companies are finally waking up. They are building relationships with talent before they need to hire people. They ask more of their company to be an active part

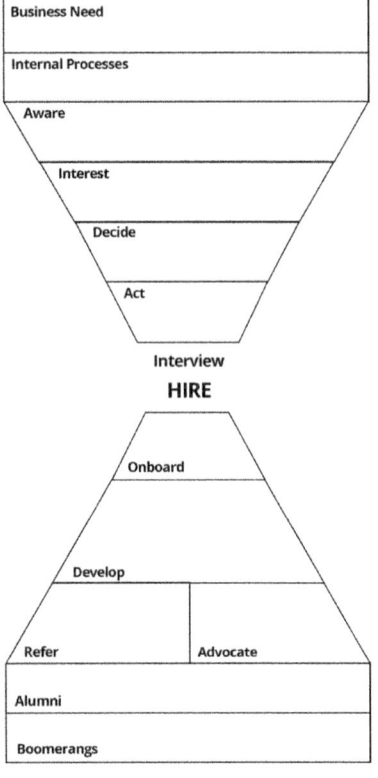

of the attraction and hiring process. They actively build advocacy for outreach rather than for compliance and reward those who build their own followings on behalf of the company.

So you're at a crossroads.

On one side is the road you've already been following. It is a well-worn path, but it leads to diminished returns and unsatisfied leadership. It leads to commoditizing the talent process and the people who oversee it. It leads to obsolescence.

But the other side of the road, the path that requires a little more work, leads somewhere else entirely. I can't even be sure I can say where your version of the path leads, as you'll end up blazing a good bit of it yourself, but I can tell you that it will allow you to engage talent that can change your company for the better, talent that has no interest or incentive to engage with the old process.

So if you're willing to trust that I and others before me have found success on this new trail, let's walk it together.

ᴇ⳹

PART TWO:
EMPLOYER BRAND THINKING

*E*mployer brand (and employer brand thinking) is the lever
that will change the recruiting and talent world. In an industry
obsessed with best-practice tactics, the coolest tool to plug in, and
a focus on filling roles without a care to long-term quality, thinking
systemically is heresy, plain and simple.

Like any good heretic, I have a healthy skepticism for doing
anything the way it's always been done, and I would ask that you do
the same. The last section should have made it clear that no one can
reasonably justify funding such a broken system. This next section
should provide a roadmap to help you dig up old thinking and see
the possibilities in front of you. Later on, you will get some tactics,
tricks, ideas, and hacks to use immediately, but first, you're going to
have to change the way you see what's in front of you.

When you change your mindset and perspective, there is a period of adjustment. I think of it like a plane taking off. Everything is smooth until you hit the turbulent cloud layer, where air temperature changes jostle the plane pretty significantly. But beyond the clouds is clear sky and smooth flying. You just have to trust that a steady hand on the yoke will get you to a place where you can really make an impact.

Ready? Super. Fasten your seatbelt. All flight attendants to their seats...

CHAPTER THREE:
DEFINITIONS AND
JUSTIFICATIONS

DEFINING EMPLOYER BRAND: WHAT IS IT (AND WHAT IS IT NOT)?

B y my measure, if someone doesn't think employer brand matters these days, the primary reason is because they don't really know what it is.

Employer brand is still very much a broad, vague, and amorphous idea to most of recruiting and business, so it becomes easy to dismiss it out of hand. It doesn't help that there are hundreds, if not thousands, of companies who label their offering as an "employer brand solution," suggesting that theirs is the one-stop shopping for implementing an effective employer brand strategy. Put ten employer brand professionals in a room and you'll discover ten different definitions. Some will see employer brand as marketing ideas applied to recruiting, some as a means to extend recruiting into something more cerebral and others just want to fill the top of the funnel. These ten people will have ten different ways of seeing, describing, and even understanding what an employer brand is. No wonder most recruiters don't really "get it." We haven't done a great job defining "it."

That's partly because the concept of an employer brand has grown exponentially in the last few years without frameworks to build upon. We all ended up taking our cobbled-together ideas and models and called it employer brand to get the ball rolling. Let's fix that now.

It's a good idea to start by defining what employer brand isn't.

It isn't about ratings sites. It isn't recruitment marketing. It isn't a web site or portal. It doesn't live on Facebook (even if you work for Facebook). It isn't a video. It definitely isn't your ATS or Candidate Relationship Management tool (CRM). It isn't your content marketing strategy. Just like a hammer, screwdriver, and saw aren't carpentry, these things are the tools professionals use to shape, direct, promote, activate, and amplify a company's employer brand.

Don't let the fact that it's easier for people to sell you a hammer than it is to conceptualize carpentry get in the way of how you perceive the job.

Definition:
An employer brand is the perception that lives in an individual's mind about what it might be like to work for you.

Employer branding answers the question, "Why would I want to work for you?" This means that an employer brand isn't something you or a vendor can own or control. It isn't a function of your org chart. Instead, it is how an individual perceives you as an employer based on myriad inputs (which we'll get into later).

As you can't get into someone's mind, an investment in employer brand doesn't dictate what the company stands for so much as how to influence people to consider new information, new stories, and new facts about the company to shift that perception.

Like a bird building a nest, an individual will build their understanding of the brand from whatever information is laying around them. That bird's nest idea will feature heavily later in this book, but for now, see the brand as being created via a million tiny choices around experiences and information that already exists, more of which is being created every day. Now realize that that's how much work goes into building a single nest, and how much work goes into building thousands of perceptions in the minds of your thousands of candidates.

Employer branding is 100% tech stack and industry agnostic. It doesn't require a budget (though a budget gives you access to tools and channels you wouldn't otherwise be able to use). It can live in any number of departments or across departments, either as an aspect of someone's job or residing in an entire team.

It can be all of these things because it isn't a tool or tactic. It is a strategy of influencing others to think positively about working for you. Which is both an oversimplification of what you'll do, but also a pretty good guideline of how much work it takes to do it right.

WHY YOUR COMPANY IS BEGGING FOR AN EMPLOYER BRANDING STRATEGY

We are in a world of staggering choice, and it isn't to your benefit.

There was a time not that long ago when people would apply almost blindly for a job. They might see an opening for a nurse, an accountant, an entry-level salesperson, a clerk, it really didn't matter. Who they worked for wasn't as important as getting the actual job. But those days are gone.

Now, if you search for a "project manager" role, you can see results from almost every conceivable company. Google is hiring them. So is Facebook. So is the Wisconsin Department of Transportation. So is a start-up. So is an architectural firm. And an ad agency. And a hospital. And a bank. Because you can find that job almost anywhere, because so many more jobs are remote-based, and because you will move for the right job, the number of jobs a person might apply to is effectively infinite. The job isn't local to the region or the industry anymore. The job is just by where the job lives: the company you'd be working for.

So with the amount of job choice for a given candidate skyrocketing, the candidate demands one thing: the information with which to make an informed choice.

Candidates with choice seek information they can rely on.

Twenty years ago, it was easy for a company to hide who they were. If you wanted to know what it was like to be a project manager at that hospital, you had to find another project manager at that hospital and ask them (and as there was no LinkedIn yet, I'm not sure how you would have found them). The hospital might have a PR team and recruiters to help say nice things about the hospital, but you didn't really know much about the realities of the job until you got there.

The business held all the information, and there was no incentive for them to open up the kimono. If your culture was toxic, it didn't take much to throw non-disclosure agreements (NDAs) at everyone to ensure that secrets stayed secret and the business could go on hiring blissfully unaware candidates into their toxic culture.

Twenty years ago, executives and managers expected to get away with sexual harassment. They expected to get away with discrimination (which is why we had to write laws making it illegal here in the US). Even when things got crazy, management could sweep things under the rug via payoffs, NDAs, legal threats, etc., and few would ever know. "Fixers" would fix things and you would never know that you were applying to enter a snake pit.

But it has gotten much harder to hide who you are. As great and cool as Uber seemed in early 2017, eventually the CEO/founder was recorded screaming at a driver. Someone else blogged about rampant sexual harassment. Stories seemed to come out every week about the bro culture and trips to strip clubs and escort clubs. To crib from Jeff Goldblum in Jurassic Park, you can't contain a company's culture. Eventually, culture will find a way of getting out. People talk.

Candidates want more than "what's the career site look like" info.

The candidate who is considering applying at your company wants to know why they should work for you. Remember, they have almost infinite choices, so you need to provide a reason. Perhaps they find an opportunity to work within such a toxic culture attractive (for all the scandals, let's remember that there were thousands of employees who were happy working at Uber, and the company has maintained a 4+ Glassdoor rating throughout the ordeal), or they were willing to overlook that aspect of the company, because it provided something they valued more. If so, this information makes the brand more attractive to those people. If not, it makes it less attractive. Ultimately, the information helps the candidate understand and decide rather than guess. Without this information, it's unclear as to what the candidate is applying for beyond "a job." Information is the fuel for decision-making and the ability to make an informed decision is what drives A and B talent to apply. A lack of information neither attracts nor dissuades C-grade people, so they will apply in higher numbers.

When the company doesn't feed talent's need for info, talent looks elsewhere.

In cases where great talent isn't applying, the go-to is often a deeper investment in ads and marketing. ("Make more haystacks!" the managers demand.) These are effective means of driving prospects to learn about your company, but if what they learn turns them off, isn't that wasted investment? If you are driving them to a weak answer to their question "why?" they won't be any more likely to apply. They won't be any more likely to engage than before, so what was the point? Ads are amplifiers, so be careful of what you're amplifying and what information you're making more people aware of.

When recruiting feels the talent pinch, they often look for better internal processing tools: a better ATS, more channels to engage on, simpler ways to disposition candidates, a faster means to screen and score applicants ("Process haystacks faster!" the manager demands.) Tools like these are great for optimization and speeding up processes, but do nothing to engage "better" talent. An A or B player isn't excited because they can now get your weak message faster and as a text message. They aren't going to apply simply because you made the application process faster. In fact, a faster and easier application process often attracts C-grade players— people looking for just any old job will appreciate the ability to apply at more places in less time, since all that matters is getting some job, not necessarily getting this job.

When talent migrates away, everyone thinks the answer is

money. But the answer is rarely money.

And there's the question of money. Assuming C-grade talent are mostly interchangeable parts in a big corporate machine, they will command an average salary for average work. In fact, the more interchangeable they are, the more you can push costs down (commoditized goods and services are always a race to the bottom). But if you are looking for a better grade of talent, you might assume that the only answer is to raise the compensation.

Yes, people with skills and expertise should expect to be compensated for the value they bring to the table, but salary is only one means of compensation. If two people make $50,000 a year, but one worked 60-80 hours a week and one works 35, are they paid the same? If they make the same salary but one is feeding a personal passion, or their personal mission aligns to yours, or you are helping them become famous in the space, or you offer more flexibility and remote work options, the salary you may offer is the same, but the value the candidate derives from it is radically different.
Successful companies give candidates two crucial things: enough information to make a decision and a reason to apply.

This isn't about adding "benefits" like remote work and flexible schedules. Work that supports the employee's own "why," where they feel better aligned to the company because they have the same why, the feeling that comes with feeding one's own personal motivations, is powerful stuff. It attracts a high level of talent, who are willing to miss out on what premium their skills might drive in other companies. That is, if they feel like they are doing something worth doing, they won't demand to be paid what a Google or Facebook might be willing to pay them. They will take a salary far closer to the median because they are getting a bonus of professional and personal satisfaction.

And as we will soon see from the employee perspective, salary and compensation are only part of the picture when weighing a job offer.

Which leads us to a deeply unpleasant truth: It's a good thing great candidates care about more than money, because you can't win the money game. Unless you are Google/Facebook/etc., one of those companies seemingly able to print money as needed and have no fear of offering salaries at the bleeding edge of the curve, you can't spend your way out of the problem to hire real talent.

From the employer side, the case for employer brand can be summed up thusly: Companies who value a higher grade of talent, but don't want to spend more money begging them to apply and don't have to have to pay too high a premium for their skills will see that a more clearly understood and communicated "why" will help them reach their goals.

INTERVIEW: DEBORA JOHNSON

I got to spend a lot of my agency time with Debora. My team delivered a lot of employer brand activation to her clients. And while clients are always picky, Debora is a different breed. She could see things that weren't exactly right, twenty paces away. She could see how not delivering perfection today would lead down the slippery slope to mediocrity in short order. It's not perfectionism, it's that she's got an eye for what's simply "correct." I look at it as a clarity of thought and approach that I find absolutely amazing, let alone uncommon. Currently, Debora manages the employer branding side of one of the best known consumer brands in the world. It is a daunting task, but honestly, I can't imagine anyone else at the reins.

How do you define "employer brand?"

Employer brand is how an organization brands and markets itself as an employer of choice, with its north star being an employer value proposition (EVP), which is the articulation of the company's purpose, vision, brand, benefits, and culture that creates an overarching sense of belonging and fulfillment of the employee's needs during and beyond their employment.

What do most people get wrong about employer branding?

Creating an employer brand without a plan to ensure it evolves with the company culture. A lot of times it is viewed more of a creative campaign that gets developed and pushed as a one-time branding campaign for external talent. There needs to be a robust internal activation, internal and external sentiment monitoring, and recalibration to ensure authenticity and connection to the employer experience. Otherwise, it's just another branding campaign for external recruitment.

What advice would you give?

Ensuring you have the right people at the table to effectively develop the unique EVP for your organization. Creation of a project team that allows insight and collaboration from HR, Marketing, Communications, Design, and employees creates an authentic employer brand that the organization can embrace. It is also important to have an influential executive sponsor that is connected within the organization and understands the company culture. And lastly, be open to insights and feedback throughout the organization to ensure you've encapsulated the employer experience.

What is one surprising thing you've seen or done that worked?

My favorite part of the employer brand development is showcasing the employee experience and meeting all the exceptional people that are so passionate about their work. I find that a lot of organizations tend to showcase the same employees, and internally the employer brand is viewed as more of a corporate PR campaign. When I select employees, I randomly select employees based on their experiences and background, which can articulate the tone and themes of the EVP. I don't do a lot of prep for the employees prior to a photo shoot but do spend a lot of time prepping the agency and photographers, showing them how to put the employees at ease and ensuring they keep the employee talking during the shoot by asking what they love about the company or projects they've had the most success with. When people talk about what they love and feel a sense of appreciation for, it creates this magic on camera and lets them be their authentic selves.

What is employer branding's biggest challenge?

Ensuring that the employer brand is connected enough to the consumer brand but still creates its own identity within the organization to inspire current employees and attract top talent to the organization. With a consumer brand you create a brand perception to create or satisfy a need or want. With an employer brand, it has to be authentic to the brand and the organization, because you have a whole organization of experts that can refute its authenticity.

WHY YOUR RECRUITERS ARE DESPERATE YOU INVEST IN EMPLOYER BRANDING

We have to come to terms with the fact that the "standard" means of recruiting is deeply flawed. That is, a recruiter, posting a job opening far and wide, collects 50-250 applications from people willing to engage at some level around a poorly described role in a company they may not know much about. That recruiter skims the resumes and runs phone screens on dozens of them to find 3-5 people worth bringing in for an interview, an interview driven by the hiring manager, who has a very loose (or even tenuous) interaction or collaboration with the recruiter. Despite not knowing what the job market looks like, the hiring manager may demand better candidates or suggest the starting comp be pushed up or down. The candidate, getting only the tiniest trickle of information about the job or company from overworked recruiters and hiring managers, looks for whatever scraps of information they can glean and is asked to make a life-altering decision without having much information.

Recruiting is begging and baiting strangers to trade their attention and time for a chance to talk to another unrelated stranger to potentially win a job that may or not make their life better.

Neither the candidate nor the recruiter or hiring manager is able to make smart decisions because no one has enough information. The only people who like this process are vendors who can sell tech to support a broken system and make it marginally less broken. And while tools and technology look to make this process slightly faster or smoother, they support the underlying broken process, and thus can have only limited impact. It's like putting a spoiler and racing tires on a Camry. Sure, it'll make it faster, but it's not going to be able to compete with a Porsche, let alone a Formula One racer.

Get a good recruiter a little tipsy and even they will admit that it's a rigged game that no one likes. It puts them in a situation where they are the unwitting bad guy, making neither their candidate nor customer happy. And yet, here we are.

If you reinvented recruiting today, it wouldn't be about ATS and job postings. It would be about building relationships. There isn't a recruiter alive who enjoys working within their ATS. They do it because the business told them they have to and that it is the only way to process candidates at scale. This is only true if you're always processing blind strangers and not trusting any of the information in the application, which is how most companies operate.

Recruiters should be focused on building relationships with hiring managers to better understand the role they are trying to help fill, what success looks like, and how to help plan for the next hire. They should be focused on building relationships with prospects and candidates and learning more about potential applicants, well beyond what is put in a resume in anticipation of that opening materializing. Instead, we make them run on treadmills that go nowhere while yelling at them.

Recruiters love employer brand (once they see it isn't a tactic, trick, or tool of the month) because it moves them away from being order-takers, subservient to the hiring managers' whims with open requisitions, and becoming consultative talent experts. Employer brand makes recruiters more successful.

WHY CANDIDATES AND PROSPECTS NEED YOU TO INVEST IN EMPLOYER BRANDING

E mployer branding isn't just something that businesses and recruiters should see value in. It is something that your candidates, especially those with higher levels of talent, want you to invest in. In fact, they are desperate for it.

In less than twenty years, the world has been upended. Technology, which at first meant everything could be a little faster and easier, has begotten huge changes across almost every element of a business. The current wave of tools allows us to sleep in strangers' homes, drive in strangers' cars, invite strangers into our own homes to build furniture, and work from wherever we want in the world 24/7. Technology isn't just the supercomputer in our pocket, it is the means of commodifying trust, so I can sleep in a stranger's home or let a stranger drive me somewhere. It is communities on call 24/7. It is on-demand entertainment of every variety. It is the ability to put our kids to bed a continent away.

That much change has also changed us. In an ever-evolving set of options, we have grown to expect a near-infinite number of choices in every industry, space, and place. We demand it. (Think back to the last time you got your driver's license or passport renewed, and you saw all the ways technology could obviate your need to stand in an endless line to have your picture taken or to answer questions whose answer already exists in some other database.)

But the ability to make a choice assumes we have enough

information necessary to make that choice. This is our life, not to be determined by the flip of a coin. This is a time when you can know exactly where your coffee bean was grown, you can locate a rating on that seller from Amazon and Etsy, and you can do a complete house tour and see tax records about that house you're thinking about buying before you engage a real estate agent.

So why would anyone expect us, the people who expect choice and the information on which to base it, to put our collective heads in the sand when it comes to our next jobs? If I can know the name of the farmer who grew all the cacao beans for my chocolate bar, if I can know how many trips my driver has made and what their rating is before I step into the car, why can't I know about the company I may be considering working for?

We're not talking about the self-serving, spintastic information that a company's marketing and communications teams generate about themselves to present themselves in the perfect light. Everyone knows that while they are giving facts, they rarely tell the whole story and are paid to present a self-serving narrative. No one's angry at that, but no one believes the marketing team is providing anything like "the whole truth." In the same way that if you understood cars purely from their commercials, you'd think every car is best in class, is stocked to the gills with tech to make you safer than you are in your own home, will make you feel great, will keep the kids happy, and probably isn't as expensive as you think it is. Which is why we read a lot of reviews and talk to friends and family before spending a second in the car lot. Marketing is great at getting attention, but it rarely gives us enough information to make a decision.

It doesn't matter what the ratings of the drivers are. You can't choose between Uber vs Lyft to get to the airport unless you know what the costs are going to be. It doesn't matter how pretty the space is. You can't pick between Airbnb options unless you see where they are on the map. Companies offering jobs who work hard to stifle or limit the information going out about them and their reputation aren't going to succeed like the ones who are willing to open up. Because that's what A- and B-grade talent want: to make a choice with all available and relevant data at hand.

Companies can't pretend they can hide. When a candidate wants that information, it's already out there. Not just on Glassdoor and other ratings sites, but on Google, and in the minds of people we know via LinkedIn, friends, and family.

The desire for candidates to have access to all potentially useful information tends to stop just short of questions regarding salary. Should the company be making salary ranges for a role available to job shoppers? Doesn't that lead to talent jumping ship every time they see a new higher salary? If the goal is to attract talent by giving them the ability to form a more complete and clear picture of what working here might mean for them, wouldn't open salary ranges lead to price wars and bidding? Does that effectively lead to an end of everything employer brand thinking was supposed to manifest?

Those questions are valid, if we assume all people work to maximize their paycheck. But if all that were true, we'd all run hedge funds. It is far more common for people to seek to maximize our lives in the broadest context. That means, making sure the choice we make allows us to feel fulfilled, both personally and professionally, in whatever way we measure those objectives.

To build relationships, no matter how transactional, you need information on which to make decisions. You can't build relationships unilaterally or blindly. Weed out people who don't fit (like those seeking to maximize their salary when the company pays roughly the average, or the people who are driven by freedom and opportunity while you are in a deeply regulated industry) and find the people who do. Connect to what candidates care about and show how you can offer it to them.

Think of it this way. Assuming you got paid something fair (roughly the median for the industry and location), would you rather take a job that let you go home at 5:00 p.m. every day or one that paid you 10% more? Would you take a job that was invested in your development and growth (tuition reimbursement, professional certifications, dedicated development budget, etc.) or one where you got a 10% higher salary? Would you rather work for the company that surrounded you with a great and supportive team or one where you made 10% more? What about a shorter commute? Remote and flexible work? What about a company with amazing maternity, paternity, and parenting benefits?

Yes, some people pick solely on the basis of maximizing their salary. But just some. And those people were always motivated purely by money and the motivation it feeds. People who give up a short commute and a supportive team for a 10% raise were always going to demand the high end of the scale and push for raises and promotions as soon as possible, no matter what job they took. So even if they were talented, were they ever going to choose you? If they chose you, would they have stuck around when they realized they could make ten cents more somewhere else?

People have a number of different motivations, and they aren't all money-driven. In fact, most people would happily lose the 10% salary bump to get something beyond a paycheck at the end of the day. These people are looking for something that makes them happier and more satisfied. They might not take a 10% cut to get it (people are deeply averse to giving something up, far more so than not getting it in the first place) and they might not be willing to be paid far below market value for it, but they would willingly choose it if they knew they could pay their bills and satisfy a deeper need within them.

Do you think people working at nonprofits are fools? Are school teachers idiots? They are if salary is the only measure of job satisfaction, but what if you're saving the world—in whatever means you interpret that? If you knew you were making a fair salary, would you forego a 10% bonus if it meant making the world better for your kids or for something you believed in? Smart and talented people make that choice every day, so the question isn't "why would someone do that" but rather "how can I leverage this idea and get people to work for me when I don't offer that salary premium?"

Transparent salary ranges are not a way to compete for the most valuable person, but a way to show your cards and prove that you are paying a reasonable salary while you make a pitch for something more, something beyond total compensation. Without that validation, you'll come across as someone trying to sell magic beans. You can't expect talent to engage with you when you only offer magic beans.

The more information and transparency you offer, the more credible you become and the more willing someone becomes to consider your brand promise as they make their choice. But their level of choice is determined by their level of talent. If someone is amazing at something companies want, there will be lots of choices. If they are a commodity-level C-grade player, there will be far less choice. The incentive for someone to become amazing at something is that they have more choices and options.

But talent can't take advantage of those choices if employers won't provide enough credible information on which that choice can be based. And as someone with choices, they will choose one of the many other competitors who know what they offer, what they stand for, and prove it day after day.

A WORLD OF RELATIONSHIPS: YOU DON'T HOLD HANDS WITH STRANGERS

The kind of evolution that comes from embracing employer brand thinking is a shift that starts as a transactional-driven recruiting model (putting butts in seats) and becomes a relationship-driven model. And while "relationship-driven" seems like a pleasant enough term, we need to see what it would mean for recruiters in how they approach their work and how it will impact hiring managers and the rest of the business.

Most of modern recruiting relies on the "post the job, review the applicants" model of recruiting. It works in so much as it has always worked: as a matter of convenience for the recruiter and the business, where the job could be posted and reviewed asynchronously, once a number of apps rolled in. In a world where having a job was the most important currency, job applicants were asked to follow some basic rules: Watch job boards for openings, apply as prescribed, and wait days or weeks for the recruiter to go through the applicants. Recruiters, in turn, identify potential candidates, treat the applicant as a complete and total stranger whose application is deeply suspect, and take 4-6 weeks to screen and interview all relevant applicants before deciding on one and offering a job to them.

See how all the power of this process is on the recruiting side? The candidate applies in the manner as they are told (attach a cover letter, send salary expectations, give references, complete this equal opportunity survey, etc.). They should expect to wait days or weeks before being given a blanket rejection statement that says nothing of value. God forbid they try to contact the recruiter before being contacted, or engage with any other part of the business. Applicants do as they are told and wait their turn while being processed like so much grain through a mill.

Aside from the fact that every book written in the last 30 years about the job search recommends avoiding such processes whenever possible—with advice like build a network of people to help get your name to the hiring manager and do everything you can to bypass the applications and recruiter—this machine only works when the company has all the power. But over the last decade, things have changed. Try to dictate a process to someone who is an expert at your coding language, or has years of success in their field and watch them walk away. They are choosy. They get to ignore your processes that exist only to serve you and not them.

The end result is that the people being brought into the interviews via this machine aren't the best talent. They are those who were trolling job boards when you posted, who followed the rules and couldn't figure out a smarter way into the interview. There's a joke here about having to pick among people who apply is often like having your fate determined by people who couldn't figure out how to get out of jury duty, but I'll let you put it together yourself. Like an IKEA "JÄKE" you assemble on your own. Their talent isn't in doing the job. The people we often hire are because of their talent in getting the job.

And when these people show up in the interview, you can tell in a heartbeat that most of them haven't given anything more than a cursory glance at your website or spent more than five minutes researching you. And yet you as a recruiter maintain the facade that their lack of effort is acceptable, so long as this person is qualified enough to put in front of the hiring manager.

It makes recruiting a kind of sitcom rerun, where the same lines are repeated to the same people and nothing ever seems to change: The applicant puts forth their best possible career history, and the hiring manager keeps trying to peek behind it. No one knows much about the other, because there's just not enough information on either side, thus forcing recruiters to be professional divining rods, predicting who will be a fit and who won't, based on little more than a sense or hunch. No wonder companies have a 30% attrition rate for new hires: Decisions are based on nothing.

Recruiting, in response, has attempted to bend a few processes (texting as a means of communication, an expectation of feedback from an interview, a commitment to no "black holes," etc.), but the machine remains the same. Every time a hiring manager wants to hire, they proceed from square one with a list of people who happen to be looking at job boards the month your posting goes out. The process from business need to offer acceptance can take months. It demands recruiting throws out the baby with the bathwater, sending second-place candidates the same blanket "thanks but no thanks" email they send to people who couldn't even spell their own name right on the application. The process is broken, but there is a solution.

What if you collected candidates before you needed them? This isn't some sorcery of workforce planning or precognitive magic. This is about building relationships with people who might one day make for a great candidate. In sales, this isn't so much a new idea as the way things have been done for years: It takes time to get someone to learn enough about you and for you to learn enough about them to find a match, so rather than trying to force the issue, take your time, but do it before the clock starts ticking.

What would that look like from a recruiting lens? Well, one or two hours of every recruiter's day would be spent talking to and engaging with interesting people without an agenda. That might mean a tech recruiter reading and sharing an interesting article on data science with the data science communities they are a part of (Facebook and LinkedIn, for example). It might mean reaching out to people in their space who have made interesting comments or posts and saying how impressed the recruiter was. It might mean following potential prospects on social media. It might mean answering questions on Quora. It might mean collecting lists of great articles and sharing them en masse. It's the business of building relationships with people online, something recruiters should be comfortable doing already.

As part of that relationship building, recruiters would also be sharing content about the company. That might include blog posts, images, articles, and white papers. This isn't the same as sharing jobs, which is transactional. This is sharing useful information to people who would get value out of it. Connected to all this content sharing would be a way for people to raise their hands and say they are interested in getting even more information about the company. Again, this isn't about getting applications. This is the process of turning strangers into leads, warming those leads over time, and helping those prospects understand what the company is all about before anyone reaches out for an application.

The result of building a pool of warm prospects is that when the hiring manager has a requisition approved, the recruiter might have a great candidate in their pocket that very moment. This would be a candidate who's already seen the employer brand video, already read profiles of successful managers within the building, understood the kind of research and production being done, and seen the awards and maybe even a simplified version of the benefits package. They are candidates who have built a relationship with the recruiter, know what the company has to offer, and are still interested in engaging.

The knock-on effect is not just that recruiters have ready-made candidates, but that they have a network within the industry, people they can tap and ask to spread the word of a new opening, people who can speak positively and authentically about the company in a way that a recruiter can't. If you want to reach nurses, don't ask a recruiter who hires nurses, administrators, orderlies, non-medical support, and other recruiters. No, if you want to reach nurses, ask a nurse who knows lots of other nurses. If you have that kind of network developed, you can eliminate the cold outreach that seems to define desperate recruiting these days. But you need to develop that network before you need to leverage it. You can't eat if you just planted. You need to plant months before you get hungry.

Even if the recruiter can only fill one in ten new roles this way, it would cut the time to fill numbers dramatically. Success will breed success and recruiters will spend more time building relationships and less time pitching to strangers.

What does this have to do with employer brand? Relationships are very hard and slow to build one-to-one. That's likely what moved us all to the "ATS/Machine" model we see today. But employer branders can facilitate content creation, ensure alignment towards a core motivation and brand promise, and are in the right spot to help manage the CRM systems that support a relationship-driven model. That is, employer brand thinking and relationship-building go hand-in-hand, supporting each other.

Recruiters will be happier and more effective, time to fill roles will drop (positives for both hiring managers and candidates), and everyone will have a far-better sense of what working there would be like.

THE NARRATIVE ADVANTAGE: STORY (NOT FACTS) CONNECT TALENT TO YOUR EMPLOYER BRAND

Stories rule the world and our imaginations, but more importantly, they are the driver of our choices. When you look at a nice watch and think about buying it, somewhere your brain wonders, "am I the kind of person who spends that much money on a watch?" This isn't crazy. This is the power Apple leverages when it launches a new product, to know that people who love Apple products are the kind of people who would buy the new thing. They don't want to be seen as missing out, or falling behind. They are willing to pay the premium (money, standing in line, etc.) to tell themselves the story about how they are on the cutting edge, that they are the kinds of people who "think different."

These stories are not strictly rational. Have you ever looked down your nose at someone because they didn't have the latest smartwatch or white earbuds? Maybe. Maybe not. But the people choosing to buy them tell themselves their own story. And more than feature set or price, the story is what drives those people to buy.

The same holds true for the jobs they take. Your job says so much about you, the same way that my job says so much about me. What job someone decides to take feeds into their own personal narrative of how they see themselves. Developers and coders dream of working at one of the various high palaces of development, so it's going to take a lot more effort to get them to consider working at your hospital or bank. Why? Because they tell themselves (and each other) the story that "great coders" work at Google and Facebook and Apple, not at a bank or hospital. And the story they tell themselves becomes the foundation of how they see the world.

It's interesting that the stories we tell ourselves drive our choices, which in turn, feed and validate the story. It's a feedback loop, a kind of self-fulfilling prophecy, one you need to break a little in order to be heard.

As Seth Godin succinctly puts it, branding fosters the idea that "people like us do things like this." People like us (recruiters) do things like this (get LinkedIn Recruiter seats). People like us (people who care about our code) do things like this (use tabs rather than spaces). People like us (arborists) do things like this (take pride in how much time we get to spend outdoors). It is the underlying thread that helps people feel like they are connected to something larger. It is the story people tell themselves as they make choices.

Money is another story we tell ourselves. We may wonder: What do I think the money I earn buys me? Security? Freedom? A better retirement? More toys? This in turn, may get us to ask: Is this what I want? What do I care about? What's really important?

Companies that can't offer premium salaries are still attracting great talent by changing the story that money tells. If the candidate thinks money buys them the chance to change the world, offer them the time to change the world as a substitute. If they see money as a means to show their success, offer them status and a platform on which to become famous. If they see money as a way to feed their own development, offer them mentorship, coaching, and feedback.

Great employer branding professionals, consciously or not, approach their jobs very similarly. They spend time wondering: What story do we want prospects to be telling themselves as they apply? Are they applying for money? Status? Opportunity? The chance to feed their side hustle dream? A career ladder? The story you tell attracts the people who align themselves to that story, reinforcing the story they tell themselves. Connecting these dots leads to higher quality candidates, better interviews, higher acceptance rates, and better talent.

Stories stick, while facts rot. Which is the biggest company in the world? Well, it depends on the moment you look at the stock market. The answer is always changing, as so many other facts change, much like people's perception of who the "best" employer in your area is, who got a big recent investment, and who won an award or made the news. These are the facts that too many companies rely on in shaping their brand, not realizing how tenuous those facts are and how little they impact candidates.

But tell a story of how much you care for your employees, how hard you work to launch a product, how successful employees become because of their time with you, and those stories live effectively forever while the facts shift under your feet. Ever see a company touting that award they won for "great employer" four years after winning it? Should that make the candidate feel positive towards the brand, because this is a company that once had the capacity to be a great employer, or negative, because those days have long since passed?

Your employer brand is the "why" in "why should I think about working here?" It is the answer to that question. It's a formula in two parts: Why should I think about working here? The two sides (the I and the here) need to be considered at the same time. Half of it is told by the company in the form of what they do and sell, how they recruit, and what stories are told to prospects (see: career site, social media, job postings, content and videos, etc.). This is the half that the company controls. It decides what stories to tell and how compellingly they are told.

The second half exists in the candidate's mind. It is how they take all the touchpoints (what their friends and networks say, news about you, interactions with your consumer products and customer service, etc.) and merge it with your story to create their perception.

An employer brand is the sum of what you project and they absorb. It is a collaboratively told story. If you insist on saying how innovative you are and they see a 10-year-old ATS, how innovative will they think you are? If you say you care about your employees, but everyone knows they work 12- and 14-hour days, what will they believe? If you say you care about women employees but your maternity leave is the legal minimum, what will they take away?

This means that in order to give yourself a chance to set the frame of your story, most of the storytelling has to happen before they apply. But that's a good thing. Talent doesn't surf job boards. They aren't trolling job postings. They are busy doing their jobs and learning how to be better. Your goal is to build such a great story that it is compelling enough to reach and impact the prospect before the recruiter even reaches out. How, where, and what story you tell should be true to the company, but it should be meaningful enough that someone not interested in learning more about you finds it interesting.

Storytelling isn't useful just as a means to attract prospects. It provides recruiters deeper tools to entice the candidate to apply, to research the company, and to accept the offer. The story becomes the lens through which all other recruiting efforts are seen, making each recruiter more effective.

THIS IS MORE THAN "CANDIDATE EXPERIENCE"

You have a dream job. I have a dream job. Everyone probably has a dream job in their minds, or, at the very least, a dream company they would love to work for. It's a company you've thought about, read about, researched, and maybe even networked towards for a long time. Maybe we have a job alert for it. Maybe we are following the company on social media. And during that time, we have built a picture of what that company is, what it offers us, and we are just waiting for the stars to align.

But what would happen if, during the application process for that dream job, you had to retype your resume into an ATS? Would that stop you from applying? What if the career site was a little outdated? What if the recruiter was five minutes late to the phone screen? Or if the office tour preceding the interview wasn't very enlightening? Or they didn't give you some swag on the way out the door? Or they took an extra day or two to get back to you with a decision? What if the offer paperwork had something wrong and had to be redone? Would any of that stop you from being thrilled to take that job?

Of course not. But we belabor the concept of "candidate experience" as if it makes someone who is deeply interested, who has researched the brand promise and value proposition, who can see how they would be a great fit and add value, who might find long-term success at that company, would balk at a wonky candidate process. Would someone who "gets you" and sees that you might "get" them reject a job if at an interview where you weren't offered water, or the interview room wasn't sleek and shiny? You don't judge the restaurant on whether or not the waitstaff gets rid of crumbs on the table between courses, do you?

If you survey candidates to ask what they wanted in an interview experience, and the clear answer was a great candidate experience. And when talent acquisition leaders hear that, they assume they need to provide some kind of "white glove" service, like the candidate was getting their Bentley tuned up or checking into a suite at the Plaza. But that's not what candidates want at all.

That kind of picture of "candidate experience" is some really shallow thinking. It shows how low the bar is. There are so many more things candidates really want, but simply don't always realize they could have. The most important thing is a feeling of connection to the brand, of understanding what the company is all about and why they want to join it. It's like asking people what they want from a prospective partner and coming up with answers like, "they shouldn't snore," or "they should be tidy." No, what you want is to fall in love with the company, to understand what the company is driven by, and know how you can help the company achieve it. You want to have an impact in a manner congruent with your own motivation.

In the face of no transparency, no understanding of the why, no clear sense of values, and a meaningless mission statement, focusing on a candidate experience might yield some results. But in the face of love and a future vision of professional satisfaction, candidate experience isn't important at all.

An amazing restaurant doesn't need white table clothes to deliver an epic and memorable meal. An amazing car doesn't have to come in your favorite shade of red to make you feel confident. A new house might be missing that two-sink bathroom, but it doesn't feel any less pride in owning that new home.

Candidate experience is what you invest in when you are too scared to talk about what you really care about. It's about creating the best window display without products to go in it.

But now you know better. You know candidate experience is helpful, but nowhere as powerful and impactful as a strong employer brand.

INTERVIEW:
AUDRA KNIGHT

Here's the problem with Audra: She smiles too much. With her purple hair and punk cover band side project (with her husband, no less), she just looks like she's having way too much fun. Way, way, way too much fun. And that's a problem, because it's easy to miss the fact that miss punk rock sunshine over there is an absolute expert at this stuff. She thinks strategically and conceptually, but her true superpower is making complex tactics look easy. She's every employer brand pro's favorite employer brand pro.

Full disclosure: Audra is the very first person to say nice things about my podcast The Talent Cast online, which led me to sharing a panel with her and going to conferences together and being on a board together, and so on and so on. So this book is at least partially her fault (and thank you again, Audra).

How do you define "employer brand?"

It is your reputation as an employer. It is not good or bad. It just is. What seems like a terrible workplace to me is the perfect company for my neighbor. There is a lid for every pot.

What do most people get wrong about employer branding?

Most recruitment content is boring at best. We are often competing with corporate and product marketing teams for a person's attention and they are winning. So many recruitment stories are generic and safe. The message is not targeted to a specific audience and meant to attract everyone. In the end, it attracts no one. More importantly, it does not provide any value to the target audience. The best content solves a problem for that audience and brings them to you (inbound marketing).

What advice would you give?

For companies, I would suggest they either hire someone with a marketing background or encourage the person(s) to take marketing courses. There are free ones online. There are also some great marketing conferences like Inbound by HubSpot.

For employer brand nerds like us, I would suggest that they know their target audience for that specific piece of content, solve a problem of theirs and then make sure they see it. I have seen some very expensive employer brand videos lie dormant on YouTube and the bottom of a Career site. And don't forget that your job postings are very important recruitment content. Most job seekers are sent to those pages from Google or job boards, by-passing your one million dollar career site. If your ATS does not allow for photos/videos to add some spice to these, then you should think of a marketing tool that does.

What is one surprising thing you've seen or done that worked?

Old school marketing can still work. We had a very nice company event and I noticed so many happy faces. I stood up in front of everyone and asked them to leave an honest review on the popular review site. Our score went way up and stayed there. Happy engaged people usually don't think about leaving a review but they often will if you just ask.

What is employer branding's biggest challenge?

Engagement, leads and hires are nice but tying the work back to revenue or solving problems of the business can be very tricky with this kind of work. That is a challenge we need to rise to and will.

COUNTERFACTUAL #1:
A WORLD WITHOUT
EMPLOYER BRANDING?

If you've gotten to this point and still aren't convinced, let's flip things around and provide a counterfactual argument: If employer branding wasn't useful and effective, no one should use it. So what would it be like if no one invested in or developed their employer brand?

First, how would candidates choose between potential opportunities? Based on the thin self-serving copy the marketing team built for talent acquisition in their space time? Based on the horribly written and non-descriptive language in a job posting or description? That's the equivalent of changing your life based on the copy that accompanies laundry soap. All or Tide or Gain? Google or Uber or the Wisconsin Department of Transportation? At least all the detergents will whiten and brighten, but those job choices won't be offering similar salaries, lifestyles, or levels of satisfaction. This is a choice with meaning.

Instead of choosing between brands, candidates won't choose at all. They will instead sit back and let recruiters come to them in droves, making pitches and offers. Recruiters, tired of using the same self-serving undifferentiated talking points, will be reduced to making up their own, anything to get a candidate to respond. This means that not only will no one be sure what candidates are being told, what they are being told won't hold water.

Those recruiters, whose work is now devalued to the point

roughly that of a boiler room call center, won't be able to show their value. So their salaries drop and businesses will start outsourcing those calls overseas. (At least this way the callers will stick to the mandated talking points.) Companies will have twice as many bodies pointed at the problem and get half the value.

Effective recruitment marketing gets more expensive to compensate. As the product gets commoditized, the marketing around it has to get more complicated, creative, and expensive to stand out. By way of proof, look at the Tide commercial from the 2018 Super Bowl. Laundry soap, the most commoditized of products, gets a celebrity spokesperson starring in a deeply creative one minute ad ("It's a Tide ad," which wasn't just expensive to ideate and film, it cost $10 million to show on the broadcast).

The result is that game-changing A-level talent never chooses you because they don't understand why they should. Their information ends up coming from formal and informal networks you can't tap into, so you're left to fight over what's left. And since to them all the jobs and companies are the same, they flip a coin to choose which opportunity to take. Your company, rightly or wrongly, is the same as any other company.

Think this is crazy? I continue to get regular outreach for jobs I can't do in places I don't live (contract, of course) based on a skill I once put on a resume 15 years ago. I bet anyone with a well-completed LinkedIn profile get these messages, emails, and phone calls, on a regular basis as well. These are spammers at best, and scammers at worst. This is the future of recruiting you should be desperately trying to avoid.

COUNTERFACTUAL #2: WOULD YOU RATHER COMPETE AGAINST A COMPANY THAT INVESTED IN EMPLOYER BRAND OR ONE THAT DIDN'T?

The second counterargument is simple. If employer branding wasn't impactful, your company shouldn't have any problem competing successfully against a company that is investing in its employer brand. In fact, one might suggest that if employer brand isn't useful, you'd have an advantage over a company spending money on their brand, because you'd have more resources free to spend on "more effective tools" like job boards and hiring recruiters.

Great! So go to a big job board. Go search for a job, something lots of companies need, like inbound sales or project management or recruiter or front-end programmer or graphic designer. Tell me how many jobs pop up and how many of those companies you recognize. How many would you trust with your work history, home address, cell number, and references?

Or go make a fake LinkedIn profile and put that you are an expert in autonomous driving cars, Hadoop architecture, blockchain, or AI. Then count to 10. That's how long it will take before a recruiter will find you and ping you with a fairly rote outreach message. And then watch the avalanche of similar messages come in fast and furious. In a week, you'll see dozens of messages, almost all of which will sound the same. (What are the odds that some recruiters have figured out how to automate this process as new people pop up on these channels?) Now go find the outreach from your own recruiters and see if you can pick it out of a lineup.

Is this how you want to compete? In the face of a tsunami of recruiters vying for your attention, is getting to the candidate faster an advantage? Is having a personalized message going to help you stand out? Is having a pretty career site going to help? Or will you only respond to brands you already know something positive about?

So let's say you beat the odds and get someone's attention and you make a pitch. Assuming you aren't a huge commercial brand (and even if you are), the next step anyone with any talent will take will be to Google/Glassdoor/Indeed you. What do people say about you? What do your employees say? What does the news say? The recruiter didn't give much to go on, except to use words like "great opportunity for someone like you" and "we have a great culture" as if those words mean anything at all.

But then you come across a company that publishes its code publicly. Or showcases its commitment to the community by staging and running in a charity fun run. Or sets up open source training to help boot camp grads make the leap to real coding jobs. Or takes a fun picture every day of someone's desk (oh look, they really seem to bring a lot of personality to this, huh?). Or they publish a new Snapchat filter every Friday so staff can take fun selfies and share with friends. Or they give the reins of their social media to a new nurse every week. Or they point to what people say about them on Glassdoor or Fairygodboss. Or they talk about how 85% of all staff have asked a family member or friend to join the company. Or, or, or.

These are companies who are opening the kimono about what life inside the building is really like, creating meaningful, authentic, and compelling content. Meanwhile, you are waiting on help from your communications team, the one that took three weeks to review your social media editorial calendar (Facebook only) and killed anything resembling personality. Or maybe you're waiting for your marketing team to jump in, even though they still haven't responded to your request to borrow their video camera to shoot a quick movie about what it's like to start the day.

Yes, the things these companies do are maybe a little silly or ephemeral and only appeal to a small slice of their potential audience, but those people are building an emotional connection with the people in that company, and you're trying to fight with generic 200-word job postings.

Who do you think wins? When the fight isn't to water down your brand and make your working experience more palatable and inoffensive to everyone, what's to fall in love with?

Try it this way. There's a woman who just made a huge breakthrough in your field, the kind that puts a business ahead three steps and puts everyone else in the dust. The company she works for is going to all but name their new sales offices after her. Everyone else in your industry is sending her muffin baskets and offering to take her on a tour of their offices to try and woo her away. Why on earth would she give that up to work for you? What do you offer her in your stock art career site and beige personality social media? The chance to be bored? Is that what you think she wants?

Now take that and multiply it by 100 (or however many open recs you have right now). That's how far behind you are when you don't invest in your employer brand.

PUNCHING ABOVE YOUR WEIGHT: EMPLOYER BRAND AS A WAY TO COMPETE AGAINST FAR BIGGER AND SEXIER COMPANIES

Everyone wants to work for Google. Isn't that what the surveys say? Google has been seen as the (or one of the) most attractive employers in the US and most of the world off and on for more than a decade. When it comes to recruitment and talent perception, Google is the 800-pound gorilla.

Or so you might think.

Why does everyone want to work for Google? It's probably because they've heard the stories about free lunch, great snacks, coffee bars every twenty paces, each with 10 different coffee offerings (and six kinds of milk). They've heard that SF employees get a shuttle bus to work that has Wi-Fi. That there are beanbag chairs and nap rooms and someone who can give you a massage when things get tense.

On top of which, we all use Google as a search engine, direction tool, directory, news aggregator, email, calendar, and word processor. Many of us use Google phones, routers, virtual assistants, and even have Google as our mobile carrier. People love the products and love the idea of so many perks.

Sure, it has a great Glassdoor rating, but there are plenty of negative reviews, too. They had multiple mass walkouts over the last year. It's probably a deeply satisfying place to work…for some people. And that's true of pretty much every company. There is good stuff in every job, and there is bad stuff in every job. Pick your poison.

Off the top of my head, I can think of plenty of people who could get a job at Google who wouldn't be happy there. Entrepreneurs, people who want to play by their own rules and run in the direction of their choosing and are willing to bear all the risks in the process, come to mind. How about someone who needs to feel like they are connected to a mission bigger than themselves? Google does a lot of cool stuff around organizing the information of the world. It might be said that there are knock-on effects that are globally positive, but their mission isn't focused on saving the world. What about someone who needs the spotlight to feel like they are important and doing great work? And that doesn't count people who prefer to work at different paces, who like to take more or less risk. What about people who are already at the top of their game and need to be seen as the top dog? What about people who need work-life balance? All those great perks were designed to keep Googlers at their desk working longer hours.

So for every person who would be happy at Google, you can find one (maybe even two) who wouldn't be. So when you say you're competing against Google (or Facebook or Procter & Gamble or whomever) you're not competing for a talent in the aggregate. You're trying to tell a compelling story for the right person, an individual. You want your message to be heard by many, but it needs to spark the imagination and soul of a single person who wants to hear it, who needs to know that you have something that may make them far happier and satisfied.

I am not trying to pick on Google. I adore Google. There are lots and lots of people who are happy there, because what motivates them internally is what's appreciated and rewarded by the company. They are a perfect fit, with the company rewarding the employee for good work, encouraging good work and returning further rewards.

Think of all those companies who are listed as "best places to work." To whom? You can't assume anyone would be happy at all those companies, because those companies are all very different.

This is why it's so crucial to know what you're about and to communicate it clearly. You are the set of the dog whistles or bat signals you send to people who appreciate what you have to offer, that your company rewards their motivations when others do not.

If you can't afford nap rooms and free food, don't try to compete on lavish perks. Instead, show how they will be more satisfied working for you. They might see one of those obvious companies and assume that's the best company. But as there's a good chance it's not the best for them, this is your chance to compete. And win.

FINALLY, THE ULTIMATE ARGUMENT FOR EMPLOYER BRANDING

O K. Here comes the swearing.

Investing in your employer branding tells great candidates that you give a crap about some aspect of your staff and what specifically that aspect is. Your employer brand is what you give a crap about.

Maybe you give a crap about their success, their satisfaction, their happiness. Maybe you give a crap about the planet. Maybe you give a crap about their compensation. Maybe you give a crap about helping them become the best employee they can be.

Employer branding is the signal that the company has figured out who they are so they aren't showing up all willy-nilly saying any old thing to whomever walks by. An employer brand suggests some measure of intentionality.

Employer brand thought and execution say that when this company brings you on, it isn't with a hope and a prayer that you'll add value and get something out of it, but with a reasonable expectation that they will be satisfied with your work and that the employee will be satisfied with what the company is providing. In the same way that investing in social responsibility projects that you are successful and care about something more than the quarterly financial results, employer branding tells candidates that both parties are looking to create mutually beneficial relationships, because those are the most valuable, last the longest, and lead to business success.

And isn't that who you really want to hire?

James Ellis

CHAPTER FOUR:
WHERE YOUR EMPLOYER
BRAND COMES FROM

YOUR EMPLOYER BRAND ALREADY EXISTS

Let's return to the idea that your employer brand is the sum of what you project and they absorb.

All your outreach, news, social media, job postings, reviews, ratings, products, customer service, etc. are already "out there" in the world. You're already selling goods and services. Your salespeople and customer service teams are interacting with the public. People can see the reviews left by staff and how (or if) you respond. They see the news. They have Google. They have friends who work there.

You may not think you have an employer brand, but you absolutely do. The fact that you haven't invested in clarifying or amplifying it doesn't mean it isn't there and making a deep impact one way or the other on how hard you have to recruit people.

When security escorted someone from that United flight two years, do you think more people applied to work there or fewer? When someone buys a pair of sneakers and just falls in love with them, do you think they'd be more or less inclined to respond to a recruiter? When the recruiter outreach shows that the recruiter really researched the prospect and wanted to offer something valuable to the prospect before engaging in any deeper conversation, do you think the prospect felt an emotional connection?

All of your company's output, from every team, whether core to the bottom line or ancillary to it, impacts your brand. When you network, when you tell stories about working there, you are spreading your brand around.

Ignoring your employer brand doesn't make it go away (as much as you'd like it to some days). People still see you, learn about you, make judgments about you, and decisions about whether to apply no matter what you will do. The question isn't "should you have an employer brand?" Instead, ask: How will you decide to shape it, what efforts will you put into clarifying and distilling it to make it clear to people what you are trying to be, and why someone might want to work there?

WHAT IS AN EMPLOYER BRAND:
A DEFINITION WE CAN ACTUALLY USE

It is well-trod ground to state that the brand is not the logo. It is not the product. It is not the tagline. It is not the commercial. And all these things are true. The brand is none of those things. If a brand was as simple as a logo or tagline, you'd simply have to relaunch a logo or tagline to solve all your brand troubles.

But you have to start any conversation on such well-trafficked territory to find a definition of a brand that we can actually do something with. To say that it isn't a logo or commercial helps us see the concept of a brand as "bigger" than a logo or commercial, but then what? If you don't understand what a brand really is, how can you be expected to fix it?

As we've already discussed, an employer brand is what people think working for you might be like. Ford's employer brand is what people would expect when they join Ford. Do they expect the interview to be friendly, rigorous, or something else? Would they expect the onboarding process to be well-designed and comprehensive or expect new hires to just "figure it out" after being given an employee manual and a video-taped message from the CHRO? Do they expect to work a focused 8–10 hour day in a cubicle while wearing a tie, or is the atmosphere more relaxed, with people working from home or shifting their schedule to fit their own lives? A person can't actually know the answers to any of those questions for certain, so they make guesses based on the brand. Understanding where the information lives that creates and supports those suppositions is also part of understanding the brand.

But that's a pretty soft description. If we're going to wield this tool to evolve our entire hiring model from the ground up, let's start with a definition that supports good work. If your brand is what people think it's like to work for you, let's break that down into pieces that we can change and impact.

First, we have to assume that if the brand is what someone thinks it's like to work there, it is a personal and individual perception. Think of any consumer brand, from Cheerios to Nike. You may love that brand and someone else may hate it. Someone may see a Toyota Camry as a safe, reliable, efficient, and comfortable sedan, and someone else may see it as boring, slow, and common. Same car, same brand, but as it is perceived by those two people, we get two radically different feelings about the brand.

To be clear, a brand isn't a thing. You can't touch it. You can't put it in a box and ship it to another office. It is a concept, one held (slightly differently) in each individual's mind. So if that brand is an individual perception, what inputs are occurring to create that individual impression. In the case of that Camry (full disclosure: I used to own a Camry and thought it was a great car; my wife hated it), both people saw the car driving around the streets. They saw commercials for it. Some of those commercials had celebrity voice-overs, and people have different opinions on how they feel about celebrities. Maybe they saw a news story that rated them highly, or a news story that listed them as one of the most common cars to be pulled over by police (perhaps a function of its popularity). Maybe they took it for a test drive. Maybe that neighbor they hate just bought one. Maybe their boss just bought one. Maybe when they Google the car, a car crash video is the first search result. Maybe the last time they were on a car lot, the sales person struck them as smarmy and kept pointing them to the Camry for some reason. Maybe they heard how rarely they need service but that parts can be expensive. Maybe a Camry bumped their car two years ago. And maybe the person driving that car was a jerk. Maybe they know someone who works for Toyota who raves about the culture and design. Maybe they met someone in a bar who said they were ugly cars.

This list of inputs goes on and on. It includes the product, the companies that make and support the product, the sales materials and processes around the product, the news, word of mouth from people who work with the company or own the product, search engines, ratings and survey sites, and personal experience. All of those inputs are filtered through that person's mind to create a brand impression, one specific to that person alone.

This suggests that a brand isn't so much built as it is revealed. That's not to say it can't evolve or be encouraged in a specific direction, but our first job is to find what already exists. We ask what someone thinks of the brand and we get the end result of all those brand impressions. So long as the brand is known, a brand impression exists. It may be strong or weak. It may be positive or negative, but the brand is already there.

The same is true for the employer brand. There are just as many ways that a prospect or potential candidate might absorb things about your employer brand as it is for someone to absorb things about that new car. Beyond obvious sources of information—such as the career site, job posting, and ratings site—they can form impressions about your brand through the recruiter, ads, videos, blog posts, consumer interactions, news, search engines, and the interview process itself. Everything your company does, intentionally or unintentionally, fuels the sense of what it might be like to work at your company, thus feeding someone's sense of what the employer brand is to them.

INTERVIEW:
ALLYN BAILEY

You know that friend you have who makes things seem so effortless, but then when you turn around they've done something spectacular? You're standing there agog, and they just move on to the next thing like it's no big deal? Yeah, that's Allyn. She is the talent acquisition transformation leader at Intel, one of the companies directly responsible for transforming all of our lives over the last 30 years. No biggie, right? She's also the inventor of the Talent Acquisition Infinity Loop and co-hosts the RM Rebelcast podcast with Tracey Parsons, which is like listening to two friends goofing and drinking while planning to overthrow an entire industry. Like I said, effortless.

How do you define "employer brand?"

The employer brand is what people say about you as an employer when you aren't around. It is what they tell their friends and peers about their impression of what your company is like as an employer.

What do most people get wrong about employer branding?

We tend to focus on what we want to "tell" people about our company versus what it "feels" like to engage or work with the company. Employer brand is rooted in the experience people have with us, no matter how flowery or wonderful our language is on our website. Talk about the benefits and coolness of working for our company, but if the experience candidates and employees have does not reflect our words, then we just look like smarmy car salesmen.

What advice would you give?

Before you pay a big agency to create your EVP for you, spend some time talking to candidates and employees about what it is like to work or engage with you as a company. Make sure you talk to people who have left the company as well as candidates who were told "no" during the process of applying. You need a full picture of what people experience, how they feel about it, and why they want or do not want to connect with you as an employer. Use that info to start making the experience changes you need to make and to help you refine the messages you need to share and talk about with candidates.

What is one surprising thing you've seen or done that worked?

Reworking our ATS disposition messages got us more goodwill then I could have imagined. We knew we needed to make them less robotic, "thank you but no thank you" message, but we had no idea how making a simple disposition message sound human could impact how people felt about their experience. We saw more uptick in positive social sharing based on the appreciation for the tone of those emails than we have seen on any marketing-based social media campaign.

What is employer branding's biggest challenge?

Finding a way to partner and play nice with corporate marketing. We have so much value to offer each other, but it is so hard to find common ground to work from where everyone appreciates the value that is being added.

THE BIRD'S NEST: BUILD YOUR EMPLOYER BRAND ONE STRAW AT A TIME

Building your employer brand bit by bit is all well and good from a philosophical or architectural or even academic point of view. But let's get real. Where does the employer brand really live? Great question.

Your employer brand is the sum of what you project and they absorb. It is not something you can control, because you only control one half of the equation. If you try to tell the world that the Camry is a fine sportscar, if you make commercials announcing it, if you enter it into car races, if you feed the communications channels with pictures and videos and testimonials about how the Camry is an amazing sports car, you aren't changing minds as much as trying to influence them. To someone who once owned that car, they may have never considered the Camry as a sports car, so all those messages are rejected. Or worse, seen as so incongruous to their perception of the brand, they make the viewer think less of the brand.

This means that as someone tasked with managing the employer brand, not only do you not have any control over half of the equation, you actually also have little control over "your" side. For all the good work you may be doing building videos and elevating your Glassdoor rating, someone in the marketing team might publish a tone-deaf tweet. Someone in customer support is about to enrage someone thinking about applying. Your product team might be about to announce a new product that has some flaw.

The news may publish a story that claims that leadership fosters a culture that tolerates sexual harassment. Each of these things will have a clear impact on how people perceive what it's like working for you, but you have no control over any of them.

In a way, your brand is like a bird's nest. It gets crafted from whatever materials are lying around. If the bird lives in the forest, the nest will be made of twigs and grass. If the bird lives in a big city, its nest will be mostly cigarette butts, coffee stirrers, and bits of plastic bags and paper. If you want the bird to change their own nest, you can't tell the bird to change the nest. But if you change the materials the bird has access to, the nest will change.

Brand management is about focusing on the inputs and less on worrying about the outputs. Right now, plenty of people are building that "bird nest" about you and you haven't paid attention. You know that when bad press comes out, it impacts applications. You know that when a new product gets launched, applications go up. You also know that when leadership makes an unpopular change in policy, referrals drop. Are you in charge of any of those things? Nope. But their ripple effects will make your life easier or harder.

Your job as an employer brand thinker is to not change the brand, but to try and influence it by influencing all the people and teams whose work impacts your brand. It's a huge job, but you need to see the whole picture in order to accomplish your mission.

I want you to understand that this is a big job with a million plates to spin. That knowledge that you will be trying to influence people well above and below your pay grade will help keep you from abdicating the process. You will be spending a lot of time asking people to be more intentional about everything they communicate because you have shown them how it drives the brand. You need them to see that when they leave that coffee stirrer out, it's going to end up in someone's bird nest.

There are twelve major ways the bird's nest gets built in talent's mind. Each one is a massive bucket with dozens of touchpoints and tactics to change the brand, but this will help you see the bigger picture without going blind on detail.

The first five buckets focus on the impressions that are created before a person really becomes a true candidate. They are passively absorbing these touchpoints and creating an almost subconscious brand perception that doesn't manifest itself until they actively consider your brand for employment. This means that a lot of the work of developing that brand impression, of building the 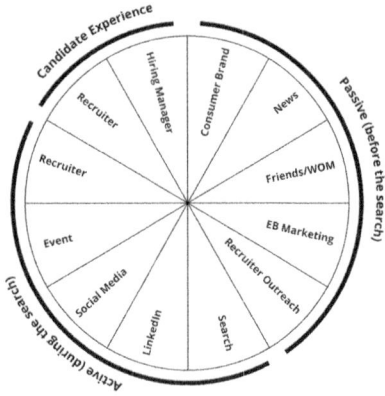 bird's nest, occurs before that great talent even starts looking for a job. If you focus all your energy on building a gorgeous career site, but someone already dislikes you when they see your logo pop up on the job board, you've lost the game before you thought it started.

Bucket One: Consumer Brand

When someone interacts with your products and services, they begin to create positive or negative brand perceptions. For most businesses, the consumer side will have a far wider reach than anything the employer branding person does, giving this element plenty of reach relative to its direct impact. Look at net promoter scores and Yelp and Google reviews to get a sense of what people are saying and where your employer brand perception might be starting.

Bucket Two: News

The best brands in the world have bad days, and some of those days end up recorded and broadcast for the world to see. For example, did you win an award? Open up a new office in a new town? Acquire another company? Have multiple consecutive quarters of growth? All those things can add fuel to a positive brand sentiment. But fraud, accusations of sexual harassment, layoffs, the mistreatment of customers, and any other newsworthy stories will have a downward impact.

Bucket Three: Network/Word of Mouth

What do people say about you? What do your employees tell their friends and relatives about working at your company? What stories are being spread organically via informal networks? As any marketer knows, word of mouth (WOM) advertising is far more valuable than anything you can pay for, and while the reach might be low, the impact is high, especially when you consider that if your lead nurse is bad-mouthing your brand, it is mostly being absorbed by other nurses who will see your nurse as far more authentic and credible than anything your marketing team can say.

Bucket Four: Employer Branding Marketing

Billboards, posters, digital ads, videos, and stories all have the power to reach people who are not actively looking. In fact, budgets are predicated on the fact that these tools can reach passive candidates and encourage them to engage. So don't ignore the channels you have direct control over when looking at your messaging plans. Depending on your spending, the reach might be high, but its impact might be low, as it is usually designed to nudge people to learn more about a product rather than rethink their ideas of the brand.

Bucket Five: Recruiters

When a recruiter does a cold outreach to someone who isn't currently looking for a job, what is the message? When they reach out, are they saying something interesting, useful, or positive that broadly aligns with and supports your employer brand? Or is it the same old, "Dear [firstname], click here to learn about a job opportunity I think you'd be perfect for!" spam message? While you might assume the reach here is low, the reach is cumulative in that sending a spam message today will leave a bad taste in the candidate's mouth and keep them from considering your brand for years.

That second set of five buckets occur during the job hunt process. At this stage, prospects aren't just actively seeking an opportunity to apply for, they are actively considering your company. People don't hang out on Indeed and Glassdoor for fun. They only visit those sites when they are in the process of looking for and considering a new role. That subconscious perception built passively now makes itself known. If that prospect has clear reasons to dislike your brand, it's likely you won't get a chance to influence them. However, if the perception is weak or bland and they see an opportunity to consider, this is when the channels you control come into play.

Bucket Six: Search and the Web

At this stage, information is being sought, and every touchpoint is more impactful, but it no longer exists in a vacuum. Candidates will search for you knowing something about you, perhaps even already having a positive or negative perception of you. The smart move would be to open an incognito window and search "what's it like to work at [brand]?" and see what comes back.

Bucket Seven: LinkedIn/Networking

When a candidate gets serious about a potential brand or role, they want information from the inside, not just the marketing spiel. So they will look at their own networks and see who they know who works there or used to work there. This is why treating alumni positively is such an important element in the talent funnel. These people will be impacting your candidate brand perception for years after they leave.

Bucket Eight: Social Media

Not just Facebook and Twitter, this bucket includes the stories you are pushing out on Glassdoor, Instagram, LinkedIn, and elsewhere. But treat these stories as marketing stories to establish some basic perceptions (or, as we'll talk about more next chapter, to "set the frame"). The reasonable expectation is that candidates will start looking for the "real" information behind your posts via the hashtags, reviews, and photos, so consider both elements when you are scoring the impact positively or negatively.

Bucket Nine: Events

Beyond recruiting events, this is any time the candidate has a chance to engage socially with your company, be it an open house, an education event, or a recruiting party. In a digital world, being comfortable in person means something to candidates if they choose to seek it out. Face-to-face means the impact is much higher, but the reach is limited to how many people you can get to attend.

Bucket Ten: Recruiters

Again? Absolutely. To a passive candidate, recruiters are annoying sales people. To an active candidate, recruiters are the most important connection to the company most candidates have. It is their source of information, news, framing, and job structure. Recruiters should be sharing appropriate content, framing it up for the candidate, and keeping the lead warm until everything lines up. Recruiters who see their job not as building relationships are telling candidates, "I only care about you as a means of hitting my numbers," which does show through to the candidate. Be aware of your interview exit surveys and how candidates see their recruiter interactions.

The last two buckets occur during the interview process. Some might call this the "candidate experience" stage, where the candidate gets a lot of firsthand information with which to craft that perception of the internal brand before making the final decision to work there or not.

Bucket Eleven: Recruiter and the Recruiting Process

It's fascinating how the role of the recruiter evolves over the course of the candidate journey, now taking the role of facilitator, confidante, and supporter. At this stage, the recruiter is incentivized to convert that candidate into a hire, so they will be sharing more information to ensure the candidate has all the details needed to nail the interview and make an informed decision about the job. This means the recruiter has to be on their game, responding quickly, sharing information, coordinating steps, and making sure the candidate feels appreciated and valued through the arduous process of offer and negotiation.

Bucket Twelve: Hiring Manager and Interview

This step is likely the most crucial and often the least invested in. Think about it: For every person a hiring manager meets, there could be 50–150 applications the recruiter had to drive, making this candidate insanely valuable. And now you have the valued person and put them in front of someone commonly not trained to interview, who already has a busy day job that has nothing to do with interviewing, is being pulled in multiple directions at any given second, and has to make a positive impression on the candidate. On top of that, in my experience, most hiring managers don't realize how tight the talent market is and generally take an old-school, "I have a job to offer, so I have the power" position and turn candidates off. Your mileage may vary, but the last thing to tell every hiring manager as they walk into the interview room is to turn off their phones and engage with the candidate like they were a customer. Just that little bit can increase your offer conversion rate significantly.

WHERE DO ALL THESE
PERCEPTIONS COME FROM?

If you looked at all those sources of employer brand touchpoints you may have thought to yourself: How can anyone actually manage the employer brand when nothing is in their control? All these touchpoints that feed the perception come from every level and department of the company. Some, like the news and rating sites, are 100% external. It may feel like taking control of the brand is the same as trying to map a cloud as it floats through the sky.

But these touchpoints, regardless of what channel delivers them, come from a single core source. Every product decision, every customer support interaction, every news story, and every recruiter interaction stems from, or is a reflection of, your company culture.

"Culture" is one of those words (like "strategy" and "innovation" and "caring") that people tend to throw around with an assumed meaning, but ultimately have none. Many businesses equate culture with posters on the wall, or the size of their foosball table, thinking that allowing employees to share a beer on Friday is their culture. That's not how that works.

Your culture is your company's DNA. It is the self-reinforcing machine that dictates what the company likes and dislikes, regardless of team, level or role. It is the connective tissue between individuals, usually only becoming obvious when decisions are being made by groups (or even when individuals choose to not make a decision and allow something to happen or continue).

When the CEO decides that the company will focus on hiring a more diverse workforce, that is the decision of an individual. But when no change is being made on the number of underrepresented audiences being hired, that's the culture. When the CHRO announces a zero tolerance sexual harassment policy but people still perceive that the company is a boy's club, it is the DNA driving that perception, regardless of what the stated policy is. If you build a highly funded marketing campaign around how much you love your customers, but don't get customer service teams to embrace it or offer them the resources to help customers? If you keep their metrics and promotions tied to how many calls they take rather than net promoter score, it's not just that your marketing will die on the vine, but that it won't be real.

Think of it this way: Culture is what makes decisions when no one person is making the decision. Sure, the CEO wants a diverse workforce, but he or she isn't there to select the next candidate. The CHRO might decide on a new policy, but are all the managers making similar choices?

The culture is often unseen, but it drives so much of the company. The culture helps elevate people who align with it and drives out those who don't. When great talent decides it is time to move on, they may not be able to point to a boss or an inciting incident. Perhaps it was the perception that the way that talent likes to work isn't valued by the company. For example, if a hard-charging employee is getting great work done, they may feel like they are fighting against a "be nice to each other at all costs" culture that values feelings over impact. The culture of the company tells that employee that long-term success won't be found there. And as that person leaves, it reinforces the culture by the people who remain.

The culture isn't magical, but it is effectively spontaneous. When you put three people in a room together, a culture exists, no matter how tenuous. Put three sales sharks in a room, and you'll feel how competition-driven the atmosphere becomes. Put three lawyers in a room and the culture is far more risk-averse.

Culture starts with the founders. Who are they, what are they like, and what do they value? If they are trying to save the world, they will hire more of those who are interested in saving the world. If they are fame-seeking, they will naturally find themselves attracted to like-minded folks. The culture becomes self-reinforcing as people are promoted and rewarded who align and others held back and leave who do not. The decisions by leadership, of who to hire, who to reward, and who to promote tells everyone else what it takes to get those rewards. And people adjust their plans accordingly.

Want to tell women that you value their leadership? Say it all you want, but until you start promoting women, the culture overrides any one person's desire. The collective feeling and proclivities move the company beyond a single leader's mandate. When they say culture eats strategy for breakfast, this is what they mean: The unwritten laws and drivers determine the future, no matter what the leader decides.

This explains why change is so hard to create at companies. Not only do you need executive buy-in, but every element of the company needs to buy in. Incentives have to evolve. Talking points and language have to change. One key employee digging his or her heels in can kill the best-funded, best-promoted, and best-communicated change by virtue of how they embrace and extend the culture.

This is why good employer brand thinking starts by trying to understand the existing culture. This is the engine that creates the product, the customer service, and the leadership decisions that end up in the news (or don't). It is also about how a recruiter does their job, how a hiring manager talks about the new role, how current and former staff talk about their jobs, and how satisfied they were. All of the channels that drive employer brand perception (on the company side of the equation, anyway) start with the company culture.

Let's go back to the aforementioned Camry. If you wanted to sell more Camrys, you might try telling the world it's an amazing sports car. But if people don't see it as a sports car, not only will sports car buyers reject the premise, people who were looking for a safe, reliable, and comfortable car will also question if they should consider the Camry. They were looking for something reliable, and you're saying it's a sports car now? Trying to build a brand that doesn't align to the DNA of the product is a fast journey to destroying positive brand awareness.

The same goes for employer brand. If, at the height of Uber's issues in 2017, when the CEO was caught screaming at a driver, when various reports of rampant sexual harassment and a culture of visiting strip clubs abounded, you couldn't launch an employer brand campaign about how much Uber cares. It wouldn't have stuck. It would have felt like a desperate attempt to try and slow down what everyone already was seeing in the news and ratings sites. At best, it would have felt like a half-hearted whitewash rather than real change. Leadership might dictate the new way of doing things, but culture drives all those touchpoints.

The employer brand manager has a choice: Align the employer brand message to what was happening or pray for a change in culture and leadership. Uber's employer brand could have fostered a locker-room atmosphere, a ribald and sexually aggressive workplace. Why not? There are plenty of people, some of whom are talented, who would have seen that as a fun place to work.

In the end, Uber leadership was very publicly changed and the new CEO has done a lot of work to change the culture, but it isn't something that is mandated away. Sure, being known as a place where sexual harassers regularly escaped punishment lead to some serious consumer problems, but trying to build a brand impression that had no basis in fact, or had any connection to what was clear to anyone, would have further killed the brand.

Put another way: No matter how many Drake or Post Malone T-shirts I wear, I will never convince anyone I am 23. Or cool. The smart play is to lean into who I am and attract like-minded folks.

THE BIG PICTURE: THE ENTIRE EMPLOYER BRAND ARCHITECTURE

At some point, you will be (or already have been) faced with this seemingly simple question: What kind of video should I make to attract more people to apply? Or maybe you wonder what you should post on Instagram. Or even if you should be on Instagram at all. Or you are about to write a staff profile, but you don't know what angle to take.

We've spent a lot of talking about what makes up the brand, but when it's time to make choices that will influence and change the brand, where do you start? The process of building the materials to attract and validate someone to your hiring process requires answering questions like these dozens of times a day, the answers to which will determine the success of your recruiting initiatives. So, you know, no pressure or anything.

So how do you go about making any of these decisions? There are a couple of standard ways of doing this. First, you could simply look at what the "big companies" are doing. If I had a dollar for the number of times I heard a recruitment leader try to make tactical decisions by asking, "Well, what does Google do?" I could print this book on a stack of twenty dollar bills. But you can't play "follow the leader" because what makes them great isn't what makes you great. You can't out-Google Google, right?

No, you can't out-Google Google. Do you know why? Because you aren't Google. You don't have their resources. You don't have their brand recognition. You don't have their customer reach. You don't have their reputation. You might not even be trying to hire in the same place or the same roles as Google.

That's not a bad thing, because the reverse is also true: Google can't out-you you.

Other people listen to the vendor or the recruiting ecosystem for what's "cool." I'm convinced that no one in recruiting or HR who bought a blockchain-driven solution actually understands blockchain enough to explain it to their child, but bought it because that's what all the blogs and social media are talking about. Will blockchain help them hire? Well, if you don't understand the technology, if you didn't have a clear use case, if you didn't have an intentional metric to measure it, how can you answer the question?

So how do you make a choice of what to build or buy? You could always ask me, but you won't like my answer: I don't know, because I'm not in your shoes.

"What should I make a video about to support the brand?" is a seemingly simple question, and yet it seems literally impossible to answer. Questions like these are akin to "what should I do when I grow up?" or "who should I marry?" Trying to answer a question like this starts with another question, which leads to more questions, until it just feels like it's questions all the way down without any kind of resolution.

But people make decisions on these questions all the time. How? Strangely, the fastest way to answer this question properly is to slow down and understand the nature of the question. The people and professionals who are great at answering this question haven't tried to skip to the end of the book, and they see the solution as if it was glowing in the dark. If you grabbed a mystery or thriller and jumped to the last few pages, you might discover that they all killed him, but you don't know why or how. That's how you realize the value of the book comes not in picking the answer, but in unraveling the mystery.

I once found a thread on the internet that very literally dissected and showed the answer to the Zen riddle: What is the sound of one hand clapping? Not just some example of highest-level thinking, this is an actual question that Buddhist monks ask their students to measure the students' progress. The answer is fraught with meaning and intention, so knowing the answer isn't at all valuable; whereas, understanding how to think through the riddle is everything. Just because I know the answer (fascinating though it is), I am no more enlightened than anyone else, let alone a monk who has contemplated the answer for months and years. It is the process of discovering and understanding the answer on your own that creates enlightenment, not the answer itself.

Your employer brand is not dissimilar to these kinds of mysteries. If I understood your employer brand, I might be able to tell you that the video you should make next should focus on leadership, but that doesn't actually help you understand why. It just means I know the secrets, and you have to ask me for answers. In fact, if you try to take that answer as gospel and make a video about leadership, it's very likely that the subject isn't as important as the message inside the video. You can do everything "right" and discover you no farther along than if you did it all wrong. Or flipped a coin.

But before I put on saffron robes and chat about how the secret to your employer brand is within you (I mean, it is, but how does that information really help you?), let me assure you that you can determine the answer, but only once you understand all the "stuff" that creates the question. The answer to the question of "what video do I make" begins by understanding the complete architecture of your employer brand. Once you see that, the answers become far more obvious and come quickly. Invest in this process and you'll be equipped to make decisions easier for years.

Here is the brand architecture. And while the architecture seems like it starts at the top, you can use it to answer your questions by starting at the bottom of the system and working your way up. Let's break it down.

Tactics

So at the bottom of the figure, we have the tactics. Tactics are the things you do that people see. They range from videos and referral programs to redesigning your career site and your content strategy. Tactics are actions, with an intention and purpose behind

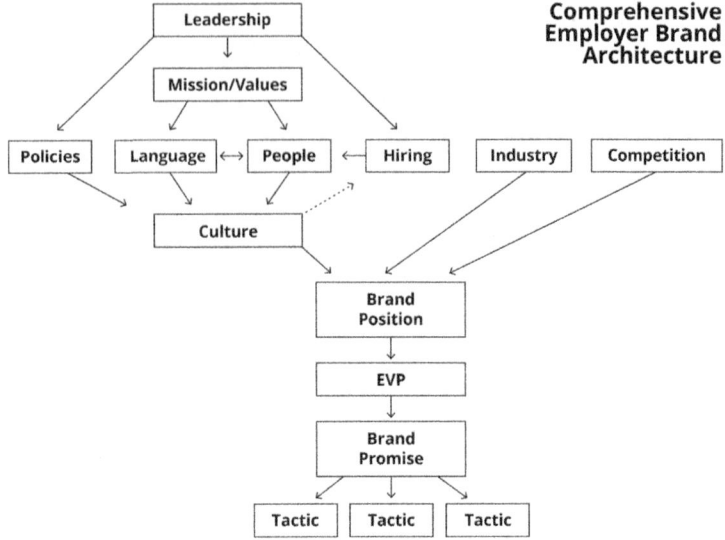

Comprehensive Employer Brand Architecture

them. They are, if we are to be brutally honest with each other, the things you spend money on. They are the things your boss thinks you do. Which tactics you use, what message you deliver via these tactics, which audience you decide to reach, are all bundled up into this area.

If you were selling donuts and you wanted to increase sales, you could lease a billboard. That's a valid tactic. But if you don't have a purpose and intention behind it (a strategy, if you will), how would you decide which billboard to lease or what messaging to put on it? Should you focus on making people halfway across town hungry for donuts in a general sense? Okay, but will they know to come to you for donut satisfaction? Or should you put it next to your store with a big arrow pointing to your front door? Okay, but don't people walking by you already know you exist? And how do you decide between the billboard and a guy in a donut outfit handing out flyers? Maybe you should buy radio commercials. Or skywriting. Or a coupon. Or or or... If this is your approach, you are flipping infinite coins to land on random results to the point where doing nothing might have been more appropriate. At the very least, doing nothing would yield one less invoice to pay.

Brand Promise

The answer to which tactic (and how) comes from the purpose of the tactic, which starts with the brand promise. A brand promise is what you are telling the prospect or candidate they can expect when working here in a broad sense. Perhaps you're promising them stability and support. Perhaps it's innovation and perpetual change. Perhaps it's fame or maybe a mission to work towards. We'll break these down later on, but what's happening is you're being very clear and cognizant of what the business is all about to its staff and communicating that broad idea via focused and specific tactics.

In the case of the donut store, is your brand promise that you offer donuts worth crossing the city for? Or are you promising donuts that are good enough but available right now? That brand promise directly answers the question of "where should I put the billboard and what should it say?"

Most companies have one of two big issues with their brand promise. Either their brand promise isn't well known or everyone already knows the brand promise so much, it never gets communicated outward.

For example, at a big box store or in a customer service role, what's the promise one company has versus another? Aren't they all 90% the same? Companies who don't have an obvious means of differentiating themselves get stuck in the proverbial mud, talking about all the same things everyone else talks about, because they are all so similar, leading a candidate to take more of a scattershot approach, applying blindly to stuff and hoping for the best. Without a differentiator, there's nothing on which to choose.

Conversely, a company may be so obvious to itself that it never remembers to spell it out. That local company that thinks it has to compete with Google and forgets to talk about how great a team they have or how short the commute is. Or the nonprofit that forgets to tell candidates how good it feels to make a difference. It's like that old joke about how fish don't talk about the water, because they're always surrounded by it. They don't think about it, because they forget about it. They see and think it every day for hours and assume you already know it, too.

Employer Value Proposition

Sure, the post office isn't promising adventure and excitement, and that hedge fund isn't promising a chance to change the world, because the post office has no adventure to offer and the hedge fund is focused elsewhere. That promise originates from the company and what that company offers to its people as an employer. That is its employer value proposition. The post office has only stability to offer. And to some people, that is exactly the thing they value.

You might object here by saying, "what people want is a paycheck." Try not to get hung up on salary and benefits, as those are often roughly similar across companies. Think of them as table stakes, or the thing you can increase when all else fails. (This book is designed to keep you from doing focusing on salary unless you see it as a strategic advantage). We'll break the EVP down even further in a little bit, but just thinking about it as the underlying promise you make to all staff is enough here.

Brand Position

So where does your EVP come from? The value your company can offer comes from its brand position. The brand position is the flip side of candidate and employee motivation. If there are people motivated by stability, you might be a company that offers stability. You can attract people motivated by status, because that is what your company is built around.

People who are not in the marketing field tend to get hung up at the position, because it is so broad and vague. To them, I refer to the Mad Men episode "Man with a Plan" where the creative team talks about the differences in margarines. Margarine is a butter substitute in which each brand is functionally identical to all the others. So how do you market one over another if you can't tell them apart?

In the episode, creative director Ted Chaough uses Gilligan's Island as a metaphor. One margarine is the "luxury brand" like the Howells. One brand is the hard worker like the Skipper. One brand is the brainy one like the Professor. The same goes for the goofy brand (Gilligan), the sexy brand (Ginger), and the attractive-yet-still-attainable brand (Mary Ann). These archetypes allow us to understand, at a glance, which brand is for us. If you see yourself as a smart consumer, you pick the brainy brand. If you see yourself as first class (or want people to see you as first class), you pick the Howell brand. And so forth.

While Mad Men saw the seven castaways as different positions, I see eight, and we'll dive into them in depth later on.

Industry

Your brand position, the core idea that determines the motivations you reward, is a function of a few elements. The first is the industry. Image you reward people who spend an extra hour in the office burning a little midnight oil. In some companies, that extra hour here or there is an example of people trying to develop themselves or taking a little more ownership over their role. But when that same extra effort gets put in a legal setting—an industry where employees are expected to put in 60, 70, and 80 hours a week until they make partner, only doing a 50 hour work week is what constitutes work-life balance—you have a very different example of how much the company supports its employees. You have the same reward for the same effort, but the industry context drives the meaning. So when you're looking at your industry, ask what the expectations and standards are of the industry before proclaiming yourself any particular position. You may think of yourself as a company that offers deep support for its employees, but if a competitor in the space outshines you in that regard, maybe it's time to rethink your position.

Competition Set

Once you understand your industry standards in the aggregate, consider your direct competition for talent. There are two ways to look at this. This can be a means of focusing on one or two competitors for talent within the industry, or looking at the competitors for talent outside the industry. For example, if you are a bank looking to hire a project manager, great project managers don't have to come from other banks. They might come from hospitals, startups, or telecom companies. If you are in an oil and gas town like Houston, your project folks are going to be people used to working at large energy companies. That expectation will color your ability to position yourself one way or another.

Culture

While each driver of brand position has value, the most important driver of your brand position is your culture. Culture is an often-cited but rarely-defined topic in HR and business. Everyone kind of knows what it is, but no one can point their finger exactly at it. As we discussed earlier, your culture is the mysterious stuff that makes decisions for a company in the absence of a clear decision-maker. Like gravity between two objects, it is impossible to see, but easy to see the impact of it every single day.

For example, think back to the last time your company launched a major internal initiative, be it "diversity," a focus on employee engagement, a call for kindness or mindfulness, a drive 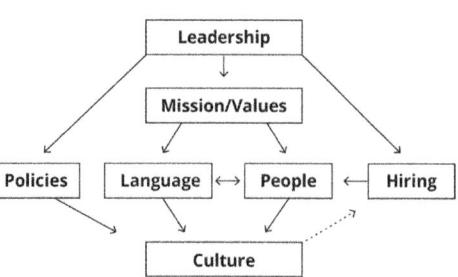 towards excellence, or something else. Leadership made an announcement, maybe some posters and flyers got posted. An email went out to everyone. Comms did their job and made it very clear how important this initiative was. But did it get any traction, or did it fade away to be replaced by something else, or was it business as usual? That's culture deciding that this idea wasn't going to stick. Or the culture did support the initiative and changes occurred. No one person decided yes or no, but the culture that exists either embraced it or rejected it. When a company announces that sexual harassment is anathema, and all employees will be treated the same, regardless of gender, the culture is what decides to stay the same or be willing to create change.

Culture is semi-magical in that it can be attributed to so much of the power or weakness of a company. In my interviews with employees at different companies, people are happy to state that they love the company and stay in the company because of the culture. As it is an important driver for what happens every day, we need to figure out where it comes from.

The three primary drivers of culture are the corporate policies, the people who inhabit the company, and the language people use on a regular basis.

Policies

Policies impact culture by providing boundaries rather than sparking it. For example, you can't create a culture of work-life balance, but if you create appropriate policies (lots of paid time off [PTO] and maternity/paternity leave, recognizing people embrace effective work without killing themselves, rewards in the form of vacations and breaks rather than just cash, etc.), you can foster and encourage its development. At the same time, policies can kill culture quickly. That same culture of work-life balance quickly decays when PTO is limited and strictly enforced. Unrestricting dress code doesn't create a more informal and familial culture, but demanding suits, ties, and heels is a great way to ensure informality never happens.

Please note that while this is the fastest and most direct means leadership has in changing and influencing culture, it is not direct control. If leadership is trying to make a specific change, they can build policies that incentivize or disincentivize that aspect of the culture, but the actual culture change is out of their grasp. Any attempt to mandate a culture from the outside leads to corporate schizophrenia, where people are encouraged to pay lip service to an ideal, but their actions suggest something very different. You can ask a shark to act like a sheep, and you can incentivize sheepy behavior, but each shark makes their own choices as to their behavior.

People and Language

Which means that the people and the language they share are the most powerful factors in creating and maintaining a culture. To wit, without people, can you even say you have a culture? The people you have hired to accomplish goals and complete tasks have personalities, proclivities, motivations, desires, frustrations, personal baggage, and occasional medication (prescribed, or off-the-shelf, as it were) that come to bear towards, with and against, all the other people. The sum total of those interactions, feelings, and personalities create the culture. Take ten people who are generally introverted and are most comfortable when the team succeeds instead of when an individual shines, and you can guess the culture pretty quickly. Each additional person you add makes a relative impact on the culture, so in a company of three, the fourth person makes a huge impact, but in a company of one thousand, the next person generally doesn't even make a ripple.

Language isn't spontaneously generated. It comes from the people. Ask yourself: What are the words they use most often to describe themselves and each other? What words do they chose to describe their work? What words do they use when trying to solve a problem with people inside the company? Words are choices, and those choices reflect the culture. If you noticed that people at a company talked about "sparking and instilling wonder" within a customer, what would you think about them? If in the same situation, what would you think about the company if you instead heard "drive demand" or "target the message" or "disrupt the prospect's worldview?"

Language tells others how we see ourselves and the preponderance of certain terms showcases and reinforces a given worldview within the company. Imagine every day you heard the term, "move fast and break things." It wouldn't be long before you found yourself taking more risks and being more accepting of failure. That language attracts and supports the culture of the company, reinforces alignment to it, and tells new hires what is valued and how to behave.

Mission and Values
The people and language are direct outcomes from the mission and values of the company. That is, what the company espouses about what it does and why and how it does it attracts people who have aligned belief systems. If you believe in saving the world one recycled glass bottle at a time, you should expect that an inordinate number of applicants will be recycling true believers. If your mission is to become the number-one pen maker in the world, people who want to be there are people with ambition and drive who share a growth mindset.

Much of the late 1980s and early 1990s could be called "the mission era" of business. Hundreds of books and thousands of pre-blog magazine articles espoused the power of a clear mission, the flag you would wave that all employees could salute. A strong mission was supposed to lead to clear lines of strategy and stated mechanisms of competition. Whether it was a reaction to watching video of Japanese workers doing calisthenics before work to achieve company goals, or the breakdown of the "one company for life" expectations in the US and Europe, every company came up with a mission to mount as a plaque on a wall somewhere to collect very expensive dust. My personal favorite mission was from Pepsi, who didn't beat around the bushes with fancy words or ideas and announced to the world that their mission was to "Beat Coke."

But that's not the mission and values we're talking about. Avoiding business school terms and five-dollar words, the mission is simply the intention and purpose of the company. It's more like: Does this company exist to help other companies move cargo across the continent? Is the company trying to put a drone in every kid's hands? Are you looking to revolutionize how people think about dim sum? Seth Godin says that businesses exist to make a change in the universe, however small or niche. What change is your business trying to make? Write it down. Perfect. You're done.

If the mission is the "what," then your values are your "how." For example, if you are trying to change the way people think about dim sum, are you doing it via empathy? Are you trying to make dim sum accessible to Kansas by making it ubiquitous? Are you aggressively putting it on shelves and spending lots of cash on celebrity endorsements on commercials and media buys? These answers show what you value: process, people, outcomes, the willingness to try new things, stability and steady success, etc. Some companies proclaim these values, but in my experience, the company that builds posters of their values is the company trying to convince the rest of the company that these are everyone's values. They aren't so much statements of shared values as they are well-printed red flags.

Please note that while you're mapping out your employer brand architecture, it is imperative that you check to make sure your company's mission and values align with your brand position. There's no direct line connecting one to the other, but you should treat it like a litmus test and ask yourself if and how the two align. If your company's values involve empowering employees, your brand position should concur. If it doesn't, that means either you've made some mistakes in distilling the brand, or your company is organizationally schizophrenic. Either answer suggests that no amount of employer brand thinking (or spending) will fix the underlying problem.

Culture is powerful, because it becomes self-reinforcing. If your culture is respectful, it tends to attract and hire people who also value respect, thus staffing the company with more people who are respectful. Those people slowly help the language evolve and can ask leadership to change policies that support the culture. With such a well-embedded idea that has its own self-reinforcing feedback loop, I'll leave it to others to talk about how to change culture. But suffice it to say, culture change is hard. Really, really hard.

Leadership

Everything in the employer brand architecture is ultimately driven by leadership. Leadership makes hiring decisions, determines company policies, as well as selects and promotes the company's values. But, as should be clear by now, leadership does not have a direct line to the employer brand. They do not dictate what the brand is or means to the prospect. Leadership makes choices that build people who cultivate a culture that determines the position that becomes the brand. It is a Rube Goldberg machine, to be sure. But that's why they have you.

Your goal is to know when and where leadership has a direct line of sight to some part of the architecture and then leverage it. For example, if you see an opportunity to make your company the place where people are empowered to become their best professionals, and the policies in place encourage supervisors and managers to micromanage people, a conversation and argument that relaxing those policies supports a stronger brand which ultimately helps the company. Your role allows you to direct leadership's attention to the problems of the company that limit or hinder your brand narrative. You don't change policy, but you can draw attention to policies which are detrimental to the brand you're trying to build.

Conversely, you can't ask leadership to change the language. It's not something they have control over. At best, they can lean on a new or refactored value that begins to use a certain language, but there's no guarantee that people will embrace the language. Leadership doesn't have that kind of power.

LET'S TALK TO THE MARKETING TEAM

Building out your architecture is opening a Pandora's box. On the one hand, it helps you understand all the things that drive your brand and help you decide what tactics to choose and how to implement them. But on the other hand, building out this kind of brand architecture means the company likely has two competing brand architectures, one for employees and candidates and another for consumers, investors, and even corporate audiences.

A company with two competing or misaligned brand architectures is a brand that will spend its time in endless meetings trying to figure out (sometimes softly, sometimes passive aggressively, and sometimes just straight-up yelling at each other) whose brand is "right." That is a horrible waste of time, one that you will ultimately lose.

Here's the real solution: You're both right.

You can see that despite the brands being seen very differently and being understood by potentially two very different audiences, there's a common source of the employer brand and all other aspects of the brand, be they consumer, corporate, investor, etc. The leadership determined the mission, purpose, and values of the company, which, in turn, drive what the company sells, how it sells it, and what it offers employees. Think of them as the rudder that directs the ship: Even if marketing is at the front of the ship with the best seats, that same rudder moves your both.

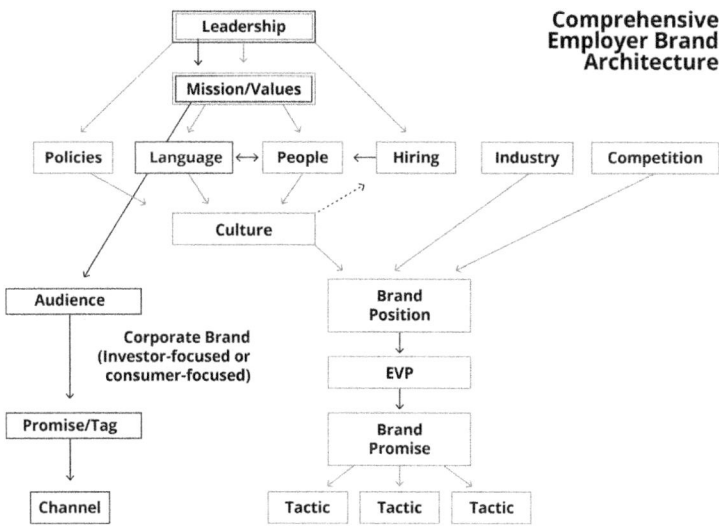

While many candidates can also be customers, seeing two parts of the brand, there is a clear difference: Consumer and investment audiences do not live within the company. Their paychecks and livelihoods do not come directly from the company. They are not using the company to support their own personal and professional identities. They may like what having a specific car, mobile carrier, or shoe says about them, but those things don't influence someone's sense of self, like what they do for a living and who they work for.

That's why the employer brand is so much more complex a diagram than the consumer brand. The consumer may only interact with the brand for 0.001% of their lives, which allows marketers to tell consumers what the company is all about. They can use a commercial or celebrity spokesperson to spark interest and drive intent to buy in just a minute or two. Compare that to an employee who spends one third to one half of a workday in the office, surrounded by others in the company. They see the company from a deeply intimate perspective. They see the decisions leadership makes. They see where the machine is held together with paperclips and dreams. There are few illusions; thus, it is impossible to tell an employee what the brand is, because they see it every day.

This kind of understanding has a few valuable outcomes. First, it makes it clear that the employer brand is different from the other aspects and must be handled differently. Second, it shows marketing and comms that while you are trying to manage an aspect of the brand, you are going to stay aligned to the brand mother elements, ensuring that you aren't trying to build some separate and cacophonous brand that will distract or hurt the consumer brand. And as the consumer brand funds your paycheck and budget, you should be very committed to not getting in the way. This makes it clear that there's room for everyone to support the business without stepping on anyone else's toes. Third, it gives those players the sense of security that you understand your part of the brand and take it seriously. Marketers and comms folks take their jobs very seriously, and they don't want to carry "some dilettante recruiter with a cute idea about marketing" as they do their own jobs. Finally, it creates the beginnings of the ground rules upon which collaboration can occur, which is something you should be working towards.

And yes, collaboration and connection with marketing and comms is a very good thing for you indeed. In fact, as they see you as a peer, they may start to consider using the employer brand as an aspect of their consumer brand, giving you an even larger platform from which to work.

James Ellis

CHAPTER FIVE:
POSITIONING AND
DISTILLATION

THE POWER OF MOTIVATIONS: WHY PEOPLE DO WHAT THEY DO

As candidates are drawing conclusions about what it's like to work at your company based on all these things your company does, we need to ask how those people are absorbing those brand impressions. I'm not talking about which social media channels will be more believable. I'm interested in how people make decisions on the information being shown to them about the employer brand.

Let me start here: Is there a job you would consider taking, even if it meant a 5% salary cut? Is there a great-paying job you'd reject, because the company mission didn't align to your worldview? I'm willing to bet you said yes to both those questions, destroying the idea that the only thing people weigh when considering a new company or offer is salary.

Don't get me wrong. People need to be paid a fair wage for the work they do. Taking a job shouldn't mean that they can't pay their rent or mortgage. Unless they are in a tenuous situation, no one will take a job that offers an unfair wage. And if they do, they will leave the second another job materializes that pays closer to the market rate. People have an innate sense of fairness, and if they don't feel like they are being treated fairly, they leave.

But if we assume that salaries for a given role follow a standard deviation bell curve, that some pay a bit more and some pay a bit less, but mostly they clump in the middle, then any given job title should expect a base salary at almost all companies. (FYI: This means your hiring manager's thinking that the recruiter can just find an unpolished gem of an employee who doesn't know the going rate or their worth is not a successful hiring strategy.)

So if all jobs pay roughly the same, how does a candidate choose their next job among all the options?

The fact that you would take a job that doesn't pay the most means there are other underlying reasons that are not as directly connected to salary (for most people, anyway). You might choose a job, because it gives your better work-life balance. You might choose it, because it has a substantially better commute. You might choose it, because it rewards your intrinsic desire to build something new. You might choose it, because it will give you less interference as you pave a path forward. And you might choose it, because the brand's status in the industry feeds your ego.

We are all motivated by different things. Some might want fame while others want a supportive work environment. Some want to save the world and some want to build their own career. Some want to show off and some want to be taken care of. The DMV manager and the hedge fund manager are equally talented, despite having vastly different salaries. But each will be driven by very different motivations and seek roles that satisfy those motivations. No one looks for a job at the DMV to make a lot of cash, and no one looks for a job at a hedge fund because of its stable and calm environment.

Do you know a teacher? Are they an idiot? Because in a world where everyone is driven by salary, teachers must be fools to take such hard jobs with such low pay. But if you know a teacher, you know they aren't stupid. They simply care more about working with kids than cashing out at age 50. These are people who are driven to grow young minds, who want job stability, and who make sacrifices every day, because helping people learn feels better than an extra $100 a week. It's not that they don't want more money, it's that they want something more.

Any one person's motivations might be all over the map, and thinking about the motivations of a large group of people even more so. Because of this, it makes sense to establish some kind of motivation framework to understand who we want to talk to. There are any number of ways to bundle up these kinds of motivations and the cultures that align to them. Harvard Business Review has a great one on the eight types of company cultures, but the framework I use (deeply influenced by Rob O'Keefe) is based on people's eight intrinsic core motivations.

Basic Human Motivation (What drives people to act)	Professional Motivation (What drives job choices)
Autonomy	Empowerment
Advancement	Innovation
Purpose/Meaning	Mission/Values
Knowledge	Development
Progress	Career
Accomplishment	Performance
Recognition	Status
Social Interaction	Support/Team
Safety	Stability

Empowerment
These are people who want to have roadblocks removed and who need and respond to less managerial oversight. They want to be given as much authority, responsibility, and opportunity as possible to work at their own pace and standards. This candidate may have been frustrated in other jobs and wants to prove themselves.

Innovation
These candidates want to have access to, or expect to create, cutting-edge innovation in the workspace. For some, it is the ability to use the latest and greatest tools in their work, but for others it is a reward structure based on what they build and develop that breaks new ground. They are looking for a willingness by the company to manage high levels of risk. This candidate wants to invent the new.

Mission/Values
People who are mission- or value-focused will seek out companies whose internal values align with theirs, where everyone is in it to save the world, the ferns, the rights of others, the university, etc. These candidates are more focused on doing great work by joining the ranks of others who feel the same. They want to know their work is serving some higher purpose than just commerce.

Development
These candidates are seeking a structural focus on training, education, coaching, and mentoring. Rewarded for more certifications and degrees, they see their growth and satisfaction as a function of how much training they can get. They want to know that development isn't just "an offer" but rather encouraged and expected.

Career
This candidate has a focus on moving up the career ladder, a willingness to take roles that support promotions down the road, a desire to get on the partnership or tenure track, or a long-term goal of being CEO. This person wants to know how this job will move them forward in title first.

Performance
Performance-focused individuals thrive in an environment where they can showcase their talents and are rewarded for excellence. They want to be surrounded by other people who perform to the highest standards, to push and be pushed by them, and to discover new levels of performance. This candidate wants to be all they can be and to show that off.

Status
People who derive satisfaction from how impressed others are by the company they work for are status-driven. They want to be seen as being at the top of the pecking order and see perks and salary as a function of working at the best company. These candidates are a little more defined by what others think about them, allowing you to leverage that ego to spur action.

Support/Team
These candidates are looking for a team environment where

they can be supported and do their best work with a minimum of uncertainty, risk, or politics. These people don't enjoy the spotlight as much and are more comfortable succeeding by helping everyone around them succeed.

Stability
Because I ended up grouping Autonomy and Responsibility as "Empowerment," it makes a gap somewhat obvious. Some people are driven not by growth, but by safety and security. Some call it loss aversion or fear, but some slice of the world thinks working for the county or the postal service is a dream job, because it provides deep security. That is, the job is the same almost every day, is managed by well-defined processes and metrics, and will likely be around next year.

First off, do you recognize yourself in any of these motivations? Perhaps you see what gets you out of bed in the morning, or maybe you immediately see that because your motivations and those of the company you work for are misaligned, you're often frustrated at work. The litmus test remains: Would you be willing to take a 5% pay cut if you knew that taking that new job would better meet and support your motivations? Then that's the one (or ones) that drive you.

These motivations are not mutually exclusive. You can be motivated by multiple things. And that goes both ways, as a company will meet many different kinds of motivations. But to establish yourself in the talent market, it is far more effective to begin a conversation with a candidate by stating and validating against a core motivation. Being focused on your mission doesn't have to make you any less supportive of stability. But in a crowded marketplace, having a single, clear message to spark a conversation drives attention and attraction. For example, if you are telling a story about performance to attract attention to that motivation, you can talk about how supportive an environment you have later on in the interview to share an additional motivator.

No one motivation is "the best" or attracts "the best" talent. Equally talented people can be driven by vastly different things. Being (for example) driven by values, driven by ego, and even driven by spite, doesn't make someone more or less talented. But if you are a values-driven company, you probably won't get the value of the person driven by ego or spite. And vice versa.

When I work with companies, their initial instinct is often to want to be all these things, to have employees who embrace the values, who want to be empowered to be the best, but also appreciate a supportive culture. If we go back to the Camry, we choose the car, because it is safe and reliable. Is it cheap? No. Is it expensive? Not particularly. Is it fast? No more so than similar sedans. Is it attractive? That would depend on who you ask. Point being the car can be many things, but a brand manager wouldn't want to build a campaign around it being cheap (undercutting any sense that it is well-built) or expensive (as it might be a higher value than other cars in its class).

Compare that to the Volvo. Is a Volvo fast? Maybe. Or affordable? Sure. It probably goes a long time without repairs and looks good, too. But for decades, every commercial focused on and reinforced its commitment to safety. Sure, it might have been a reliable and affordable car, but no one else was talking much about safety, so Volvo planted its flag in that space. In return, people saw the Volvo as the safest major-name car (regardless of what crash tests or other research might say). If they were looking for a safe car, they started at the same brand. It was the hook that got people in the door, where once inside, they could learn about reliability and affordability.

For every motivation, however, there is a dark side. Stability and safety tend towards stagnation. Status tends towards cutthroat behavior. Performance isn't often aligned to teamwork. So if you claim that what you are motivated by and reward is a given driver, you need to be aware of that dark side.

For example, most start-up companies tend to attract risk-comfortable people. But there's an assumption that the willingness to do "whatever it takes" to make the company succeed will lead to long days and little free time. For some people that is a compromise they are willing to take, because they are innovation- or status-focused. But imagine if you had a start-up that made it very clear that no matter what, everyone would be expected to go home at 5:00 p.m., you may not be any less innovation- or status-focused, but your point of differentiation is now about work–life balance, thus attracting a very different kind of talent. They aren't any less talented, because they won't stay at the office for 18 hours. Instead, they are attracted to what makes you different.

This is the core of brand differentiation: not trying to be like everyone else but establishing and communicating over and over again what makes the product or job special.

In effect, you can be either the most something in a space, or you can be the only one in a space. In this start-up story, you can be either a company who stops at nothing to make innovation happen (being the most innovation-focused), or you can be the company where people go home at a reasonable hour (being the only innovation company to be support-focused). If you can own either space, you can compete effectively for talent. If you can't, you'll be stuck sounding like every company who is neither the best at something nor the only one who does something. You'll fall back into that commoditized brand space where you lose all your advantage.

INTERVIEW:
CHARU MALHOTRA

I'm absolutely stumped on how to introduce Charu. First, go look up her LinkedIn and scan the logos. Cool, right? But that's not the thing that makes me revere her. Charu is a thinker and a do-er in equal measure. Like some warrior priest of employer brand, someone who is able to change the oil on your car while composing an epic poem about how the oil came to be in the first place. She is fighting a larger fight than might first be evident, championing the needs and honor of all workers, and is using employer brand to do it. She's seen it all and done about as much. If she has a flaw, it's that she hasn't written her book yet. Because I want to read it!

How do you define "employer brand?"

To be glib, it's the fine line between an organization winning or losing its ability to attract, retain, and engage the right talent. An employer brand or talent brand, which is a phase I prefer, is a distillation of the functional and emotional benefits plus the "why" of working for an organization, with a focus on communicating these consistently with a clear, apparent link to the corporate brand, underpinned by the culture of the organization or the microcultures of the function/country/team. It cannot be created but can be nurtured and amplified by employees and leadership focus.

What do most people get wrong about employer branding?

First, thinking it's all about broadcasting messages that the organization thinks are "cool" or "attractive" to candidates versus researching what actually differentiates the company from its competition.

Second, chasing the shiny new fad (e.g., a VR game, video, an app, a TikTok channel, launching an Instagram channel, etc.). That is, forgetting the "why" in the quest for awards or a shiny new toy. Asking your employees what they wished they had known or what they wished they could have seen on social media or the career site is one of the easiest ways to cut through fad culture.

Third, most organizations fail when it comes to activation, as all the energy, time, and money has been focused on the creation of the EB, while careful thinking, planning and analysis of activation gets scant attention

Finally, my personal bugbear, people forget about employees' activation and implementation. If employees are not being courted about their reason to stay and if they are not engaged and reminded of the great things going on, there will either be a retention issue or, even worse, an engagement issue. Remember, the receptionist at the front desk, the customer service call center operator, and the overworked recruiter are all part of your EB, so invest in them first.

What advice would you give?

Plan systematically what outcome you are trying to achieve: Is it an employer brand problem or something else?

Create a shadow team of employees across functions, demography, and tenure to test your ideas. Along the way, these become your activation leads and pulse check as to how things are landing.

Know your baseline before you start anything.

Make friends with communications and employee engagement teams so you can access any outreach they do with surveying employees, such as data insights and EB questions.

Don't make the employer brand an HR issue. Always, always, always couch it as a business problem, because it is.

What is one surprising thing you've seen or done that worked?

In the face of the guardrails and governance that come with working in global organizations, creating a business case for video content that employees created with minimal brand input that was shared on social channels was a massive win. We were able to give employees a voice and candidates insight into how diverse the company really was.

At the same time, I also created a series of videos for some high-volume roles where employees talked about the worst things about the role and why they still loved it. It was a massive risk and took six months to get everyone to sign off for fear that candidates would be scared off. In the end, these real and painfully honest videos were used in internal career fairs.

What is employer branding's biggest challenge?

Aside from not getting lost in the noise of what's new (the candidate has to be the focus here, today, and always), I'd say not forgetting that the EVP must also connect to remote workers, contractors, and third-party employees. All too often, companies fail to communicate or include these populations in their communications and strategies. It is a huge missed opportunity.

GOING DEEP WITH YOUR
EMPLOYER VALUE PROPOSITION

What's the difference between an EVP and an employer brand?

It's not a riddle, but for something so foundational to our understanding of helping attract and retain talent, it seems like EVP, employer brand, brand position, and brand promise are almost never well-defined. I've been guilty of using them interchangeably, or just mirroring the terminology used by my customer to get to the work of crafting and communicating the brand.

Even very experienced and smart employer brand practitioners don't (or can't) properly explain the difference. They just use phrases like "the way I like to think about it is…" and go off on some flowery bit of poetry.

So let's nail things down right here once and for all. What's the difference between an employer brand and an EVP?

The employer brand is the big picture. As we've said before, take the sum of all the touchpoints and experiences someone may have with the company that builds a mental concept of what it's like to work at that company. Those conceptions are collected across everyone and called the employer brand. While it can initially feel like a messy idea, it really isn't. You just have to let go of the idea that it is controllable, because it isn't. At best, it is influenceable.

The EVP is the tiny bit of DNA of the company that makes all those experiences happen. It defines how the company does what it does, why it does it, and how it does it. Those behaviors, decisions, and actions are what people are registering as they build their sense of the brand. Which means that you can't separate the employer brand from the EVP: They are two sides of the same coin. One is the instruction set of what is done and the other is the outcome of all those behaviors and actions. The EVP is the tent pole supporting a much bigger and wider employer brand tent.

But while the employer brand can be described in many different ways, your EVP should be expressed as structure, because that's what it is. It is that core idea around which you support taglines, stories, videos, websites, reviews, tweets, images, job postings and a host of other deliverables.

Think of an EVP as a concept "organizing the world's data." That might sound familiar, because that's the mission of Google. Using that simple concept, they make large and small decisions every day. Should they try and map every road in the world? Sounds like a project of organizing data, so yes. Should they build a mobile operating system? Sounds like a means of helping people organize their own lives and personal data, so yes again.

Did Google think about mobile operating systems and real-time traffic data when they announced their mission of organizing the world's data? It's unlikely, as even the most basic mobile technology and data plans were hardly in use. And yet, with a strong central idea of why the company existed, they could define the shape of their company for years and potentially decades.

That might explain why Google has never really succeeded at social media, because social media's power doesn't come from organization, it comes from connections and communications.

The same is true with your EVP. What is the core reason your company exists to your employees? What is the reason they work hard and push boundaries and give extra effort? What are they getting (or expecting to get) out of it?

With that concept nailed down, the employer brand is everything your company does with that idea and how it interacts with people.

178

(Remember, it is the underlying idea of what it must be like to work in your company, an idea that lives solely in their own minds.) You can take that concept and make better decisions around what social campaigns, videos, job posting language, and career site to put your jobs out into the world.

Having read all about motivators and positions, maybe you think your EVP is all about how you develop your staff. Great. But that becomes one-dimensional very quickly. If a company decided that its EVP was "move fast and break things" that sounds like chaos. Are they breaking rules? Laws? Each other? Without context or other information, any single element of an EVP may sound a little psychotic.

So we flesh that idea out with additional ideas that provide more information. Here's an example of what a brand might look like. It is a core value proposition being supported by four secondary value propositions we call pillars.

At this point, you might think I'm trying to make things as complicated as possible to justify my salary. And I can see why you'd complain like that. But the pillars are a necessary means to frame the core value proposition correctly, but also make it flexible and applicable to the entire company.

We offer our staff the chance to do the work they want to do, to push themselves and grow themselves **[EVP/Brand positioning]**			
All ideas are considered, but the best idea wins	We have a deep appreciation of our company's history as we invent the future	Everyone at every level is accountable for their work and actions	We treat each other with respect no matter their background
Pillar 1	Pillar 2	Pillar 3	Pillar 4

It's almost like food. The core EVP is the protein, but fish or beef all by itself is pretty boring. So we pair with a sauce, some vegetables, and maybe some carbs. In that way, a piece of beef can become beef Wellington, Chinese beef and broccoli with rice, or a steak burrito. Any one idea is boring by itself, but if you combine ideas and you can create a complete dish, one that stands apart from others, even when they might share ingredients.

That's important when there are millions of companies trying to differentiate themselves using a limited pool of value propositions. The combinations and way they describe those combinations is what makes their EVP unique.

Beyond Flavors: How Pillars Make Your EVP Work
But the second purpose of the pillars is to make the EVP work for all aspects of your company, to create a brand that resonates with the facilities team as much as the sales team, or the Melbourne office as much as the Seattle office.

The cardinal sin of employer branding is trying to be everything to everyone. Remember: The goal isn't just to define your brand, but to differentiate your brand from other companies. This is easier said than done.

In the process of developing your brand, everyone will want to be heard, but they will also want their perspective baked into the brand. If your company has a strong brand, it will tend to hire people who align to the brand, but since you don't have a strong brand, your talent will have a wider variety of interests, motivations, and drivers within the company. You will be tempted to try and draw a circle around all of them, but the wider the circle, the less clear it becomes.

But don't stop at one or two. Think of a brand as a personality: Every person has forward-facing traits as well as those they tend to keep in reserve. As real people, they have complete personalities, not just a trait or two. The comedian who can't stop telling jokes is that kind of personality, the one who feels less than human or fractured, because there's not enough "there" there.

So the rule of thumb is to have three to five pillars. Any less is a fairly thin, bloodless brand. Any more than that and you show that you don't really stand for anything. There are exceptions, but really, keep it around four.

Pillars Aren't Values
The other big mistake is to confuse pillars with values. I see how people do that. We talked before about how values are a huge part of the total brand structure, but we can't confuse them with pillars.

Instead, you can think of pillars two ways: like facets or modifiers of the larger brand position or how you present your values to candidates and employees.

As modifiers, pillars solve the problem of trying to make the brand too singular. Let's bring back the Volvo example. If they said their brand was safe, but left no room for other pillars, they would be one-dimensional. Sure, Volvo made a safe car, but it also valued reliability and efficiency. The pillars flesh out the core brand message and allow you to give it more life and to give people more handles with which to grab onto your brand.

The other way is to take your values and see them through the lens of your candidates and employees. For example, if one of your company values is that you are innovative, how does that look to non-consumer audiences? (I ask, because "we're innovative," aside from being weakly written, sounds like consumer marketing copy.) Remember, you're trying to convince people who may soon try to apply in your ATS that you are innovative. How is your HR team innovative? Or your legal team? Or compliance? The value of "we're innovative" was designed to extract more money from a customer, not get someone to apply, so you need to re-describe that value to this new audience. Perhaps you'll talk about how you're always testing new ideas, that you are always optimizing, that you're open to ideas to grow, regardless of where they come from. Those are more employer-brand focused pillars.

Remapping the values is the safe approach, because you are riding on the comm team's (or whoever codified the values) coattails. They are preapproved; you just need to explain why you have to present them through a different lens.

See the Big Picture
Just keep in mind that your job is to describe the company, not just to get a brand "done." There are shortcuts you can take to expedite the approval process (whatever yours is), but don't do it. The task of capturing a complete brand, of giving it life beyond you, isn't an easy one. But there's a real impact if you do, so don't try and skip to the end.

LIKE FINE WHISKEY: DISTILLING THE ESSENCE

If you understand what motivates some people, you can look within your company and see which of these motivations you are rewarding. Are you rewarding people who innovate and drive change, or are you treating them like rabble-rousers and trying to silence them? Are you promoting the people who cultivate your "together" culture, or focusing on the ones who do the best individual work? When you say you are trying to save the world, are you recognizing the people who work towards that goal or the people focused on developing their own career ladder?

Remember: A culture is built and fostered on these decisions. These cultures align or are counter to people's motivations. If you are rewarding the people who best align to this culture, you are reinforcing this culture and telling like-minded people this is a great place for people like them.

If you reward individuals who excel at individual achievement, you are reinforcing a culture where teamwork isn't valued but rock stars and divas are. Since that is what people will talk about, you will attract more divas and rock stars, reinforcing the culture set by what you choose to reward.

Your goal is to take all the elements that make up your company and distill them until you craft a simple positioning concept. Then ask yourself: Of all the motivations you could support, which do you do most meaningfully, most effectively, and in a way that separates you from your competitive set? Just as Volvo could have said it was a reliable car, or an attractive car, or a car that made you look more appealing to others, it focused on a message that others ignored. It carved a place out of a crowded market for itself without having to pay a premium to do so. This is your goal, too.

But there's a chasm between the idea of your positioning (what motivations you feed) and the message you tell the world. You have existing corporate and consumer branding. You have an existing perception of what your company is like to work for. You have channels and forces driving your employer brand that you have no control over. It should be becoming clearer and clearer how this job is about influencing ideas, not stating them. But to be effective as an influencer, you have to work with the existing structure. You have to be aware of all the current brand architecture if you're going to change the shape of the building.

Fleshing out the brand architecture is a long and arduous conversation, primarily because every element and function is abstract. When I talk about mission and vision and pillars, even if I define them, there is so much wiggle room (unless we're talking about a specific brand), that it doesn't take long for everyone to end up with different understandings.

This isn't about you. This is the nature of a brand. Even when I have conversations with other brand and marketing professionals, I find myself making and demanding definitions to ensure we're all on the same page. It can feel like a game of improv without stated rules or boundaries, as you expect to land on some solution. Quite frankly, you might be better off playing imaginary marbles. The only way to play is to remember that no matter how serious you get about the size and location of their marbles, everything is still imaginary: Everyone is making it up as they go along. I promise.

So when I discuss this particular concept of architecture, don't treat it like a set of instructions. See it more as an example of how to start and where to head. It's your map and compass for the trail you're about to explore.

DISTILLING THE EMPLOYER BRAND WHEN THE COMPANY IS COMPLEX

I want to be very clear: I know it looks like I'm simplifying something very complex. How is it possible that a brand or position can be boiled down to basic ideas, especially for a large and diverse company? It can't be that simplistic, can it?

Of course not. But, like so many things in life, what might look simple at first glance can become incredibly complex. First, while we might have eight motivations, no two people's motivations are truly identical. You and I might both be driven by status as a concept, but where that motivation comes from or how that motivation expresses itself can be very different. So as we consider working at a company, I might be attracted to a company looking to put me on a stage, but your drive for status might be about being able to say you work at a given company. Or even if we are both looking for the ability to say we work at a different place, my experiences say that company A is more beloved and respected than company B, where your experience might disagree. For example, if you ask: Which brand drives more feelings of status, BMW or Aston Martin? Apple or Nike? Berkshire Hathaway or Goldman Sachs? There's no right answer, so don't try to look for one. The goal is to develop a brand that triggers those feelings of status (or your core motivator) to spark that emotion and build from there.

Second, because these motivations are so deeply embedded and intrinsic to who we are, they can be expressed by a million people a million different ways. If your company is mission driven, look at your HR and sales teams. These two teams may have completely different cultures. For example, HR is often risk-averse and sales is often risk-loving. HR can be collaborative; whereas, sales is more competitive. Despite these differences, they can all be focused on a common mission, whether it's changing the way people think of travel, or saving the seals, or something else.

If your company is all about empowerment, the same polar opposite teams can find ways to empower themselves. Within HR it might be a willingness to be more deeply partnered with the business and be a part of more business decisions instead of on the outside looking in. For sales, it might be about sharing tactics and ideas across the sales floor, sharing what's been working and giving every salesperson a chance to push the rest of the team further.

Or if you have teams in different locations with different cultures, they all operate under the same umbrella of mission and values. The New York office might be a 24/7 sales floor and the Minneapolis office might be more chill, but they can all be working under the motivation of Support or Performance.

The idea can be simple, but how people live it can be as complex as fractals. Don't be afraid to dig below the simple concept. Your goal will be to find that unique way of expressing that concept down the road, so getting specific and concrete with that concept will allow that.

And don't forget to use the pillars.

The brand isn't meant to be applied equally in every case, every time. It isn't a label you stick on everything to claim it as yours. The brand is more complex than that. Once you've established the pillars, you should see them as a set of tools to use as needed. That is, you can apply the pillars in different weights in different situations. For example, you can use the idea of respecting your company history more at HQ than at the brand offices, where you might lean more on another pillar. And perhaps you can have the sales team focus on empowerment and HR focus on respect.

The pillars can help you localize your brand to different contexts. In a company with just 10 people, you can't assume all 10 see the company the same way, so imagine what happens when there are 100 or 1,000 employees or many, many more. You are essentially trying to create a framework that helps those outside the company understand what it's like on the inside.

INTERVIEW:
LISA CERVENKA & JASON SEIDEN

Look up "Talent Strategy Power Couple," and I would expect you to find Lisa and Jason's picture right there. Together, they built Brand Amper, one of the very first employer brand platforms, before making a successful exit with The Muse. They have advised hundreds of companies on their talent, recruiting and employer branding strategies in various capacities so they have chops on top of chops. I'd list their titles, but by the time this comes out, it's likely they will have added more, so why bother. Individually, they are lovely, smart and kind people. But since they share a home, I thought it would be interesting to have them answer the interview questions together. So here we go!

How do you define employer brand?

Lisa: At their best, employer brands are the sum of all the brand contact points related to what it's like to work someplace (for a candidate, employee, and alumni point of view), expressed in a way that could not be identically true for any other organization. It is a memorably specific–yet flexible, iterative, and evolving–way of expressing what the employee experience is at an organization.

Jason: I agree that employer brands are like a composite view of a company's employment experience, built from a mix of what's been expressed–intentionally and unintentionally–to the outside world. And while employer brands would ideally be differentiated and values-driven, ultimately, I think the thing that matters most about them is that their truth is entirely determined through the

187

eyes of their beholders.

What do most people Get wrong when it comes to employer branding?
Jason: The biggest mistake I see people make is thinking that a company has only one employer brand.

I stumbled into this while looking into why I found such a massive disconnect between company and employee messaging on LinkedIn. Very early, I looked at how the top 50 marketing companies positioned themselves online, versus how their 52,000 employees represented them on their LinkedIn profiles (the only vehicle for sharing company at the time), I found that, on average, only 10% of employees had employer brand messaging on their profiles.

In other words, if you just looked at sentiment, you'd see a very positive picture, because the 10% who shared company messaging did so in a positive way, but the real brand was being told through silence: 90% of prospects wouldn't interact with the brand at all unless they went to the company's page—something very few of them were doing (at the time, employee pages at the time were getting 6-7x the traffic as company pages).

Even amongst Best Places to Work, employee engagement with the employer brand would average about 20%.

The question this led us to was, how do we close that gap? And that's where Lisa's marketing background was brilliant. She understood immediately that unlike products, people have free will to share, modify, or reject an employer brand, and that we needed to test what would happen if we gave employees space to make employer brands their own.

Lisa: The thing I think most people miss is that employer brands are often perceived by employees as trying to be something that's not true. I call employer branding "the most demanding brand of all" because there are dozens of brand contact points to consider, candidates are often customers, and messages that may be self-evident to one group of employees might still be aspirational to a different group.

You really have to take the time and care to reveal what employees truly feel the brand is. Being too aspirational or generic are common mistakes, yet getting real can feel limiting and risky.

And sure enough, when we embraced employer brands' dynamism rather than fight it, and let people tweak brand messages to make them their own, we found that not only were people much more willing to engage and promote the brand in a consistent way, but their actions often led us to see if there were maybe 2 or 3 or 4 brand themes that were–I'll say "more true"–than others. Using our technology, we could do this in real time, at a fraction of the cost of a series of focus groups.

All of these benefits and insights are completely lost when a company takes a copy-and-paste approach to rolling out an employer brand.

What advice would you give to someone who owns their employer brand?

Lisa: The worst thing to do with an employer brand is to try to get all your employees "on message." It's so tempting to tell people exactly what to say. It might feel like the safest way to go, but the idea that you can promote a brand and then back it up by having employees copy-and-paste supporting language doesn't work. Again, the biggest mistake companies make is forgetting that employees–and prospects, and consumers, and alumni–can (and do!) reject things they see as untrue.

Because marketers have so much experience with this challenge, I think it's really important for employer branding professionals to build relationships with the people in their organizations' marketing teams. Once some trust is established, marketing can be a great resource, in terms of sharing experience, metrics, and also in lending credibility and political heft where needed to move employer branding activities forward.

Jason: I have to echo this, Lis! And one thing I'd like to add–or reiterate–is that it's key to create a process that extends trust to employees, and gives them the space to bring their own stories to the table. After all, all of those stories are part of the company's brand!

Giving people the tools to put themselves on display is far less dangerous than companies fear: after all, employees have a natural incentive to make themselves look good.

So my advice is, instead of thinking, "We need everyone on message," we need to be thinking, "Our message is the sum total of what everyone's saying. We hired these people because we believe they're the best for our organization… so let's get them talking and see what they say!"

If employee messages aren't consistent with where we want our brand to be, then talk about needs to happen to bring them closer together.

What is one surprising thing that worked for you in influencing and shaping an employer brand?
Jason: You have to make it safe for people to engage. I've found that when something about an employer brand won't "stick"— maybe it's a message people won't adopt, or an activity they won't do—there's almost always a hidden fear that's blocking them.

Typically, companies see the lack of engagement and think that the problem is that people don't understand what's being asked of them. This leads to all kinds of wasted effort. Bottom line is, it doesn't matter how simple something is, if people are afraid of doing it wrong, they won't do it. Make it safe, and people will act. That's the key.

Lisa: Creating any type of meaningful and memorable brand takes discipline, focus, and acute self-awareness.

One of the biggest surprises for me was just how important that element of "self-awareness" is, or how rare it is! It was almost universal, with all of our clients, and with all of the companies I worked with at The Muse, that organizations would stop short of wanting to focus and talk about those specific things that would truly differentiate them and set their employer brand apart. They were so afraid of turning some people off that they'd end up with generic statements that turned everyone off.

I developed the phrase "bold transparency" to dare leadership to get real about what they reveal through employee storytelling, and encouraging them to embrace those very particular things that make a place special. It's really key that those precious particulars do not get watered-down by committee—someone has to own the brand, stand by it, and protect it.

On average, it would take about three rounds of message development to get to language detailed enough to resonate and be differentiated. Don't be afraid to keep pushing. Get peoples' fears out on the table and talk through them. Being willing to address what everyone else is afraid to address eliminates fear. It also establishes you as that person who is willing to say the hard thing, which makes you a leader and improves your influence.

What is an employer brand professional's biggest challenge, as you see it?

Lisa: The first is wrapping their heads around just how dynamic and demanding employer brands are!

Constantly taking the pulse of candidates, employees and alumni is critical. Sentiment can change quickly and being out of touch is a huge risk.

Also making sure to use an integrated approach and taking care to take into account what is going on with things like Inclusion, Diversity and Belonging efforts and Marketing initiatives can seem daunting but is critical. When you have strong alliances in other areas of the business you create the trust you need to take risks and experiment.

Jason: If you want to see just how demanding employer brands are, just try to measure one!

Inevitably, you'll find yourself several steps removed from recruiting or retention results. (If you're not, then you're too tactical.) This is the part of employer branding I've always found to be the most challenging, and also the most rewarding.

For instance, a new employer brand might be rolled out in conjunction with a new hiring process, new job descriptions, and possibly new hiring technologies. One approach to measuring impact would be to include all those changes under the heading of "employer brand," but that often leads to an impact metric that is unbelievably large.

This sends companies the other direction, with different groups trying to isolate the cause and effect of each specific change. But with so much happening at once, the numbers inevitably explode into a noisy mess. My favorite is when the sum total of all the employer brand-related changes add up to more value than the company is getting from those activities, which happens often when different teams come up with their own ways to measure impact. I call this "succeeding to death" because the lack of coordination itself erodes credibility and becomes a killer to the employer brand process.

COMMUNICATING THE EMPLOYER BRAND: SETTING FRAMES AND FEEDING PERCEPTIONS

B y now, I've likely used the phrase "setting frames" a few times, and it is very possible you have no idea what I'm referring to. Sorry about that. Let's fix that now.

Frame setting is a concept that says how you look at something is as important as what you're looking at. If you want to understand something, you see through the context to the thing, but the context plays as much of a role in understanding and judgment as the thing itself.

That is, the fact is a thing and the lens through which you look through at it has as much impact as the fact itself. So if you are trying to change people's minds, you can change the facts, or you can change how they perceive those facts. Either strategy is equally effective.

For example (and this is a famous example, so I'm cheating): Some of you are old enough to remember when rental cars advertised on TV and magazines a lot more than they do now. One brand was Avis, which was in second place in terms of market share. Hertz was the largest brand. Now, for business travelers, rental cars are a bit of an all-or-nothing game. Why have a membership to any other company than the largest one? The largest company will likely have more cars, more choices, and more locations and support more of your needs at any given time. Rather than keep memberships in two or three companies, a renter would just have one, and it should offer the most options.

In this situation, we have a fact: Avis wasn't the biggest brand or network. Can't dispute it, as it is pure fact. Now, most people would see this fact and say, "Well, it's in second place, why bother?" and call it a day. But what if you could change the frame? What if you could convince renters that being in second place was actually to their advantage, despite not having as many cars, locations, and options? How do you change the lens through which people see the facts and evaluate them?

Avis knows how, and this is exactly what they did. They ran a very long campaign under the banner: "Avis, we try harder." Think about it. At no point did Avis dispute the fact that it wasn't the biggest company. Instead of bemoaning the fact that Hertz was on top, they changed the frame. They suggested that because they weren't the biggest car rental company, they were incentivized to work harder for the customer so they could one day become the biggest. The changed the frame so that being smaller was an advantage rather than a weakness. When you change a frame ,the facts stay the same, but the frame changes, revealing the brand in a whole new light.

What are the facts about your brand? Are you big or small? Are you fast or steady? Are you risk averse or looking to break stuff? What's your stock price look like? What do they say about you in the news? What do employees say about you? What do you offer that others don't (or do, but not the same way you do)? What do you reward and what do you punish?

The frame you set changes what those facts mean. If you're a company that is risk averse (fact), you can set the frame that your customers and clients come first so you never make a move without making sure it's the right move. You can frame it within the idea that highly regulated industries have to be risk averse to meet regulatory obligations. In fact, with that frame, you can be the least risk averse in your industry, but look as solid and steady as a mountain to others. What looks boring from the tech space might look fast and loose inside the banking sector.

Are you small (fact)? If so, what does being small allow you to do? Develop more customer-centric solutions? Give more time to customers? Give employees the chance to grow and stretch themselves, because they'll end up wearing many hats? Does it mean employees get a bigger share of equity? Will people feel like they have more agency and ownership within the role? Or will it feel fly-by-night, a company this close to falling apart, or just so small that it can't service many customers? The frame determines if the fact is positive or negative (and to whom that fact is positive or negative).

The goal is to figure out what facts a candidate will naturally learn about you and accept as facts, and build from there. Are you known for being big or small? Fast or slow? Inventive or steady? Are you public or private? A market leader or an upstart? Growing fast or reorganizing? Is your stock up or down? Are you opening offices or expanding territory? These things are facts that you can build a frame around. If what a prospect absorbs about us was turned into an equation, it would look like this:

Fact + frame = Observable information added to bird's nest

This process is much easier if you start with an obvious fact. An obvious fact will likely be found by the candidate instead of being delivered by the recruiter. A fact that a candidate finds on their own has more credibility than something you team delivers, because it won't come with the same baggage a recruiter has. If you tell me you are smart, I may believe it, but I'll likely put it in the "he's clearly trying to make himself sound good" category of information. But if my friend raves about how smart you are, or I discover something smart you wrote once, I am more likely to accept it as a fact.

Think of GE as it transitioned from manufacturing powerhouse to software company. They rolled out a whole series of commercials to convince you that their core business was much more tech focused than light bulb- and appliance-based. Now, if you had investigated the company before you saw those commercials and saw that they were hiring software engineers and were no longer boasting of their manufacturing expertise, you would have come to come to your own conclusion that GE was a tech company. You would have accepted it as fact without having to be convinced via expensive commercials.

This can become tricky, as leadership tends to lead to the aspirational here in a way that may not be 100% authentic. For example, your leadership may talk about how they are at the forefront of customer service, that they put the customer first in everything they do. Leadership may talk about this so much they assume it is a fact. Stating something over and over does not make it a fact. It makes it a claim. One that anyone can support or refute with a simple Yelp or Google search.

Once you understand the facts being discovered about you and you've decided what frame you want to set that aligns to your position and brand, you're ready to begin communicating that frame to the world.

WRAP-UP

You'll start to realize that employer branders have an impossible job. They show up. They ask questions they don't always know the answers to. And they listen. They research and collect hard facts. They interview and converse. And in the process, they are thrown any number of inputs, opinions, and histories, most of which are contradictory if not outright mutually exclusive.

And in the end, the company looks to the brand practitioner to weave a narrative about a glorious future for the organization they will reach together. You are expected to make a silk purse from the proverbial sow's ear every day. But in reality, there are always new stories to hear, new inputs to analyze, new contexts to navigate, and the river is never the same river twice. In other words, the story you tell has no ending.

How can anyone be expected to tell the story of the company where sales feels milked like a cow and the product team never feels like they have enough information to create insight? How do you tell the story of a company where white collar jobs are in one country and manufacturing jobs are in another? How do you make a company perpetually losing ground feel like a place someone can win?

The secret superpower great employer branders have is perspective. They can see both sides of the coin at the same time. They can see what staff want and like, and they can see what leadership wants and likes. They see success for individuals in falling market shares. And they can build shared futures for people who vest in four years and people who are paid hourly.

At the same time, like a therapist, they learn to not project their own desires on the stories they hear. They know they aren't building a brand for themselves, but for everyone else.

It isn't easy. But it can be accomplished. One step at a time.

James Ellis

꙯

PART THREE: EXECUTION

You might be wondering how it is that a book about employer branding takes almost three quarters of its book to even get to the tactics that actually help you launch and manage an employer brand. That's totally fair.

Employer brand isn't a checklist. It starts as a way of seeing the world, both how candidates look for jobs and how your company presents itself. That overlap is a complex and ever-changing network of desires, motivations, and expectations, so you need to see things for what they are in the moment, not what you (or your boss) wants them to be. But once you do, you can see all the ways you can impact and influence your brand.

Now that you've seen how a change in perspective can expand your hiring, the trick becomes embedding that perspective into everything you and your company do. That's what makes the difference between painting slogans on a wall and fostering a culture that succeeds because rewards and motivations are aligned, since every part of the business knows how to tell the story of the culture in its own words. This is employer brand not as wallpaper, but as DNA.

This section is less an instruction guide than a basic list of tools you can call on to get the job done. There are infinitely more beyond what is included in this list, but these tools will give you the foundation you need to pretty much go anywhere. Shall we get started?

CHAPTER SIX:
PLANNING

HOW TO TALK TO INTERESTING
CANDIDATES (AT PARTIES)

The funnel makes it really clear that there is amazing talent to be found in places far beyond the job board and hiring event. Prospects are all around you. The trouble is that trying to communicate with them via job postings will only work on the limited few who are looking for a job, know your brand, and are willing to listen to what you have to say. (Gosh, when I write it all out like that, it's a wonder anyone ever applied from a job board.) You're going to have a lot better response, both in terms of rate and level of reaction, if you connect and communicate with prospects how they want to, rather than with what's easiest for you.

This isn't a new idea. When social media first started to become a legitimate channel for recruiting, it's rally cry was, "talk to candidates where they are, not where you want them to be." And while I agree, asking me to look at a potential job (assuming it was a job I could do in a city I would live in—a low threshold to be sure, but one most recruiters who try to engage me can't reach), while I'm looking at pictures of my friends' kids or a funny animated GIF isn't going to get me to respond. The medium is designed to trigger your brain into producing dopamine, while getting you addicted to the platform. And trust me, your "we're hiring!" post with a stock image isn't producing any dopamine.

While we're here, when you think about your competition on social media, you likely think about your industry, the companies that compete against you for consumer business. And then you think about competing with other recruitment marketing posts. But that's a huge mistake. When you're a recruiter and you're trying to connect via Facebook, Twitter, or Instagram, you aren't competing against other companies that are recruiting. You're competing against my friends' vacation photos, inside jokes, funny video clips, breaking news, and Ryan Gosling memes. Can you compete for attention against Ryan Gosling? No? Then you need to rethink your social recruiting strategy.

But what is a recruiter without a job posting? It's like a plumber without a wrench or teenager without a phone. These things have all but defined the role of a recruiter for so long, it's hard to wrestle them out of most recruiters' hands.

It's not so much that job posts are bad. (Actually, they really are.) Sure, a handful are okay, but the odds that any posting you might find doesn't read like a technical spec for a job translated into Icelandic and back into English by two lawyers who don't like each other are slim, like Powerball-level slim. When you see one, you can't believe it, like a four-leaf clover being given to you by Bigfoot.

Two things to talk about here. Job postings don't have to suck. They really, really don't. And the first way to increase your odds that they don't suck is to stop equating job postings with job descriptions. Job descriptions are legal documents created to keep the company from getting sued. They really are the defensive technical specs of a job written by lawyers who never had to actually do that job. They are horrible and should only be seen by lawyers, HR professionals wearing protective clothing, and the candidate once they've expressed actual interest in the job (if that's even legally necessary). The trouble comes when the overworked recruiter is handed the description and told to open the requisition. Instead of spending an hour (or three) trying to make heads or tails of the description and turning it into something useful and vaguely attractive, they just dump it into the ATS and hope people apply. And when in doubt, they ask the hiring manager, "The description notwithstanding, who are you really looking to hire?" and go from there. And in all honesty, up until a few years, that was enough. But not any longer. Your job post must be better.

The fastest way to write a "not bad" job posting is to not think of it as a technical spec, but as a marketing document, which is what actually it is. As such, you shouldn't be asking, "How do I fill this thing with so many bullets that it looks like a Michael Bay movie to make sure I'm not missing anything legally important." Did you go to law school? No? Then stop trying to play a lawyer. Just talk about what the job is like and why someone would get some measure of personal or professional satisfaction. Talk less about what you want and talk more about what the prospect might like about the company and role, removing jargon and legal-sounding terms. Just those little things put you way ahead of 90% of most job postings.

INTERVIEW:
LAUREN SANDERS

Lauren knows a thing or two about talent attraction. After spending a dozen years helping the biggest and best-known finance companies attract every kind of flavor and stripe of candidate, she became the head of talent attraction at LinkedIn. So yes, she runs talent attraction at the place every other recruiter looks to for help with recruiting. But after spending an hour in a lobby waiting for security to let us up (long story, and it does tangentially involve Lisa Rima), you really get to see someone's ability to be aware of the big picture without ever losing focus on the unshakable truth that talent is an inherently personal business. As you'll see, she knows that it's not about the big, crazy strategy or tactic, but in doing the hard things right, day after day and candidate after candidate. It might seem obvious, but that focus on execution is how Lauren creates excellence.

How do you define "employer brand?"

In the same way your personal brand is what people say about you when you are not in the room, your employer brand is what people think about your company late at night when sitting on the couch deciding to search for their next career move. It's the perception in a candidate's mind about what you have to offer as a prospective employer and one of the most critical factors in how an individual decides to approach their job search.

What do most people get wrong about employer branding?

Often there is confusion between a company brand and a talent brand. While the two are intimately connected and influence one another, I don't believe they are mutually exclusive. There are companies that have strong brands, and I might be a big fan of their products or would class myself as a promoter of them as a consumer, but they wouldn't necessarily be top of my list when I consider the qualities I am looking for in an employer. When we consider the attributes that make a company attractive as a brand, they don't always align with our personal values related to employment experience or speak to "what's in it for me" at that particular stage in our careers.

Building a strong employer brand is as much about getting someone to be attracted to your brand as it is getting people to decide that your company is not for them. We're all looking for something different in our employers and a great employer brand is one that authentically represents the talent experience on offer to allow prospective candidates to make the right decisions and help them invest their time in applying wisely when considering companies to work for.

There is no value to you or talent in creating an employer brand promise that is not true or credible to the experience on offer. Take the time to dive in with current employees and new hires to research and deeply understand their perspective on your culture and align your employer brand messaging to that, focusing on the attributes that are the top priority for the audience of talent you are trying to attract.

What advice would you give?

Do an honest assessment of your company culture and the experience of your employees. If what is being said about your company in your employer branding materials doesn't align with the reality employees are experiencing each and every day, you will be hard-pressed to have your messaging break through to candidates. Once you can identify the area of concern, build tactics that directly drive to bridging the gap and demystifying the perception of your employer brand. Credibility, consistency, and clarity are incredibly important in having your employer brand resonate.

What is employer branding's biggest challenge?

The biggest challenge employer branders typically face is how to stand out in the crowd. Sometimes, in trying to be innovative, I have seen companies stray from what is authentic to them and fail. As we all try to get more reach and compete in a challenging talent market, the ability to focus on your problem statement and build employer branding campaigns that are targeted, relevant, and honest will be the golden ticket.

THE EIGHT RULES FOR WRITING
A JOB POSTING THAT WON'T
MAKE YOU WANT TO DRINK

Your job posting is the most important first impression you will likely make to the highest number of people, so getting it right puts you on the path to understanding how to do more of this right.

For the record, no one likes writing postings (with the possible exception of Katrina Kibben) and no one likes their job postings (again, see Katrina as the exception that proves the rule). In fact, in many companies, it's not exactly clear who's responsible for building them. Some collection of old job postings, bullets from the job description, and some purloined text from some other company vaguely in the shape of a job posting just shows up, and it is published to the ATS as if Maya Angelou wrote it herself.

But that's no excuse. Especially once you see how easy and effective they can be.

Rule 1: Job postings are marketing tools.
First off, job postings are not job descriptions. Job descriptions are legal documents and unless you want to spend the rest of your days up to your eyeballs in red lines, focus on job postings. Job postings (the things that go on job boards) are, in fact, marketing documents. They should spark interest, attract attention, and inform the reader.

By virtue of being marketing documents, you are now obliged to throw out all the rules you were taught about job postings in the past. They were fifth-party hearsay about job descriptions and have no bearing on reality.

What do I mean? Well, a common misconception about job posting is that they have to be comprehensive, that they have to spell out every single duty someone might perform so you can't reject someone in a wheelchair saying you "forgot" that the job requires lifting 30 kilos of weight to a shelf four feet high all day. But I'm not an employment lawyer, so let's move on.

How do I know you don't have to be comprehensive? Because I grew up in a time where "stock boy wanted" constituted a job posting in a newspaper. Once you realize you don't have to be comprehensive, you realize that everything you do end up saying should mean something. There's no value in "filler bullets" or "stuff I thought I had to put in."

As a marketing document, they follow some simple rules about marketing, the most important of which is that the marketing document does not make the sale. The value of the marketing document is to get someone interested in learning more so they contact a salesperson. The salesperson makes the sale. Trying to make the marketing document make a sale is an exercise in frustration.

The only other marketing rule to be aware of is this: Just because marketers can lie, doesn't mean you should. So don't. Paint a picture, create a vision. But be honest when you do.

Rule 2: Develop a modular framework.
If you had to write a job posting from scratch, you'd quit and find another job as soon as you could, and that's a fate I'd like to keep you from. So I offer a modular framework.

A framework makes it easy to see when you can reuse existing copy and when you have to write something new. The longer you follow this process, the less often you'll have to write anything new. Here's the framework:

- Headline
- Job Title

- Paragraph 1: Company
- Paragraph 2: Team
- Paragraph 3: Role
- Paragraph 4: Culture
- How You'll Spend Your Time
- What Kinds of Things We're Most Interested in You Having

A lot more rules are embedded in this framework. Let's take a look.

Rule 3: Spend the most time writing the first paragraph about the company.

If all your postings follow the framework, you will only need to write this paragraph once, and then use it for every single posting, every single time. As a time-saver, it's hard to beat. But it does require some work and thought on the front end to deliver value.

Because when you think about writing the, "about the company" paragraph, it's likely you thought of something like, "Established in 1958 by P. Rickleton Flabberghaster, Esq. as the premier provider of cracker box sealant to the world, our company has…." That stuff is straight off the investor relations page and has no business on your lovely new job posting (let alone on all of them), so toss it out.

Instead, you should think of an answer to this question: What change in the universe does your company seek to make? Why does it exist? Every day, you ask people to show up and do something, so what is that something? Why do they work together? Why do they brave commutes and mediocre coffee to do this job? What is the change they seek to make collectively?

Once you've figured that out (and by the way, this concept will help guide a lot of other employer brand tasks you'll be completing soon), turn it into a paragraph that makes that purpose sound interesting. Throw in a few facts to make your company sound real, but focus less on Q4 net revenue and more on the goal the company works at achieving every day.

Take that draft to your comms team. Ask for their blessing. Hold back the tears and recriminations when they suggest edits. Have a conversation and find a common ground that keeps your original vision but keeps them from feeling like you're running a rogue comms team over in Talent Acquisition. And when everyone is comfortable with it, lock it down and move on.

Rule 4: Spend some time writing a grabby headline.
The nice thing about this being a marketing document is that you really get to treat it like one. For example, you'll realize that great marketing is really microscopic. For example, take a good look at any piece of marketing content. The picture, which is eye catching, has only one purpose: to get you to read the headline. The headline's sole goal is to get you to read the first paragraph. The first paragraph, in turn, entices you to read the second, which persuades you to read the third, which is how you get convinced to look at the call-to-action button whose text exists solely to make you click it.

Amazing, right? The rules hold for your job posting. When someone is pushing a search term into a job board, you have about a half of a second to get them to pause scrolling long enough to read a little. That task falls to the headline.

Oh, your ATS doesn't have a headline function? None of them do. Instead, wrap header 2 tags around the title so that in the HTML editor, it looks like this:

<h2>Free coffee and meeting!</h2>

That will make the text between the tags look like a headline.

Remember, you aren't trying to sell someone on the job, you're just getting their attention to convince them to skim the job title and start reading your "about the company" paragraph. That's all it's supposed to do.

It's a time-tested technique to ask a question in the title. Asking a question forces the reader to answer it, even if only for a fraction of a second, but that's enough to get them to read more deeply in the posting. For example:

- Are you ready to have your skills tested?
- When's the last time you felt engaged at work?

- What are you working towards? We're trying to…
- When was the last time you had a great laugh at work?
- Do you feel like you're making an impact at work?

Any one of these might start to frame what you are offering in your EVP. So, as the candidate validates their interest, the idea you spark with this little question will begin to take root over time.

If you search for "51 headline formulas" you can jump-start your headline ability in about five minutes. (And if you start applying these rules to your internal email subject lines, don't blame me when more people start reading your emails.)

Rule 5: Write paragraphs about the team, role, and culture.
Having written what change in the world your company is trying to make, the reader might be worried how they will help you make that change. If you are leading them onto the arc, will they be navigating or sweeping out the animal's cages? There's a difference, right?

So with the next three paragraphs, you want to write a paragraph that explains how the team or department in question is helping the company make that change happen. Then you'll write a paragraph about how the role will help the team support the company. These three paragraphs create an easy-to-understand straight-line narrative that makes it clear how this role makes a difference.

And finally, you'll write a short paragraph on the culture of the team. Having spent three paragraphs describing what and why this role does what it does, you'll now be describing how it does what it does. Together, you'll start to create a clear picture of why someone should be interested without filling it full of mumbo jumbo and legalese.

The nice thing is, once you write a given team's paragraph, you just reuse it every time this team has an opening. And you'll probably only have to write a handful of iterations of the culture paragraph to reflect teams or locations.

Rule 6: Label your bulleted sections better.
This one is the easiest to fix. You probably have two sections
of bullets. One labeled Qualifications or Requirements, and one
labeled Responsibilities. These are horrible section labels that have
not been serving you well. It's okay. You just didn't think to consider
an option. So here's your option.

Change "Requirements" to "What Kinds of Things We're Most
Interested in You Having," and change "Responsibilities" to "How
You'll Spend Your Time."

Done.

Oh, you want an explanation? Okay.

First off, these suggestions simply sound more human. The job-
hunting process is soul-destroying even for talented people, so
anything that makes a person feel like they are being spoken to by
a human is a good thing.

But the most important shift that comes from these labels is how
many more underserved audiences will apply because of them. For
example, there are studies that show, when you list Requirements,
you are saying that every bullet in that list is "required," which we all
know isn't the case. But women and underserved audiences are far
less likely to apply when they don't meet 100% of the requirements,
Men have far less compunction and tend to apply even when they
don't have all the requirements. If you change it to my label, you're
not being strict with a word like "requirements" (which might even
"feel" like a legally binding term) and you'll see more applicants,
especially from audiences you want to see more of.

Rule 7: Make bullets count.
This one is my favorite. To get your bullets to actually be useful,
write them in the following format:

You'll use [tool or skill] to [task] to [outcome].

Most bullets are listings of skills, which isn't really a useful
descriptor of anything. For example, "must know Excel." On the
face of it, that should help a candidate understand that they will

need to use a spreadsheet tool in the job. But will they be doing data entry or running VLOOKUP commands? Will they be color-coding schedules or developing complex formulas? All those very different skills can be called "knowing Excel." Instead of "must know Excel" let's write it according to the formula.

You'll use Excel to run pivot tables to find sales opportunities.

Not only is this infinitely more descriptive of what we mean by "knowing Excel," we've also established some skill leveling. We've reinforced why this job exists. In this example it's helping sales teams find sales opportunities to chase after and bring home revenue more efficiently. That's a job with purpose. You can even choose words to make sure the bullet uses language that supports and aligns to the EVP. Here's another example:

Must be excellent written and spoken communicator

Are there any other words more often used but signify less? Tell me, will this job be writing novels or haikus? Will they be drafting emails or soliloquies? Will this person be expected to perform on stage, or is the ability to tell a coworker what's going on suffice? In the initial bullet, we can't really know, can we? So we redraft it as:

You'll write emails and lead video meetings to remote team members to ensure that everyone is doing their job.

That paints a much clearer picture. In fact, it reveals that this is a company that uses video software to work with potentially remote staff, some of which will be on this team.

You don't have to rewrite every single bullet this way (as it would read tediously), but doing this to a few of the initial and most important bullets will shape candidates' understanding and interest in the roles.

Rule 8: Build yourself a library.
Give yourself a gift of time in the future and plan out a simple library of your best job postings. I highly suggest putting it in a shareable document that you control access to so you can share it with recruiters to steal from as often as they see fit, which keeps

them from changing your hard-earned content. They'll be thrilled to have a library to take from (one that you know supports the overall brand and has been appropriately vetted by comms as needed), and you'll start building advocates in the recruiters and HRBPs who normally have to think about writing job postings.

And while following these rules will ensure you are always writing solid postings, this isn't about how to write an actual useful, effective, and engaging job posting. Writing job postings is a microcosm of how to be a great employer brand professional. Only you will really understand how the word choice that describes the company isn't random, but plants the seed of the EVP. By thinking strategically, you know that a huge percentage of your audience starts their employer brand journey with the job posting, so you'll take advantage of that. You're willing to be tactical and get your hands dirty by writing copy. You're getting political by looping in comms when you probably could have hidden this from them. You'll see that you can get everything done you want to get done, and you'll be able to make and see the measurable difference because of one project, without having to explain how the magician does their tricks. These lessons will likely shape your work for years.

This is also a call to action. Recruiters: Put down your job descriptions! If they only work (when written well) on people in a certain place at a certain time, the natural next question is "Okay, so if I can't just spam people with the job posting, what do I talk about instead?"

Great question.

꙰

INTERVIEW:
ELENA VALENTINE

E veryone should have a friend like Elena. Someone smart, curious, willing to engage, who knows when to wallow and when to find positivity in the situation. But what I love most in Elena is that she absolutely and undoubtedly knows her reason for being. I like to joke that employer brand is a calling (because who would want a job with all the responsibility but none of the control), but Elena has been called. She is documenting the concept of work, creating beautiful and moving love letters to the simple idea of doing a job. She illuminates and elevates every subject without ever being patronizing. It is truly her Ikigai, which she will happily tell you about. And through it, I have become both her fan and friend.

How do you define "employer brand?"

So the short answer is thinking about elephant parts. Go back to the parable of the blind men and the elephant. The story goes that there are seven blind men in a village and they discover an elephant, a creature that no one in this village has ever seen before. The seven blind men touch a different part of the elephant: the tail, the tusk, the trunk, the body, and so forth. Because of this, they all have very different interpretations. So the blind man who touches the ear says, "Oh, this feels like it's a fan. This must be a fan." The one who touches the trunk says that it feels like a snake, so it must be a snake. And so forth.

They all are fighting over what's true, right? And while they fight,

217

the elephant is all of these things. No one was right or wrong in this situation. They just couldn't see from different perspectives than their own.

Your company is the elephant, made up of a multitude of endless stories, and everyone has their own interpretation. And it's up to employer brand leaders to be the ones to be able to see the elephant for what it is to be able to identify what those parts are, and in some ways to be able to call upon it, to show that actually, their company and their brand can describe the whole and parts at the same time.

What do most people get wrong about employer branding?

Not leaning into the suck enough. Let's get into it. You know, again, because this isn't marketing, which I'll get into, because I think that's what a lot of people also get wrong. With employer branding you are dealing with folks who are already very, not just perceptive, but skeptical about company messaging. And when they see the video or anything that feels more "unicorns and rainbows," they're questioning what's hidden? What are they not telling me? What are they not showing me? That does make this real challenging, because people are real or realistic. And so this idea that what you're saying is okay, well, there's this thing that is rewarding, but by the way, rain, sleet, shine, or snow, you're out there working.

What advice would you give?

First, I come from a design research background. So when it comes to employer brand, you have to know that you are merely a facilitator.

Second, you have to democratize the tools that enable you to engage more employees. With our smartphones and a little structure, we have to look at what we can capture together.

What is one surprising thing you've seen or done that worked?

One of the most delightful things that I've been able to work on is working with very large global companies that are tasked with the challenge of providing localized employer brand assets for their global sites. So I ask: What does that look like? How do we maintain this overarching large global brand, while still celebrating the unique kind of cultures and environments of Poland or Mexico?

I was talking with Charu about some of her work that she does in Poland. It just hit me, you know, that they're there, not here. Sure, it might be an English-speaking company with locations around the world, but what are the ads that resonate the most in Poland? The ones in Polish, of course.

Something really shifted for us, especially in working with larger global brands that have leaned into trying to be nimble enough to let the local employees at these sites advocate for their own location and culture by letting them communicate in their native language.

What is employer branding's biggest challenge?

Finding ways to involve employees early and often in the actual employer brand strategy. Some of the best ideas and products come from the bottom up, and the same is going to apply here. So then we have to ask: What are the tools that support and enable that democratization? What are the mechanisms by which we can start to do that? And how will we scale up that democratization to make an impact?

WHAT CONTENT SHOULD YOU USE?
(YOU'LL NEED A MAP)

In tenth grade health class, you learned about something called Maslow's Hierarchy of Needs. It was this pyramid thing that said, "While you might want food and sex and happiness, you're going to have to deal with that tiger trying to eat you first." There was a hierarchy of things humans wanted. You couldn't search for a comfy place to call your own when you're starving to death. If I made and delivered an amazing meal to you while you were sleep deprived, nothing I could do could convince you to eat. You'd fall asleep into that bowl of French onion soup, no matter how well-aged the Gruyere was.

Put another way, the context dictates the need. You can't know what content to deliver a candidate to engage, interest, and encourage them to apply, until you know what their context is.

So let's put the kind of things a candidate would want to learn in the order they would want to learn them.

Company or Brand
As we've talked about, the brand trumps the role. The best job opportunity in a company I loathe

isn't an opportunity at all. So as a prospect, I need to know that the company is acceptable. Or at the least, acceptable enough to learn more about the role.

Job Location
If I can't get to the job, if the commute is overwhelming, if I have to move to a city I would never want to live in, the job isn't important. Is there coffee and restaurants nearby? Can I bike or walk or bus there? If I have to drive, what's the parking cost?

These first two criteria are all about filtering out roles that are on their face bad matches. In a world where Indeed has 3.6M open roles (open search using location "worldwide"), candidates don't need to find a job, they need to get rid of jobs they would never take. But once they filter out obvious bad fits, the search process shifts.

Job or Role
Here's where candidates apply another filter: What is the job? Can I do the job? Is this job at the right level where I can expect enough pay? Is this the kind of job I want to do? What's the purpose and business need of the job? How will I spend my time and what impact will I be making?

This section is where the candidate is spending a little time actually looking at the role postings, looking for reasons to keep a role in consideration. Looking like every other job posting means you aren't competing for attention as much as you are hoping you are the first role they see.

The Work Experience
Here's where the candidate wonders things like: What is being in the role really like? What's the office like? Will the job feel rigid or fluid? Will I be expected to grow? What kind of support will be given to me to help me grow? Do you trust employees to do great work, or should I expect to be micromanaged? A lot of the motivation stuff we've already talked about lives in the section.

This is where 20–40 potential roles get narrowed down into a handful of roles the candidate feels good about. A bad rating or a scandal can still shake the opportunity out of that set, but these are the jobs the candidate will start to project themselves in, trying to see if they're a fit that makes sense.

Personal and Professional Satisfaction

Trick! This isn't a level you can build content for. It's more of an aspiration that all your content, when absorbed in total, should align towards. It's tricky, because you can't state that someone will be professionally satisfied by this job any more than a car or shoe ad can straight up say: "This will make you happy." Why? Because it can't. Being happy is a function of the person who buys the car or shoe and the product itself. And if the ad said it, no one would believe it. The ad can suggest it. The ad can allude to it, but outright saying it is like when a lawyer promises you'll go free: It's not up to them, so they can't make that promise. Neither can you. So don't get caught in the trap of overpromising just because you know what they want to hear.

WHAT KIND OF CONTENT TO SHARE

While that helps you get a sense of how people want information and in what order they absorb it, I haven't actually said what content to share with a candidate. So let's break the hierarchy up into more granular pieces and see what kinds of content you should be filling it with.

Company or Brand

If you're a well-known entity, this might not be content you have to invest much in. Google, Facebook, the Mayo Clinic, SpaceX, Nike, Coca Cola, Disney, and the like don't worry about whether you've heard of them. But be honest: How well are you really known, and what are you known for? Are you well-known in the industry but not outside it? That's great if you're poaching, but it doesn't help you connect to people outside the industry who could help you grow. Google yourself to know for sure. Start by making it very clear who you are, what your company does, and what they stand for. Talk about how big you are, if you're public or private, how you're funded, what kind of consumer reach you have, etc. This is the sort of stuff that should already be on your corporate website, but make sure you rewrite it for your career site, job postings, and social media biographies. Again, just because you know you, doesn't mean anyone else knows you. So spell it out.

For people just getting to know who you are, this is when you roll out those news stories about awards you've won, papers you've published, lists you've been on, charitable events you've supported, etc. This is the base of the pyramid, so the goal is to establish the company as credible. Give facts and details.

Location

When we talk about location, adding an address is helpful, but it's really only the first step. Location isn't about what zip code you're in. It's much more about the commute, the move, the environment, and how a prospect's day-to-day life might change if they work there. You might start by adding a Google Map to your career site to let someone figure out in seconds what kind of commute to expect and what kinds of travel options you'd have. In Chicago, a place right off an El or Metra stop is far more desirable than a place where the only option is to drive. Your office might be a mile farther away from my current job. To a car driver, that might be an extra minute on the highway, but for public transit folks, that might mean an extra bus transfer, adding 15 minutes each way.

And what about asking people to move? If you are trying to ask someone to move from Cincinnati to Toronto, what does that mean? The distance isn't much, but it's a different country, different costs, different rules, etc. Without that kind of information, it's way too easy for a candidate to shrug off the suggestion without a second thought. But if you deliver a package that talks about the city, what the perks of being there are relative to their current city, and testimonials from people who have made similar leaps, you've got a shot at getting them to consider learning more.

When someone is at the office, what's around? Is there day care? Shopping? Food and coffee? If the candidate has to manage child care, how does this office change things? Will they have to bring food, or will there be options close by? Will there be only fast food? Do you offer in-office options? Remember, if you're asking someone to spend 8–10 hours with you each day, where they spend it is as much a matter of location as it is environment. A page on your career site that shows off a dozen pictures of the building, local amenities, and atmosphere really allows someone to picture themselves there.

Job or Role

You might think that leaning on your job posting is enough to explain what the job is, but that's only true if you have amazing job postings for each job, and I feel pretty confident that you don't. Sorry. It's my job to be honest. But even if you did, there's so much more you could be doing to explain what the job is and how someone might succeed in it.

Did you ever do that activity in second or third grade where you had to write the complete instructions on something simple like how to make a peanut butter and jelly sandwich? Then the teacher would try to follow those instructions exactly to the letter to illustrate how much information the writer assumed was shared and didn't need to be expressed. No matter how descriptive the instructions, the teacher would end up trying to spread peanut butter with the handle of the knife because you hadn't said how to pick that up, or would smear jelly over an unopened bag of bread because you forgot to say to remove a single piece of bread. Or ended up putting peanut butter along the crust edge because you weren't clear what part of the bread the ingredients should go on. I think of that activity a lot, because it makes it clear what we know to be true in our heads is very, very easy to mess up as we put it out in the world, especially when we're only using words. (Said the guy trying to write a book…)

When you say in the job posting that the applicant should have excellent written and speaking skills, you might be trying to say that a lot of this job is communicating with individuals about how to do their job, but it also reads like they'll be expected to speak in front of an audience or write the user manual. They both fall under "excellent written and spoken communication skills," but those are two very different jobs, attracting two very different people.

If you're a lawyer, you might assume you can lawyer up the posting, giving so much description for every possible context and situation that something as simple as "wear appropriate attire" will turn into a three-page contract the candidate will need his or her own lawyer to unravel. Think I'm joking? Go look at any of your vendor contracts and find the pages of the rules that exist for situations that only occur every seventh blue moon and you'll see what I mean.

224

Remember, this is a marketing document, not a legal document. So instead of trying to cram more words into it, find ways of describing the role that allows candidates to put themselves into the role and see themselves becoming successful.

One way of doing this better is to annotate this post with photos and videos. Ask the hiring manager to take their phone and selfie stick, walk from their office to the desk of this hire, and explain who would be successful in the role and why someone would see this as a huge opportunity. It fills in so many gaps with visuals and non-textual cues a posting by itself can't do.

Secondly, you could ask people doing the job to describe it in some interesting fashion and turn it into a page for your career site. Get three accountants to describe their job using only Excel and bookkeeping terms, and you'll have a page (or video) that puts me to sleep but will feel like a hot new Netflix series to an accountant. Stranger things, indeed.

The goal isn't to recreate the entry in the "these are what jobs are" book the government puts out, but to make someone (the right someone, remember) feel like they've found a place to grow and thrive, where they have something to add to the growth of the business, where they can see how they make an impact. This means emotion and projection play a lot bigger role here than anything a lawyer can add.

The Work Experience
When people in our profession(s) think, "We should make some content!" this is what they are thinking about: They want to make Instagram pictures of folks having fun at the holiday party, show what a team celebration looks like, shoot a video of everyone surprising Jane at her baby shower. This content is okay. It checks the box marked "made some content." But what does that content say? What should it tell the candidate? What should it make them understand about your company?

As every good content strategist knows, content for the sake of content, without a strategy or intention, is wasted time and energy and should be stopped at all costs. I'm not saying that these content elements are bad, it's just that they have to fit into a strategy that all things align to. A baby shower video is amazing at supporting an idea that everyone at this company supports one another. However, it doesn't reinforce the idea that you are innovative or 100% focused on performance. A picture showing a team celebrating a success shows a team that has clear goals and works hard at attaining them, but it undercuts the message that you are mission driven or develop your people (unless the success you are celebrating is clearly connected to some professional development and should be framed and stated as such). Your holiday party photos might help support a message of performance if it's clear that you are also celebrating the successes of the year and not just the various collections of religious and secular winter holidays.

At some point, agencies fooled us into thinking we needed to build editorial content calendar frameworks and then fill them up every week. I should know. I used to manage a team of 19 people who were tasked with exactly that. It stoked the sense that every hospital needed to have #NursesWeek content, or it somehow was missing out, but never did the research or even asked if the nurses being communicated to had time to browse the #NursesWeek hashtag. We helped the client expect regular content, then filled that need, whether it helped move the needle or not.

Let's start by breaking free of the tyranny of the editorial calendar as a bucket to fill instead of as a model to focus our thinking on what we're trying to say. In fact, in the next chapter, I'll show you how to ideate new content. For now, focus on looking at the content you have and how it can attract applicants and validate candidate interest. That starts by knowing your position (like we covered in the last chapter) and building content that supports that position.

Don't be scared to throw away or reject content that doesn't directly support your position. Unless, for political reasons, it makes sense to put the holiday picture up where your CTO is doing a goofy dance, because they think it's funny. We all make short-term compromises to create long-term wins. (Just tuck it towards the back). That also means looking at the content that does reinforce your position and finding lots of different ways to reuse it over and over again

The fastest way to recycle content is to reformat it. That is, take the interview article and turn it into a podcast, a series of animated GIF quotes, or a short video. Take quotes from five interviews or articles and turn them into a page about how committed you are to a single idea that was touched on in all those various interviews. (This is easier as more and more of the company embraces the employer brand and they naturally talk about similar things.) Turn that article into a video. Tale a transcript of a video as the raw material for an article. And all of these things can each be turned into a dozen tweets, Facebook posts, and Instagram photos.

Think a candidate will get bored seeing the same stuff over and over? They won't. Candidates almost never go back more than a few weeks to look at old content. Look, your stuff is pretty good, but it isn't competing with Ryan Gosling, is it? So don't be scared to look for ways to repurpose old stuff in new packages.

Find the intersection of what the job feels like (emotion, emotion, emotion!) and how the job makes an impact on the people who work there. The goal isn't to sing the praises of how great the coffee is, but how the company spends the money on great coffee, because that's how it supports its people as they do some amazing things. Those are the stories that hook onto people's minds and don't let go.

The tricky part may be trying to use these content pieces as a means to attract attention AND be a part of the hierarchy. As a part of the hierarchy, you are assuming the reader knows the brand, has approved the location, and can see themselves as able to do the job. In this model, the intention of the content is to get someone to start to think of the job as a means of professional satisfaction. They project themselves into the job and see how six months later they are doing things that make them feel good about that choice. Get the prospect thinking like that, not only will they apply, they will become excellent interview candidates and have a higher likelihood of accepting the role.

But if you are trying to use this content as a means of attracting cold prospects' attention, these folks will not have the benefit of knowing the brand or the job. That shouldn't stop you. A great story can have multiple uses. Just be sure to look at, and evaluate, each

Talent Chooses You

piece of content based on how you are using it. That story about how you only serve your staff great coffee is a form of support for employees, which works great for a data scientist interested in understanding how a company treats its data people. You can use that same story as a way of attracting the attention of a cold prospect that loves coffee. But just throwing that video on Facebook and thinking that people wandering by would enjoy it is an invitation for problems. Without the context of why that video is indicative of your company, people might just wonder, "Does this company sell coffee?" and wander away. Make sure you are properly framing the content for success with the intention of moving the prospect to the next step, regardless of what that next step is.

Personal and Professional Satisfaction
I've already said flat out that it would be a mistake to try and build a piece of content that says, "You'll be very happy and successful here!" Maybe if a marketing genius like George Lois or Lee Clow took a shot at it, they might be able to make it happen. But for the rest of us mere mortals, it almost certainly won't work. You will be far better served by focusing elsewhere.

But knowing that this is what you want great talent to feel is still a useful aspiration. I see too many videos and articles that are clearly trying to prove how cool or fun or interesting they are, forgetting that cool is attractive, but it's all frosting and no cake. Why pick a cool company? No cool company stays cool for long, so what's after that? You can ride a scooter in the office? Cool, but how does that make you happy? How does that make you excited to wake up every Monday morning and get to work?

Think of this as a manifesto to stop building empty content and to stop praising things that don't matter because they are easy to praise. What if you started telling stories of people who had bounced from job to job who were smart and talented and just never felt at home? They never really fit. They were too curious about the wrong things and too focused on results in cultures that were process driven. You aren't saying, "Here is proof that you will be happy here." You are instead saying, "This is the kind of person who found happiness and success here when other places didn't work. Your mileage may vary, but what would professional

228

satisfaction look and feel like to you?"

People can't be given happiness, but you can point them in a direction where they can find it themselves. Because that's what keeps people around.

INTERVIEW: TORIN ELLIS

I've spent the last two years making the joke that Torin and I are brothers, which is a pretty good joke when you see us standing next to each other. But the funny thing is that I really do see Torin as my brother, a wise, kind, and humble human trying to elevate other humans, driving a message about diversity that gets into the emotion and fear underneath those conversations. He has a level of bravery I am in absolute awe of. Oh, and he'll blow you off the stage. That's a promise.

How do you define "employer brand?"

It is something layered in feeling, interest, and reputation experienced by the engaged. For instance, when I think about a clothing company that I support, I wonder what it's like to work there? Is the office quaint and attached to a design and manufacturing facility? I wonder if they give two thoughts to diversity and inclusion, because I often support emerging/off-the-radar clothiers/designers. As a consumer, I experience these thoughts differently, yet try to think as a current employee or potential candidate. I go on to define EB as not needing to be unique but genuine. That an organization can share a mantra, mission, and tenets of being that are similar to other organizations but that employees and candidates should find such to be authentic and genuine.

What advice would you give?

To remain present. That depending on the organization size, the employer brand may be different in a business unit or department and not clash with the brand associated with the company logo. It's one thing to see the Nike Swoosh, and it's something different to work in material science where there are less than 5,000 people in the country doing that work. I'd suggest a new person to employer brand remain present and flexible to developing brand management and messaging that is honest with the business unit or department.

What is employer branding's biggest challenge?

I see EB as being more organic, self-generated. People have access to so much information that they are closer to forming their own opinions and aren't as influenced as much by the messaging. I believe the market will look favorably on brands that continue to express reality and not "staged messaging."

CHAPTER SEVEN:
BUILDING

WHY IS CONTENT SO IMPORTANT
TO EMPLOYER BRANDING?

Let me tell you about Dave. He's a great guy. He'll do anything for you. Just ask, and he'll do it with a smile.

What do you think of Dave? Despite a glowing endorsement, these are just a bunch of nice words that don't really mean that much.

What if instead, I told you about the time that Dave was running late in the morning, knowing full well that he had an interview candidate coming in for the final round of interviews with leadership, but on the way to work, he stopped to help a women with two kids in the back seat change the flat on their car? When Dave made it into the office twenty minutes late, there was a huge smear of grease across his shirt and his jacket was likely ruined. The candidate, who had been oscillating between nervous and annoyed, suddenly changed, wanting to hear Dave's story, which Dave told laughing the whole time.

What do you think of Dave now?

The power of a story has been written about many times before, but there is a core and undeniable truth: People believe stories. More than that, stories have a depth and complexity that claims simply cannot. In Dave's story, was he someone who was just an auto enthusiast or someone who really worried that the kids would be stuck in the car for a long time? Was the grease smear an indication of how hard the task was, or the fact that Dave wasn't really an amazing tire-changer? You can read and project so many things into a story, creating new depths, connecting you to the characters and developing emotional bonds like nothing else.

So when you are looking to learn about a company, do you want claims, or do you want to hear the stories?

I think you know the answer. That's why content, in any form you choose, is so crucial to building your brand.

The Roadmap for Building Content
Don't forget that this is a hierarchy. Candidates need this information in the correct order. Trying to explain the work environment (let alone their level of anticipated professional satisfaction) without going through the first steps makes even the best recruiter look tone deaf and lacking in credibility.

So now that you know what content to give a candidate, how do you know what content to build? If you have a photo of the holiday party and a photo of a product launch, which one do you use? This is a framework that lets you answer the questions that spell out "who and what is this content for?" before you start building it, thus keeping you from going down blind alleys or building content without intention or purpose.

The first step is to start with the "Who." If you don't know your audience, you don't know what they already know, what they care about, where they are online, or...well, anything. You are effectively nowhere. So you need to define your audience before getting started. But what does "defining your audience" mean? Here are the things you need to nail down.

Career Area
When I first started sketching out this framework, the biggest part was where to start, both for myself and for the audience. You really could start at three other places on this framework with a reasonable chance for success, but in the end I started here simply because it was the safest part of the entire framework.

Safest? Yes. My assumption isn't that I have to convince you that this works. Instead, I need to get you to convince your boss that it works. The best way to get that to happen is to start in a place you already know: What your business does and who you need to hire on a structural level. (We're not going for a fit level or anything like that yet.)

You already know who you need to hire: an IT support person, a nurse, a customer service team member, a marketing manager, a mid-level account person, a factory floor manager, a director of whatever. We start here, because this is what you already know you need. Everything will get added in as we go along.

So do you really need to worry about the career area?

This is something I've thought a lot about as I developed this framework and used it for clients, and my opinion flipped a few times, I admit. In a lot of ways, you can ignore it. As we'll see in later sections, there's a case to be made that understanding the career stage is more important than the career area. And the rules and thinking behind your content is the same for every role.

But the framework is a means of focusing thought, to quickly figure out what you can ignore and what you must include. And if that's the case, the career area is important. Not just because the motivations behind those roles are so different, but because people, more than anything else, want to feel understood.

If you were looking to hire IT staff, would you send a nurse to recruit them? Of course not. Not because a nurse couldn't understand what IT does (they can), or understand the motivations to help people without getting a lot of glory (trust me, they can do that, too). You don't send a nurse to talk to IT recruits, because an IT prospect will want to feel like you understand them. Sending someone who speaks their language is one way we do that.

Starting with the career area means we can draw a more clear picture of who this prospect is, which lets us figure out what this prospect wants, which leads to compelling content.

Demographics
There was a time when Pinterest's user base was 80% female, suggesting that brotastic messages wouldn't be well accepted there. Pinterest has shifted to be far more balanced, but it makes the point that knowing your demographics helps you define what content you should be building.

Beyond gender, what are the age groups you're trying to engage? Where do they live? Are they poor or affluent? Do they rent or own? If they own, is it a condo or a ranch? Is their commute car-based or train-based? All of these questions will help you make choices down the road.

Career Stage
One of the elements of demographics is age, which, if you squint just right, might be the same as career stage. But career stage is such a driving element in how candidates make decisions, it needs its own consideration.

Ask 100 entry-level millennials (bearing in mind that at the time of this writing, some millennials could be as old as 35), and you'll discover that the most important thing they look for in a job is the ability to learn. Ask the same question to 100 people between the ages of 60 and 63 and you probably won't hear that. You'll hear that they are interested in coaching others, leaving a legacy or impact, and that they are considering the end of their career.

The position of the career stage is universal, crossing industry and professional divides. This means that an entry-level accountant has a lot more in common with another entry-level HR specialist than they do with an accountant with 20 years' experience. Both entry-level audiences will care less about pensions or 401(k)s and mentoring (giving, not accepting) opportunities than they will about growing their skill sets and learning how to navigate the local politics.

Keep this in mind when deciding what kind of message you'll be delivering.

Motivation
We've covered this previously.

Funnel Position
We've already done a deep dive on the recruiting funnel, so the simplest way to approach this question is to ask: Are they needing to be attracted, or are they looking for validation?

The funnel isn't purely an abstract model, but a way of remembering that the consideration journey is long and requires content at every stage (even if it isn't occurring on your site, it is still very much occurring). At each stage, the prospect is concerned about different things. At the top, they may be more concerned with logistical and foundational questions like, "Could I do this job?" or "Is this job feasible to reach?" Later on, these questions will shift to worrying about what the experience of working at this job is like and if it will support the prospect's career goals.

INTERVIEW:
CHAD SOWASH

One-half of the notorious Chad and Cheese podcast, Chad is an absolute character. A combat veteran and former drill instructor with more than 20 years of service under his belt, he's also the first person to stand up for the rights of the disabled, under-represented minorities, and vets in the workplace. He's one of the strongest people I know who's committed to fighting to protect some of the weakest. While he doesn't take any crap, professionally or personally, he's a prince. Just don't tell him I said nice things about him. I wouldn't want him thinking he's somehow won me over.

How Do You Define "employer brand?"

My definition has changed dramatically since talking to a bunch of consumer brand people. It's not about the company, the employer brand should revolve around how your brand actually impacts the individual. It is about focusing on the audience and what they experience.

What do most people get wrong about employer branding?

That they don't focus on the actual people that are going through the experience. Instead, they focus on themselves.

If you're in consumer branding, the first thing you learn is to focus on the buyer coming through to experience your physical or online store. But in talent branding, we think about ourselves too much in this whole process. Record an interview and you'll see the language is in the wrong direction: Why do you want to come work for us? Why should we hire you? How do you attract people to your jobs like that?

That person taking the job is making a commitment to actually spending 40 hours a week and occasional weekends and nights with you. That's real commitment. So if you want someone to join your cult (company), that means you've got to look at them as something more than just an employee. You've got to focus on what you want to be for that person.

What advice would you give?

Keep it simple, stupid. As humans, we try to make things way too complex.

What is one surprising thing you've seen or done that worked?

When I helped build a veteran hiring brand for the Ford Motor Company, working with Randstad, the main key to our success was to treat every candidate like an individual, with white glove service. We were forced to focus on the simple ways we could use technology, hiring managers, and the rest of the support system to think about and engage those individuals like people, not candidates. The surprising part is that it doesn't sound scalable, right? But it is when you have the right messaging and technology to support the process.

What is employer branding's biggest challenge?

I think the biggest challenge is really understanding what this job opportunity really means. Seriously, why is the candidate here? Not just for a job. It's more than that and if you don't understand the true reason and you're not creating value to those individuals, you might hire them but you won't retain them long. It's about understanding that you're trying to create value for the actual individual and not the 20,000 potential candidates and that you need to treat that one human being right and scale from there. That's what it comes down to.

WHAT DO YOU WANT TO SAY?

N ow that you've defined the "who," it's time to figure out the "what."

Content Goals
Classically, these are the core purposes of what content can do. It can educate, inform, entertain, and inspire (sometimes short-handed as EEII). These goals are not mutually exclusive, but they further tighten the writer's focus to content that leads to action.

Where these goals help is to help remind the writer to focus on the reader and not the organization about which they are writing. Companies are the worst kind of narcissists, with huge teams of people devoted to taking any line of information or inquiry and turning it back to the company's perspective.

Think of all the articles written about how company X won this award or that award. This is corporate ego, speaking very little to the prospect. If the goal for highlighting these awards is to make the prospect feel like their work at this company will likely win awards, this is inspirational content, a different beast than your standard "we won the XYZ award" press release on most career sites.

If you have job titles that are obscure or unusual, you need to build content that informs the reader about the job and educates them about what that role might entail. Otherwise, prospects might not know if your Marketing Manager reports to the CMO and requires years of expertise or if it's an entry-level role.

Finally, content can entertain. Not that you would guess that from most career sites. I've always found it interesting that brands spend big money for art (stock or custom) in which employees (or models) are smiling, but the copy reads like dour washing machine instructions.

Sure, perhaps your brand isn't very funny, and perhaps you pride your brand on its button-down attitudes (see Brand Considerations in the next section). But those companies are few and far between. Do you have office happy hours? Do you have a staff outing (and does it resemble something closer to "fun" than an "all-hands meeting?")? Have you heard the occasional chuckle down the hall during a brainstorming session? Then maybe your career site should reflect that level of humor. Just do it in a way that doesn't call the attention of the lawyers and the corporate fun police.

Content Hierarchy
We've covered this pretty well previously.

Call to Action
Remember: Content marketing is all about inducing or encouraging action. On most career sites, that takes the form of three major tasks: Apply for a job, contact a recruiter, and join a talent pool. There is also a fourth action that is commonly implicit on the site: Read more.

A mistake in most recruiting content is that it assumes that content with a well-defined audience and a focused message will automatically create that action. But that simply isn't true. Every book on how to look for a job has at least one page (if not a whole chapter) on asking for the job. The same holds true on our side of the table: Don't forget to ask people to take that action.

This is why the call to action exists: to connect compelling content to a meaningful action.

You might assume that every piece of content should end with a big flashing button that leads to a job application process, but that's a rookie mistake. While Alec Baldwin might get away with the strategy of Always Be Closing, your content doesn't (and really shouldn't) feel like a ham-fisted demand to close the deal. Content is there to inform, educate, inspire, and entertain as we discovered when we learned about Content Goals. Nowhere on that list is "incessantly pester" or "annoy."

Think of a specialized middle-manager role you are trying to fill. The job description requires 7–10 years' experience in the subject matter and 2–5 years' experience in management. This suggests that you are looking for an experienced dual-threat candidate, which is not an easy find. Now, let us assume your amazing content begins to give a qualified prospect a compelling reason to apply. But obviously the prospect wants more information, either from your site or somewhere else. But every time they look for information, you've got that big flashing button demanding they apply. If your recruiter behaved that way, you'd probably fire them.

Content should be an invitation to read more content, consumed like potato chips, one after the other, until the prospect is sated. Only then will they consider applying. But if you've badgered them enough, they will simply leave (remember the threshold for leaving is a simple click).

So consider where in the funnel your content exists and what kinds of applicants it is speaking to. Is this content for the beginning of the process or should it be trying to close the deal, so to speak? That thinking will dictate the call to action.

DEFINE THE FORM
With the "who" and "what" determined, you can see the context and begin to figure out exactly how you tell that story.

Brand Considerations
It is customary to start by remembering what Bezos said about branding: Your brand is what people say about you when you aren't in the room. I'll add my own as-yet-unnamed corollary: Your employer brand is what people say about you when they aren't on the clock.

That said, there are things you do every day, consciously or not,

242

that influence, establish, and define that employer brand. Are you a suit-and-tie kind of company? Do people bring their dogs to work? Is your office quiet or cacophonous? Do employees work in offices, cubicles, bullpens, or remotely? Is the culture collaborative or competitive?

Those attributes and feelings make up your employer brand. How you express them in your content reinforces them to a wider audience, one that may not have any other information about your brand. If you're a top brokerage house, you likely thrive on intense interpersonal and inter-team competition. If your content attempts to reflect a more collaborative environment, it won't align. More accurately, it will gut and hollow out the intended message.

At this stage of the content creation process, you should have a firm understanding of who you want to talk to and what message you want your audience to hear. The brand element forces you to marry these external thoughts to the cold reality of who you work for.

Subject

This might be a strange stop on the way to the end of the process, but content marketers will understand it immediately. It is the question, "Now that you know who you are talking to and what message you want to deliver, what story are you going to tell that delivers that message?" Most people do it the other way around, looking for a story and trying to figure out how to jury-rig it into the brand. To my mind, this is why so many employer brands feel like houses made mostly out of duct tape. Don't do that.

A million years ago, when I was doing competitive forensics in college, I was an "extemporaneous speaker" (which entails making up seven-minute presentations based on a prompt with only 30 minutes to prepare). I know, I was super cool. Anyway, I saw one team that had four different people use the same story of a bird flying south for the winter whose wings freeze in mid-air. The bird plummets to the ground but lands in a fresh cow dropping and thaws. Each person found a way to use that story to support prompts ranging from "You never know what the future holds" to "we thrive because of the kindness of strangers" to "our success is determined not by what happens to us, but how we react to it." That same stupid frozen bird story was told four times, but to drive four very different ideas.

The same is true for you—that story about how your year-end holiday party can show the extravagance your performance enables. It can show how you work together and support each other. It can show the culmination of working towards a shared mission, or how you've achieved great success through innovation or opportunity. One subject can tell a multitude of stories. This is when you pick the subject that best tells your story.

Format

Should your content be a video, tweet, or a podcast? Should you build an entire event around this? Maybe it would make more sense as an online streaming webcast. But once you have all your other audience and message questions answered, format selection should be obvious. For example, if you know you're trying to reach 28-year-old professional women who commute by train, a podcast would make a lot more sense than a live event.

How to Use This Framework

This framework was developed when I had a team of 19 inbound and content marketers working in the recruitment marketing space. The goal was to capture all the unspoken questions a great content marketer asks when considering the content and then building them into a structure that anyone can use to make better choices about their recruiting content. While I think I achieved the goal, I've discovered that not everyone really gets it the first go-round. So let me help you think through the process.

Let's say you are about to build some recruiting content. You could build almost anything, so start at the top. Who are you trying to reach? Are you desperate to engage Latinx salespeople? Has it been a while since you've said something interesting to marketers? Is recruiting concerned about their pipeline for entry-level data scientists? That's your "who." Just that audience definition is enough to extrapolate their demographics, their experience level, and even their place in the funnel (the more experienced people aren't on job boards or your career site, so your goal isn't to explain the job to them, but to get them intrigued by the brand).

Then you figure out what message you want them to take away. Do you want them to see you as exciting? Sexy? Stable? A place where people grow? A place where people are happy? Okay. Having read and absorbed your content, what do you want them to do? Will they apply straight away, or should you send them to more related content? Should they see you at an event or send a video answering a question?

Now that you know all that, you can figure out what story and format will best drive that message and develop it while being mindful of the broader brand considerations.

Do that a few different times and not only will the process become second nature, you'll also find that all your content has a cohesiveness and alignment, despite being aimed at different audiences and telling different stories. They will all exit (to steal a current movie trope), within a shared common universe.

Yes, employer brand is a kind of world building.

Or maybe there's an event or other "content-ripe" situation that presents itself. If you just "write it up," you're working without intention. If you walk through the framework, you can see immediately who the content would appeal to and how to present the story to them that maximizes its impact.

Happy storytelling!

MAKING DECISIONS WITH
YOUR ARCHITECTURE

What kind of video should you make? No, we didn't forget the question. But now you have a better way of answering it. So let's jump in.

Most talent teams skip past breaking down their own architecture and try to skip to what they think is the obvious answer. But they often get halfway through the content strategy process only to realize how much they don't know about what options there are, what story they want to tell, and what candidates might want to see. In trying to skip to the end, they lose the plot completely, often having wasted resources and political capital in the process.

Do you interview the CEO to get their views from the leader's chair? Do you interview staff about why they work here? What do you ask them? Do you show them working? If so, what kind of work should they be doing? Should you show when things get tough or messy, or do you focus on building something with the polish of a 30-second TV spot? What kind of music should you use, if you choose to use music? What kind of pacing? Fast jump cuts or slowly let people see what's happening in front of them? Do you capture the holiday party or everyone walking into work on a Monday?

You can say and show anything, so what will you build?

It's the same process as when someone asks you to write a bio or a dating profile. You know who you are (and you're a delight, I assure you), but how do you package up 20, 30, 40, 50 years of life into a few sentences? How do you take the work of dozens (or hundreds or thousands) of different people and distill it into a concise message of a minute or two?

This is usually what drives the preponderance of glossy videos that don't seem to say anything: No one really knows what to say. And most folks end up building that video on top of a nonexistent foundation. It becomes a glossy brochure for a product that never existed, hollow and useless.

This isn't my chance to knock around boring career site videos (that would require a whole other book), because we could (and should) cast the same discerning eye at your tweets. And your Instagram pics. And your job posts. And the letter from leadership on your career site. And that hiring event.

By now, you should realize that whatever the choice, it should be intentional. It should reinforce a core message about why people might like working there, an idea they can see reflected a dozen other ways on a dozen other platforms. But rather than cast about blindly for "whatever sounds good," you should be looking at the architecture to tell you what messages (and videos and tweets, etc.) you should be building. Like physical architecture, the foundation determines what you can build on that space. Have a thin foundation? You'll be building a one-story bungalow. Did you spend the time and money to drop reinforced pillars well past the frost and water line? Great. You can build a skyscraper.

The architecture isn't abstract or academic. It is like being shown backstage to see how the magic trick works. It's seeing the strings in the puppet show. And when you know how the trick is done, when you see the mechanics that drive the choices, you can start to build your own, which is where all the fun is.

Going back to the question of what video to make, let's look at what the architecture tells us. A video is a tactic, which means we're going to start by looking at the bottom of the framework. The decisions around what kind of video you should build starts by looking up at the brand promise. Any video you build should connect to and reinforce the brand promise. I mean, is it important to show off a pretty new office when you're really trying to explain how working there will make someone's life better by giving them the opportunity to push themselves to do their best work? Maybe if your brand promise was to provide a supportive working environment that video of the cool office would be more effective.

So where does the brand promise come from? It comes from the employer value proposition, the thing of value that the employer offers. Is it just salary? Is it stability? Is it support from a team and company? Is it connection to a mission that matters? Is it the opportunity to grow? The opportunity to test yourself? The value your company offers to candidates determines the brand promise, which determines the content of your messages.

You can see how this works, can't you? It's like that old chestnut about how the maximum size of an intercontinental missile was determined by the size of ancient Roman chariots: The chariot width determined the size of the roads Romans would build, many of which were converted into rail lines, which means the track width was based on the available space the old roads had taken up. And as missiles and other massive technology are moved via rail, you can't make a missile any wider than standard train tracks. Foundational decisions have long-lasting and long-ranging impacts.

So we continue up the framework, and we can see that the EVP is a function of the brand position, which is based on the culture, industry, and competitive set. Follow things farther and farther up the chain and you can see where leaders and values start everything off.

What does all this mean? It means that an employer brand professional who spends the time and energy to understand each element in the architecture will know exactly what video to make, what to tweet, and what to share, because they understand where foundational decisions came from and what foundation they are building upon. They can see how the culture drives the brand, and what impact a new leader might make. They see the strings and thereby know how to make the puppets dance.

Some people think the brand is what they say it is, what Glassdoor says it is, what ratings say they are. That's like thinking when you turn the tap, the water just happens, that it isn't based on a million specific and system-driven decisions, some decades old. To them, the employer brand is just "turtles all the way down." But now you know better.

Understanding each piece might feel like busywork, but it will arm you with better decision-making power and the ability to properly defend against others (marketing, comms, recruiting, leadership, etc.) who think they know better when they really don't. If you can show you understand all the choices and decisions that build the brand, it will be very hard to reject your ideas. Deep understanding of the architecture will set you up for success down the road.

INTERVIEW:
JOEL CHEESMAN

The slightly more wry (but no less opinionated) co-host of the Chad and Cheese Podcast, Joel has a strange day job. He runs Ratedly, a company that monitors dozens of ratings sites for employer brand folks. What, did you think it stopped at Glassdoor? Consequently, he gets a prime seat watching employer branding evolve in front of him, which is good for us, because he's as smart as a dang whip and twice as sharp. His candor, insights, and more-than-occasional profanity are always a welcome (and almost always jovial) addition to any recruiting conversation. I'm sure I owe him quite a few beers.

How do you define "employer brand" and what do most people get wrong about employer branding?

[Chad and I] were doing a show last month with the CMO of Yeti. We asked him what his definition of employer brand was, and he had never even heard of the term. So when you ask me my definition, I'm coming to a conclusion that I'm not sure that it exists, that the company should have a brand and the employer side of that should coincide with the vision and mission of the company. To separate those things to me is sort of inefficient. It's what is our "why" as a company, and that should drive all the employees, all the customers, all the vendors, and all the shareholders. Everyone should be on the same boat going down the same stream.

What advice would you give?

The brand starts at the top. It is a vision that has to funnel down to the management team, to the boots on the ground, the people in the trenches. They all have to get on board with that. If I look at what employer brand managers should be doing, it's taking the pulse of the organization to say, "How strong is our culture? What is our culture and what is our 'why?'" They should be making sure that everyone understands that core idea and can connect to it every day.

What is one surprising thing you've seen or done that worked?

If you look at the consumer side, you can get a perspective into the future and the past. For example, for a long time Yelp was the end-all, be-all for reviews of restaurants, dry cleaners, and pretty much all local businesses. And then Google and Facebook came along and said, "We're going to do that, too."

So reviews became commodities. No one cared if you got a review off Google, Facebook, or Yelp, because they were all sort of the same, right? It's the same for jobs. No one cares if they see the job here or there. It's the same job.

It's also the same for company reviews. Glassdoor has to avoid being commoditized. If you go to Google for jobs, part of the data that they're serving up is the star reviews on Glassdoor. Which means that Google has basically said, "We're going to Yelp-ify Glassdoor and put reviews everywhere." Which becomes a huge challenge for employer branding folks.

What is employer branding's biggest challenge?

That Glassdoor is the only place to get information about a company. We look at roughly 30 sites and monitor feedback from employees and employers. Now some of those sites you wouldn't think of as employee review sites. For example, Twitter is immensely interesting. When it comes to people talking about their employer, that's where people go. Places like Reddit, Twitter, and Quora are places HR folks and employer brand people don't even think about going to, which is a mistake.

᠅

WRAP-UP

It took me a very long time to realize why there's such a close relationship between content marketing and employer branding.

Content marketing was a kind of reaction to a world that defined marketing as advertising, that only cared how many ads they could push out and at what cost. It was a world dominated by "cost per thousand impressions" rather than by anything of value. No one was spending any time trying to differentiate products or use cases. It was just brute force attached our consciousness with more and more ads. It was a world in which you needed a lot of money just to play.

In response to all this pay-for-play, content marketing asked, "What if I have more time and creativity than money? What if I just tell a compelling story and let people share that instead?" Practitioners found ways to spell out clear and meaningful differences between products so that prospects could decide what made the most sense. The best content marketers were able to carve out a strange space between ad buyers and ad vendors, and while they had little to no power in the marketing world, they built a great deal of influence.

On top of it all, content marketers are rarely in a position of power. If they write a compelling bit of content, they can't force it on people. People have to want it, which means the game of "cost per thousand impressions" changes to "did the people who care about this stuff see it?"

The parallels become obvious. I bring this up to suggest spending a little time around content marketers now and then. There are always great tricks to learn from them to support how we tell our employer brand story and creative ways to put it in front of the right people.

PART FOUR: TURNING PRO

*A*t some point, you'll want to turn this knowledge from an interest into a job. Maybe you're a recruiter who sees the future and wants to play a bigger role. Maybe you're a marketer who wants to play in a very different kind of sandbox. Maybe you're one of those rare birds who woke up one day and went, "An employer brander! That's what I'll be!" It doesn't really matter.

But are you sure?

I'll put it clearly: Only crazy people want this job. Why? Because I can't think of another job where you have so much responsibility and expectation without the authority to actually accomplish your mandate. When they ask you to deliver mail, they give you a route and a bag. When they ask you to code, they give you a computer. When they ask you to take someone's blood, they give you needles.

Not so with employer branders. Ours is a job of influence. To most eyes, even to our biggest clients and prospects, it is very hard to see what we do or what the outcome of our work is.

When people ask me how to measure our impact, I always ask them what the ROI is of taking a brisk walk every day. A walk won't get you much stronger. It won't build much muscle. It won't burn much fat. The things you usually do to measure your body won't shift much, and it might look like nothing has changed. But if you do it every day, you'll live ten or twenty years longer. How's that for ROI?

Businesses are addicted to instant gratification, becoming accustomed to seeing immediate measurable improvements in minutes and days. But how long does it take for therapy to work? And even if you go to the gym every day, it might take weeks to notice a change.

Beyond the way we manifest change, thinking and talking in those kinds of strange, metaphorical, and abstract ways is part of the challenge. Bridging the gap between the brand and the aspects of the business that depend on it will be how you spend your time, all the while without having the authority to demand that change.

So are you sure you really want to do this for a living?

If so, here's a handy survival guide.

CHAPTER EIGHT:
TRICKS AND
LESSONS LEARNED

HOW THIS ALL GOES WRONG

As a bitter, cynical, black-hearted human, I tend to see the worst in every situation and all the ways a given idea can fail. It would be a mistake to pretend that following along with all this instruction leads to automatic growth in your recruiting and business, and I'm not going to say that. There are about half a million ways this all falls apart in big ways and small. If you do part of this wrong, you could become a laughing stock within the branding community, or maybe the whole project slowly loses momentum to the point where people quietly point to it as a failure behind your back and never let you on any other projects because this one went nowhere.

Change is hard. If it was easy, you would have done it already.

Employer branding isn't a weekend seminar. It isn't a project you check off your list. It isn't a tactic of the month. To make it work, to make system-driven changes across the entire organization that change perspectives and outcomes, and to evolve, you have to integrate this thinking into everything you do… forever.

It's like losing weight or getting fit. You can't accomplish it in a window of time. To make the change real and for it to stick, it has to become your new reality. You need to stop eating donuts and show up to the gym three times a week no matter what. Forever.

Sorry. That's just the way it is. Nothing you can do about it, so you might as well prepare for it.

To help with this, we're going to cover some of the bigger problems you're going to need to defend against to ensure your success. This isn't a comprehensive list, but hopefully it will help you see the kinds of problems that could derail even the smartest plans. It isn't enough to have the idea. It isn't enough to launch the idea. It isn't even enough to manage the idea. You need to turn your idea into the company's idea and help each person find their own place in the company's idea. Here are things to look out for.

No Executive Buy-In

Don't think that this is the most important problem to fix, because I listed it first. It's not. But it is a good place to start, because every employer brand or employee engagement needs buy-in from leadership and executives. First, because even though they have more equity and nice parking spots and better offices, they are also employees and should see this as a project they need to cheerlead and be a part of. Nothing saps employee morale as leadership playing the game of "we make the rules and there are special rules for us." If leadership wants the company to join in on this journey, leadership must be willing to make the first step.

Second, a change from the grassroots without executive buy-in is called an overthrow or a coup. When leadership says to go left and the staff goes right, the leadership is no longer in charge. You know what leadership hates? Not being in charge. If they get a whiff of insurrection or change, their first reaction will be to stomp it out like a spark in the grass to stop it from turning into a fire.

Wait, you may ask. This book is making it pretty clear how amazing and important employer brand thinking is to the health and growth of the company. Why would executives stomp that out? They are smart, so why wouldn't they see the value of moving forward?

Great question. First, it's very possible that your talking points and proof points will create their own buy-in, that leadership will see the merit of your plan and get behind it with all its resources. That doesn't happen often. Two things are far more common. One, the job of leadership is to make choices. It has to divvy up finite resources across a seemingly unending list of requests, of which only one is yours. You are competing for resources with product managers who have a great product idea, HR leaders looking to modernize systems, sales leadership looking to fund more leads, and so on. Every single request will be framed as "here's how we make the company grow!" so your request isn't exactly special. Second, people aren't rational. They are emotional, and change sparks emotions (a theme in this whole section). What if they fund your project and it doesn't work? What if you're not the right person to run it? What if you mess up and you make the company look bad? If this was such a good idea, why didn't leadership come up with it? These are all fear-based responses, and you need to be prepared for them.

You have a couple of plays here.

One: Ask leadership to lead a new idea, but to start small (with a larger plan behind it to expand over time). If you ask leadership for $300,000 this year to build this project out, you are competing against other large requests that have more obvious ROI (sales, marketing, product). Chances are, those other players will be better connected politically and find a way to freeze you out to converse resources for themselves. Instead, ask for nothing. Well, ask for your time. They already pay you to help solve these problems, so you won't ask them for a huge pile of money, but instead ask for one year of freedom to prove the point, to show what can be done with just one person (which is a trick because you're going to get a lot of help from a lot of other people). It's a meager ask. It's also hard to reject and minimizes fear. I call this strategy the "stone soup" strategy. It comes from an old story of a miser who hated spending money. But when the miser walked past a woman (it's a fable, so I hope you can forgive the outdated gender roles) cooking soup, it smelled delicious. When she offered to teach him how to make it, he refused, assuming the ingredients would be expensive. But she said, "Nonsense! This is stone soup, and it only requires one stone." He was flabbergasted, but the soup smelled so good, he agreed. She dropped a stone in a pot of water and pretended it smelled good. "You know, this would be even better if we had maybe an old carrot to throw in." The miser said, "Oh! I have an old carrot. I'll go get it for you." And he brought back a shriveled old carrot, which she tossed in. "You know, this would be even better if we had an onion." To which the old miser said, "I have one of those!" and bit by bit, the woman made soup and the miser never realized what was happening.

Two: Ask leadership to get behind an idea that is taking root (and fuel the opportunity in front of them). As the idea is in its infancy, this is when leadership can score points by getting in front of it. The value to them is that they get to claim credit for an idea that was already working and more credit for supporting it with more resources. The project already looks like a winner, so the level of fear is very low. You have to be careful not to overplay your hand here. If you show that this project is already growing and will likely grow without support, you will bruise egos and no one will want to help. But if you can suggest that this nascent idea is on the precipice of failure if not for leadership's intervention, you give them a chance to feel like a hero without putting their political credit at risk. That's a win-win and only a little manipulative (but in a good way).

Three: Ask leadership what you should do to make this happen (because they like to feel smart and know lots of things and love it when people need their help). This one sounds the most manipulative, but it isn't. Everyone likes to feel like they are adding value, so build a project that begs for that help to kick it off. You will create allies on the inside who will support their project (yes, it needs to feel a little like "their" project, but we'll talk about taking credit a little later on) for a long time to come. You don't have to come in like an idiot asking for their help to do your job. Instead, set up the problem and give half the solution (that is, the half you control). This puts the ball in their court, so to speak, giving them the chance to determine their level of involvement. They might tell you to continue your work, that things are moving in the right direction, or they may help you find money and resources to go big. Either way, they've helped, meaning they have a little skin in the game. To ensure their choice was the right one, they will be far more inclined to find more resources down the road, as you need them, and to speak up on your behalf in a meeting you'll never be invited to.

If you've got leadership buy-in, you have a lot more options and choices on how to leverage that buy-in. Ultimately, the worst-case goal is to get them to commit to not obstructing this change you are proposing. You can do a lot of great and impactful work under the radar, but not if they are working hard to stomp on you. Even if you don't get their help, ensure that you get their commitment to allow the work to continue. Maybe at the end of your pitch, as you realize that it's not going how you wanted it to, you ask, "What if you give me another six months or a year to cultivate this idea on my own and bring it back when it's got more legs? Would that be something you'd agree to?" That gets a commitment to "wait and see" that gives you another chance to pitch it again later on.

No Marketing or Comms Buy-In

No matter how you slice it, what you are doing is a kind of marketing. It isn't exactly the same kind of marketing that your marketing and communication teams are doing, but it definitely lives in their world. Launching an employer brand project without their buy-in is like starting to sell a new product for the company but not talking to the product development and sales teams first.

And there's no denying that there has often been a long-standing uncollaborative and sometimes antagonistic relationship between these teams and the employer brand. Most of it is an unwillingness by both sides to see how they are the same and to discuss the ways they are different.

For example, marketing probably owns all your commercial ads, both television spots, banner ads, in-kind spots on podcasts, branded content, images, video, etc. That's their job, to put out a consistent message to potential buyers about the product and the virtues of buying it. If you put out a banner ad about why yours is a pretty cool company to work for, it might get seen by the same audience they are trying to reach. As they didn't build or manage your ad, they can't be sure it's consistent with their message. You might be seen as potentially undercutting or muddying their message to consumers. You're not going to make a lot of friends if they see you that way.

Now, look at your internal comms team. Their mandate is to communicate to the staff what the staff needs to know. And here you come, communicating how to advocate, engage in referral programs, write testimonials, star in videos, etc. Their team has a direct line to the executive team (as they are likely the voice of the executive team to the rest of the company), and here you are muddying the waters. Again, Dale Carnegie wouldn't say that's the best way to make friends and influence people.

You need both of these teams' buy-in to get things done. For the most part, a lot of talking points and strategies will be the same as when you talk to leadership, with one major difference. The executive team's job is to distribute resources, so when you ask for money, attention, and time, you are taking it away from something else. It becomes a zero-sum game. In this space, you aren't asking to take anything away from them. You need to show how your work actually supports their work.

As marketing is trying to connect with buying audiences, they usually use a product-first mentality. That is, "Hey, look at this cool thing!" as a means of starting the conversation. What's been interesting in the last few years is that when companies have a major PR crisis (Uber and their screaming CEO, Wells Fargo creating mystery accounts for clients, Papa John's Pizza CEO claiming that players kneeling lead to falling pizza sales), they often respond with an employer brand-focused campaign to try and mitigate the damage. They show the employees doing great jobs, providing goods and services with a smile, etc. The staff becomes the face of the brand instead of the logo or the product.

Now, I'm not saying to wait until the company is making unpleasant headlines to jump in and offer to help. Instead, I would suggest to marketing that there's a lot of precedent to leveraging the staff to support a marketing message. In fact, good employer branding actually leads to sales (see the study of Verizon where bad candidate experiences led people to cancel their Verizon consumer accounts) and can give more reasons for people to feel good about the brand.

Take that once step further and say that you are looking forward not to building your own brand, but to existing under their brand umbrella. The best way to make that clear is to ask them to teach you about their brand architecture. What's the mission? And what are the values? The pillars? The value propositions? I would ask you to sit in on these or these meetings with a beginner's mind, absorbing the ideas that are second nature to them (even if you disagree). Once you understand their world (and have invested in building a relationship with them that is clearly designed to support their goals), you will have a chance to carve out a space for yourself.

Here's how.

If they show you a brand architecture that establishes a mission-driven company with pillars and values and value propositions to the customer and lots of structure on how to communicate to the consumer and potential consumer, then, as nicely as you can, ask them how much of this applies to someone looking to invest in the company. An investor is investing in the brand, so the brand architecture has to work for the investor as much as it does for the consumer. Look for an opportunity to establish that the structure makes sense, but at the value-proposition level, the value proposition to the consumer and the investor must be different, right? Great, now could we do the same thing to potential candidates? This is a delicate conversation, but you are using a brand jiujitsu to take the strength of their structure not as a weapon against you (the "we've already figured all this stuff out, so you don't need to be a part of it" mentality) but as something you can leverage ("great, so if I build out an EVP that aligns with and lives within your brand structure, it won't be dissonant, but will, in fact, support what you're doing when you talk to them as a consumer").

This doesn't happen in a 30-minute meeting. It may be a very slow process, spanning weeks and even months. Your goal is to build trust, to show that you aren't looking to go rogue and strike out on your own, but tapping into a new audience to use their tried-and-tested structures to engage them. It makes them the hero and allows you to do great work, because your brand and their brand remain very much the same.

The same holds true for the comms team. Only instead of tapping into their brand architecture, you need to show that you will abide by their rules and processes, but that your success begets engaged employees who will actually listen to the comms team.

Most comms teams live in a world where they are expected to communicate to staff, but most staff stopped listening to them a long time ago. Why? When was the last time your comms team said something interesting and compelling? When was the last time they said something so interesting that you stopped watching that new Drake video or Ryan Gosling meme to listen? The comms team passes down announcements and changes from leadership, but does so as "the voice of leadership." This means there's no room for fun, flexibility, or misunderstanding. The comms team can't be misinterpreted. Which is why great comms people tend to be half writers and half lawyers, trying to weed out any language that could possibly be misconstrued. Live in that world long enough, and you'll build up a callous and work under the assumption that no one cares about what you have to say.

But here you are, engaging staff, getting them to play a role in the company's growth, showing how their spirit helps everyone. Do your job well, and you'll help close the gap between a comms team that has to be clear and a staff that needs to understand what leadership is saying.

Everyone's experience will be different, but don't expect comms teams to jump to help you. Come to them from a more submissive or supplicant position, stating that you want to learn their rules so you can abide by them. Show them your first small ideas on how to engage staff and ask their opinions on how they can help. Over time, they might start to see employer brand not only as a supportive tool within their tool kit, but as a way of having more fun and engaging staff without having to be the "voice of management" all the time.

No Staff Buy-In
This is probably the biggest hurdle, depending on the company you work for. In fact, 90% of your time as an employer brand evangelist and manager will be to foster engagement within the staff, then direct it to where that attention and engagement does the most good. You are a firefighter, and staff engagement is the water. You don't put out fires so much as point the hose so it directs the water to the right place.

All of your best ideas need to start with a realistic testing of the level of engagement. Great ideas will never ever, ever turn a disengaged staff into an engaged one. It can't be done. It's like trying to lose twenty pounds or learning the violin in a week. That kind of change takes time, which isn't just a function of patience as it is a willingness to remove self-deception from your eyes.

It's 100% human to think the work you do makes an impact, to give yourself the benefit of the doubt, to make the leap that if you are sweating you must be doing something good. But that is self-deception. In order to motivate ourselves as we slog through work where impact is far away, we deceive ourselves. We tell ourselves that someone notices, that we are making change happen, and that input drives output. It's a great myth to tap into when you're having a bad day to keep you from giving up. I wholly support using it like a cup of coffee when you need a quick pick-me-up, but relying on it as truth is going to get you in trouble. Assuming or pretending you're making an obvious difference is a drug, and we can become addicted.

That's why you need to start every campaign or your entire employer brand project by taking an honest measurement of where things stand today. If you've ever lost weight, one of the hardest things to do is stand on the scale on day one to collect the baseline measurement. Whatever the number is, it is embarrassing, a testament that you weren't able to put down the donut. It is shameful, and I would bet it is the one moment that keeps most people from making a commitment to their health. They want to deceive themselves that it's not that bad, to let themselves off the hook of previous bad choices, and to just keep going with how things have been going.

Ironically, if you can learn to swallow the pain of establishing that baseline number, it becomes the fuel for amazing work. That first weigh-in is painful, but that pain drives action. And that action leads to initial successes. Who cares if half of it is "water weight" when you can see the scale drop four pounds on week one? It is the endorphin hit that keeps you on track for deeper successes down the road.

The same is true for your engagement baseline. Only 42% of staff fill out monthly pulse surveys? Only 56% of staff completed the annual engagement survey? Comms emails have a 28% open rate? Only 7% of all hires are referrals? Less than 2% of staff use the hashtag or even share corporate social posts? Ouch. But you know what? Your job is to move that number up, and when the number is that bad, there's a lot of impact you can make.

Knowing that baseline keeps you from deluding yourself as you launch a new program or campaign. It reminds you to start small and look for small wins you can build on. The fastest way to fail is to try and launch a company evolving program at a company where engagement is super low. Your bosses and peers will see the big launch (because you work for them or next to them) and then see how little change results. This destroys your credibility to the point where even if you're doing the right thing, you won't be able to create lasting change.

But if you know your baseline, you can establish wins, even for small projects. Your last email asking recruiters and HRBPs to retweet something only got a 20% open rate? Brutal! But if you knew it was a 15% open rate previously, you just made a huge impact! That's a 33% growth rate! Now, do it again!

The other secret to employee buy-in is to not build too many rules into your project. The funny thing about employer branding is that you are kind of telling people who they are and what they show up to work for. If you do your research and you decide that your brand positioning is all about innovation, you are effectively telling employees that the reason they get out of bed to work at this company is because of their love of innovation and their willingness to try new things and build a brand new future. While it may be true, do you think most of the staff see themselves that way? Just because that's the hook you'll be using to bring people in, what happens when existing staff see it and ask, "Is that why I show up?"

I'm not asking if it's true or not, but to ask yourself how strange would it be to get that information? If someone walked up to you and said, "You're a 30-something man of Germanic descent with a long track record of enjoying Taylor Swift songs," the question isn't "were they right?" but instead, "why would anyone tell me that!?"

So your role is to not to tell staff who they are, but to provide them the materials to project the brand to the world and to allow those materials to shape their perception over time.

If you joined a nonprofit to do some social good, you might be willing to take a nominal pay cut. Sure, but the recruiting process makes it clear that "people here are willing to take a small pay cut to do this social good (people like us do things like this)." It should be pretty clear. Along with that idea, you won't be surprised to discover that your work-issued laptop is a generation or two behind. You might discover that it is customary to print on the back of old documents to save paper. You won't be shocked that everyone volunteers on their off-hours to go to semi-related events for this common good. Even if you weren't told that people take a pay cut, all these other things would lead you to think that people here work hard to achieve some common good. The context dictates the motivation (or at least people's perception of the motivation).

If you know the position, build materials that suggest the position. If your position is driven by empowerment, tell stories of people who built things and taught themselves a new skill and ended up doing something cool. You talk about the choices staff make in service of the goal. You might make stickers and share them with a tagline about how people own their job. Surround people with this idea, and they will create the idea within their own minds. (For another perspective, go watch the movie Inception where you'll see how to plant ideas in other people's minds that feel organic versus someone telling you about the idea.)

No Defined Metrics
Do I really need to be the five thousandth writer to intone "what gets measured is what matters?" Maybe I do. So I did. But the lesson is real: One of the fastest ways to get something done is to measure it and publish the ongoing results. If you can attach a bonus to a certain outcome, that process goes even faster (sometimes to the point of management gaming the system to achieve the letter of the result and gutting the spirit of it).

Beyond that starting baseline, if you want your employer brand to be taken seriously internally, you need to establish metrics you will be measured against. This is a huge opportunity for you to establish credibility (people who show you their own metrics are saying they aren't scared of a little good faith scrutiny) and to determine where you want to focus your efforts in a space where almost any work can be said to support or impact the employer brand.

While working on your credibility, you will have to define your own metrics. They will likely come in three categories: Sentiment, Reach, and Recruiting.

Sentiment
What do people feel about you? Why do they feel that way? What fuels that emotion? How often do you have a chance to change people's emotions? How are those emotions captured? On what channels are those emotions communicated to the world?

These are the kinds of questions that support the concept of sentiment. Don't get trapped in the monometric of "do people see you as a great place to work?" because, as we've seen, that answer has as much to do with who answers the questions as what company they are describing. For example, the DMV employee may love to work at the DMV but see Google as a horrible place to work, because it doesn't support their motivations. And vice versa. So when you are measuring sentiment, stay focused. When people say you aren't a great place to work, what are they really saying? Where did that sentiment come from? Are they the likely audience or a likely mis-fit? Who are they talking to? And how long do their opinions resonate in the world?

Things like Glassdoor ratings try to be one-stop shopping for sentiment, and plenty of people take those ratings seriously. But they are focused on a good/bad model of businesses without getting too deep into the why. It's worth measuring in many cases, but you should look at the factors that drive it rather than the rating itself. Plenty of companies with objectively bad or mediocre ratings are able to hire well, so don't limit your thinking here.

Reach
How many people will see this opinion or sentiment? How many people are in the various stages of the funnel? How many people are connected to our social media platforms? How many people are absorbing brand messages right now? Are they active or passive? Where are those messages coming from? How much influence over them do you have? How much web traffic are we

getting? How many views on our outside content (including job postings) do we have?

If the question of sentiment is measuring the kinds of materials people are building their bird's nest from, the question of reach is about understanding how readily available those materials are. You might consider things like how many email addresses you have you can ping, how many social followers you have, how many people are opening your emails or clicking into content, and how much traffic there is to your career site, third-party recruiting platforms, and your corporate site.

There are a lot more metrics for reach than sentiment, but a million people hearing bad things is worse than ten people hearing amazing things, so don't evaluate them each in a vacuum.

The Sentiment-Reach Chart
One of the questions I learned to dread was, "how strong is our employer brand?" This question was usually uttered by some well-meaning middle manager after I'd spent half an hour defining the value of employer branding to their own hiring and what we were doing to strengthen the brand.

Unlike raw sales figures or numbers of downloads, there's no strict metric for employer brand. In fact, there is no discrete metric for employer branding. You can't assign a brand a 7.2, for example. But you can show the relative strength of the brand against another company. For example, if you found yourself competing with another local company for talent, you'd want to know which brand was stronger and in what way.

This is when a simple Sentiment-Reach graph makes things very clear to whomever you're talking with.

Start by drawing a simple X/Y graph. On the X axis, write Reach. On the Y axis, write Sentiment. It should look something like this:

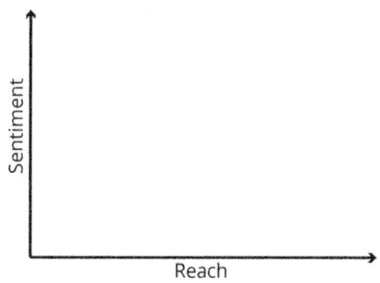

269

I highly suggest you draw it out like this right in front of the person. It works wonders.

Next, identify the competitor in question. Look at their Glassdoor reviews, their job postings, their social media and any third-party content sites. What is the overall sentiment? Is it positive? Is it weak? Is it all over the place? Don't try and turn it into a math problem. You're just going to assign a mark to how much positive sentiment you are seeing. Put a mark on the sentiment line to show that competitor.

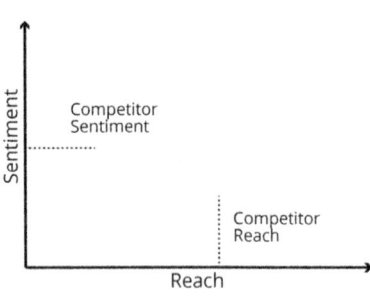

Do the same with reach. Look at website traffic, numbers of LinkedIn followers, amount of social sharing, and how they rank for a job posting on Indeed and Google for jobs. Give that information a mark for Reach.

Now, do the same for your company. Be sure to be 100% honest and open. Try to keep things as close to apples-to-apples comparison as you can. If you have access to internal data, don't use it unless you have access to correlating data from the competitor (and if you do, how?). Again, it's not about a score, but about how much better or weaker sentiment is around your brand relative to the competition, and how much better or worse your reach is to them. Then turn the marks into shapes like this:

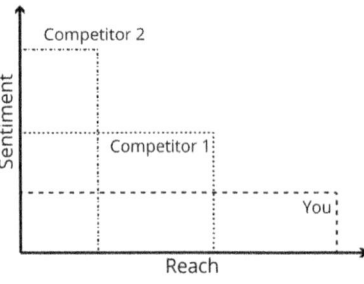

Your relative brand strength is a function of the area of the box. The bigger the box, the stronger the brand. And at a glance, you can see if your brand is relying too much on Reach (either

270

because of a strong ad budget, size of company, consumer brand halo, etc.) relative to the competition. You can see if you need to focus on Sentiment programs (Glassdoor, advocacy, social media engagement, etc.) to compete.

Recruiting

Because recruiters are tasked with engaging and attracting talent, they are your best allies to understand, shape, and communicate your brand to the world. And as most people see employer brand as a means by which they improve hiring and recruiting, bake your work with them into your metrics. Based on what you've learned here so far, you're going to be able to evaluate and write better outreach emails than most recruiters can (it's not that they are stupid, it's that their own metrics tend towards quantity instead of quality, so they can't see what you see). You can build content for them to share, either en masse or with specific candidates. You can talk to them and hear what's resonating as well as what isn't.

Without recruiters, most employer brand folks flounder, so show them that your interests align with their interests by building metrics that show how your work is making their lives easier every day.

Here's a list of initial projects designed to make recruiters' lives easier that you can use to build stronger relationships with them:

- Launch your new job posting project (see Chapter six).
- Review their outreach emails and write a few new versions for them to test.
- Launch an internal recruiting newsletter to suggest ways they can use your content to more effectively attract and close talent.
- Write up a list of shared responsibilities between recruiting and the hiring manager. Once completed, recruiters should bring it to every intake meeting and go over the list in front of the hiring manager to build credibility and establish a stronger process.
- Offer to help the most problematic hiring manager become a better interviewer by running some workshops with them.
- Attend weekly recruiting meetings and listen to their troubles.

- Identify the biggest and toughest hiring need coming down the pipe and offer to write a short profile of someone in that role (or offer to shoot a quick video).

How you help recruiting isn't something you can really measure. But if you pre-establish these three buckets of actions with your boss, they will quickly see the value of you having a well-trained and supported army of recruiters to help you get the message out in a hurry.

No Celebration
Is a victory still a victory if you didn't bother to celebrate it?

The work in employer branding is fairly subtle. We nudge people in the right direction. We spark ideas and then allow them to make decisions on their own. We influence and encourage, which means that to many, our work isn't really work.

Ours is a job of slowly moving boulders. We don't have one boulder to move, we have dozens. Every day, we come in and nudge the first boulder forward half an inch. Then we nudge the second. Then the third. At the end of the day, we've pushed each one a smidge forward and then we go home. The next day? It's the same exact thing. Every once in a while, one of those boulders lands where it's supposed to and we can call that job done. Then we add a new boulder (job) and repeat.

If this sounds Sisyphean to you, I can see why. But our job is to change systems that turn massive boats. Our work never moves the stock price directly. Our work rarely creates a new killer product feature. Our work never makes the sale happen. At its most basic, our work helps attract and hire the people who make those things happen.

So it's easy to forget to celebrate. But I warn you: Never forget to celebrate. Our work is so subtle that it demands an occasional celebration. We need to do a little victory lap when the Glassdoor scores hit a goal. We need to ring a bell when our new site launches, and another when it hits 100,000 views. We need to send the mention of our work in industry publications to our bosses and other recruitment leaders. Going to be on a podcast? Tell people.

Wrote a blog about your work? Market it internally!

If you don't, you're in danger of being taken for granted. I've spent a lot of time in roles where everyone else thought they knew how to do my job (design, social media, inbound marketing, etc.). The fact that they read an article once or know how to encourage people to apply gives them license to assume they know. Don't fight them. Make them allies instead. Show them your wins and ask them to help make new ones. Everyone wants to be on the winning team (to the point where it's a well-known phenomenon called the bandwagon effect) so showcase your successes and invite them to play a part.

Remember: Your job isn't to win, but to cultivate an environment where wins happen, even without your direct intervention. Celebrating wins is part of that.

Lastly, at some point you're going to want leadership to help you out. Celebrating your wins means telling your boss about your wins so they can tell their boss about your wins so they can claim victory. Feed them enough wins and eventually you will be welcome in any meeting and allowed to pitch any idea.

Now that's a win!

Jumping to Budget Conversations
Anyone who says you need a budget to be successful with your employer brand is probably selling you something. I should know.

I'm not saying money can't help, I'm saying you'd be smart to reject money for as long as you can, because money comes with strings. It comes with expectations of a kind of success based on the money, not based on your strategy. If culture eats strategy for breakfast, budgets determine how hungry they can be.

Here's a list of things that require no money whatsoever (beyond what you as an employee should have access to):

- Email
- Phone calls
- Team chat tools

- Video calls (if your company is distributed)
- Surveys (between Google Forms and SurveyMonkey, you can collect a lot of custom data for free)
- Your career website (change pictures, text, even learn a little HTML and make some design changes for free)
- Posters (What? Even if you don't have Illustrator or Photoshop, you have a slide-building tool and a printer)
- Dry-erase markers (Between whiteboards, glass walls and windows, I would guess something like 70% of all office vertical surfaces are writeable and visible, so use them)
- Intranet (I'm not saying anyone looks at it, but it is a tool you can use)
- HRIS systems
- Recruiter outreach emails and InMails
- Job postings
- Third-party websites like Medium or YouTube
- Social media (posts, banners, hashtags, filters, etc.)
- Video (You have a phone, right?)
- Podcasting (Again, record with your phone, save to a SoundCloud account)
- Onboarding (Most onboarding is junk and I would bet whoever is doing it now would love your help to make it better)

It should be a rule that you can't ask for more than $1,000 until you've leveraged most of the above list. The rule actually helps you, because it creates dozens of little wins that you can use to build your case that you can manage a bigger budget and you can show ROI. In the process of launching and using all these channels, you're going to have to define a clear position, create some compelling calls to action, and test any number of talking points to see what works and what doesn't. It's like training to drive on a video (and crashing the car a million stupid ways) before proving you can drive on the test track. That's when you ask for their keys.

That's not even a comprehensive list. Look at your company and see what resources naturally exist. I've been in places where they were already paying for a third-party web host. I just got an account (free), installed WordPress (free), installed a design overlay tool ($85) and started building profiles of staff. Yes, I got help from the design team to help me polish the look and feel (and keep it in line with existing style guides). Yes, I got help from the editorial team to get headshots as I needed them. Yes, I asked people I knew to be the first profiles to go live. But that's how to build a 20,000-visit site in a year for less than $100. I used what was available.

If you work at a place that builds mobile apps, ask for help to build a mobile storytelling tool. If you work at a packing facility, work with packaging to tell employee stories and have them printed right on the boxes. Work in a place where everyone spends all day in different locations? Ask them to send you cool pics from where they are and fill your social channels.

Once you do all that, asking for money is much easier. You have a track record. You have shown you can do a lot with nothing. You won't look greedy, because your needs align to the business needs, making you a very safe bet.

Making It About You

I left this one until last, because it's the scariest one. That's right, far scarier than pitching a CEO or rejecting your own self-deception. That scary thing? Your ego.

I owned the global employer brand for Groupon for 18 months, and in that time, we made huge strides, turning a brand that wasn't attracting top-tier talent into the number one rated employer brand in Chicago. A lot of what I tested and learned in that time are on these pages (so hello, AJ and John! Take a bow!). We built something like 400 employee profiles for the People site, but I never built one about myself. We highlighted success around the company on social media channels, but never our own. You won't find me on any videos or pictures, because I was always the one behind the camera (or holding the phone, in many cases). I wrote glowing stories about other teams, other managers, and other offices. I raved anonymously about the culture and office space. But you would be hard-pressed to find my name on any of it.

The thinking? We don't take our bows publicly. We celebrate victories internally, where they can do the most good. I didn't want anyone to think I was building this brand for my own benefit. It was their brand. I was only facilitating its growth. It's like being the trainer at the gym: The person lifting the weights should command the attention and kudos. The trainer should just be yet another person applauding their effort.

When I owned the brand, there was someone else at the company who was tasked with elevating the brand in their own space (independent of my team's work). It was crystal clear how their focus on promoting themselves instead of promoting the brand leeched their credibility over time, to the point where few people would take them seriously.

Sure, I made certain my boss (and her boss) had all kinds of data points to show we were doing great work and making an impact. I took my victory laps. I knew I needed their help to keep things moving in the right direction. But my position of never letting the employer brand be "The James Show" made it easier to show up to other team's meetings and suggest ways to help them promote themselves. It was never about me. It was only about them. I highly recommend embracing that as a strategy.

INTERVIEW:
RACHEL DURAN

There are three kinds of employer brand professionals. The first live in agency land, working hard to solve a client problem as fast as possible before jumping to the next one. The second go in-house, living inside the brand, putting it on like an overcoat and wearing it every day. The third is the rare bird who can do both, who knows when to go deep and when to jump to the next problem. That's why I am such a fan of Rachel. She is that third type, taking a community-first, "just let your employees be people" approach to branding (which is not easy). Currently, she owns the employer brand of a fast-growing cloud company, where she gets to think big thoughts while keeping her hands dirty.

How do you define "employer brand?"

Employer brand is the feeling you convey to candidates, and even customers, about your company culture through visuals, sound, and interactions.

What do most people get wrong about employer branding?

Most companies seem to rely heavily on professional videography and photography for their employer brand communications, even on social media. While those refined media assets certainly have their place in an employer branding strategy, it can come off to candidates as too contrived and not genuine. Employee-generated content can be an effective tool for

277

projecting authenticity in employer brand stories, and it's relatively easy, inexpensive, and quick to request and collect. You may be surprised how many of your team members are naturally gifted, or even professionals, in creating digital content with their phones.

What advice would you give?

The most important key to solving your employer brand issues is to know your audience. You can use a variety of tools–surveys, analytics, competitive analysis–to understand where the gaps in information and sentiment occur in your candidate experience, and how that differs by region, job type, and diverse backgrounds. Also, be sure to work closely with your recruiters and sourcers, as they speak with candidates and hiring managers all day and can provide a wealth of information on each unique candidate audience. Once you have a deep understanding of the gaps, you can evaluate the opportunity losses, both from a financial and quality-of-hire standpoint, and you can make a solid business case for the proposed time and money spent on improvements.

What is one surprising thing you've seen or done that worked?

The most surprisingly effective employer brand campaign I've seen that worked was a Pinterest board. It started out as an internal EB project–create printable PDFs of cutout cards with clever puns for Employee Appreciation Week gifts. We decided to make a public careers blog about how we created the cards and even provided a download for our template. We then added the gift example pics to a Pinterest board and linked each pin to the careers blog. For two years, our gift pics with the clever logo cards were in the top Google Image results for "Employee Appreciation Gift Ideas" and Pinterest was in our top 10 sources for visits to our careers site. And that's how Pinterest ended up on an enterprise software company's ATS candidate source list!

What is employer branding's biggest challenge?

I think an employer brander's biggest challenge is building internal relationships. Employer Brand requires a strong working relationship with the hiring managers and the marketing, legal, HR, and executive teams. And when it comes time to build content for various locations, teams, and events, you'll eventually get to know a substantial percentage of people in your organization. My best advice for navigating this task is to offer help before asking, be present and sociable at as many events as possible, follow every internal and external employee group you can find, and be collaborative.

THE LAUNDRY LIST OF GOOD IDEAS

"Inspiration is for amateurs. The rest of us just show up and get to work. If you wait around for the clouds to part and a bolt of lightning to strike you in the brain, you are not going to make an awful lot of work. All the best ideas come out of the process; they come out of the work itself."
—Chuck Close, artist

Random story. Chuck Close suffers from prosopagnosia, or face blindness. He sees faces, but not as "faces." But that kind of mental "glitch" is what allows him to see faces differently, leading him to become one of America's most famous living painters. He should serve as an inspiration to the weird work we do (see: Employer Brand Manifesto).

Most starting writers fear the blank page. Most beginning artists stare blankly at the empty canvas. The only way to move forward is to move. So when the going gets rough (or more likely, when the going gets strange), here are some good ideas to just help you get moving, even when you don't know what to do.

Guerilla Marketing
First, go read any of the "guerilla marketing" books by Jay Conrad Levinson. Like employer branding, guerilla marketing is a mindset that says that effective marketing isn't about marketing budgets, but about the intersection of the right message to the right person at the right time.

My favorite guerilla marketing tactic is to leverage whiteboards in an office. The assumption is that anything written on one is something someone wrote, not a marketing message. So if you start writing motivational quotes or the hashtag on random boards, it will feel like an organic expression of an idea. It will seem like people are just writing it on their own, instead of something with an intention, which will have greater impact.

When you go to an industry event where you know candidates will be, don't do what everyone else does (spend big cash on a lavish booth that no one remembers a week later). Instead, find other ways to push messaging out. Try and own the back channel or hashtag, engaging people directly, asking questions to get people talking and generally spark curiosity (you don't even have to be at the event to make that work). Or if the company is sending a bunch of staff to a big event, save your booth and swag money and tell all attendees that the cost of the ticket and travel is that they each have to make three friends each day. Strangers they can connect with on LinkedIn or Facebook. Then those staff can talk up the company directly. You could even take your swag money and use it to buy all these new friends nonbranded gifts (I'm partial to books) that they will prize. For less than a few hundred bucks, you made dozens of connections, and they all think your company is amazing.

And let's not forget stickers. For not much money, you can print up a few hundred stickers of your tagline or hashtag and use them as rewards for people who make a video, are cheerleaders on social media, complete a profile, or are just your support system. Let them put that sticker on their computer or office window. Let them show off their support for less than a few cents each.

Building Brand Ambassadors

There's an army waiting for you if you know where to look and how to unlock it. The best part is they all work at your company But it isn't easy. These people are busy with their own full-time jobs and lives so you need to give them a great reason to join your little rag-tag group of misfits.

One: Teach all new hires that the expectation is that they share social media content that you and the recruiters put out (do this after the lawyers have attempted to scare the bejesus out of them with their compliance and "privileged content" presentation at onboarding). Just review your talking points with legal and turn the "this is how you get fired and sued" part of onboarding into something productive and engaging.

Two: Identify cheerleaders at your company and ask them to share their own content (pictures, GIFs, awards) that align to your social media guidelines. Make a list of those cheerleaders' social media accounts and share these accounts with recruiters to amplify those posts. Don't know who the cheerleaders are? They are the ones who have helped you recently.

Three: Ask people to post Glassdoor reviews (at the right times). Can you embed a "congrats on your new promotion! Now leave a review" email into your HRIS system? Or request they write a review at their 90-day mark? Do it!

Four: Got employee resource groups? Go make friends. It turns out these folks are better connected to audiences you might never know about. If you want to attract more black and African American applicants, ask people in the black/African American employee resource groups to refer folks, to tell their stories, and to engage. Offer to help them tell that very specific story and amplify it so it isn't "just a diversity story" but also an employer brand story. Now do the same thing for all ERGs.

Five: Draw a line across your org chart where everyone above the line will be given a special code to hand to amazing people they meet that will act as a "golden ticket" and move those people directly to a recruiter for white glove service instead of having their resume sit. The assumption is that everyone above this line understands the business and culture and is vouching for this person as being an interesting fit. If hiring is everyone's business, this is what they can do.

Six: Shirts. Encourage all staff to wear their shirts in the wild, answering peoples' questions about what it's like to work there. Bonus points for situations where a lot of staff will be in one spot and they all have on your shirts (a local fun run, an industry event, etc.). Low cost, but big impact.

How Marketing Can Help

As a marketer myself, I sometimes assume I can do it all on my own and that isn't the smart play. You can and should work together to get your message out there.

First, don't assume anyone in marketing will talk to you until you've established your employer brand work as existing within their brand architecture.

Second, don't ask anyone in marketing to stop anything they are doing to promote your message.

Third, never ask them to share jobs. That in no way helps them achieve their own goals. But you can focus on telling interesting stories about people who work there, the kinds of work they do, how engaged they are, why they chose to work there, etc.

The goal is to find places in between their messages to tap into an audience who already has a positive sentiment. So don't ask them to give you commercial slots, but do ask if you can put the people site URL on the tape that seals consumer boxes. Don't ask them to promote you on social media, but do ask if you can deliver regular employee stories that support the idea that yours is a cool company, both for consumers and applicants.

Down the road, if you play your cards right, you can build relationships with marketers who can be your second set of eyes on your own branding and marketing messages. They can help you fine-tune language, provide better graphics, and even be a sounding board for you to bounce your crazy ideas off of. It takes time and trust to get to that stage, but it's very much something to aspire to.

How Can Internal Comms Hel?p

In many companies, comms owns the internal channels. So the biggest help they can provide is giving you access and guidance in using them.

Comms tends to be focused on the what: What someone needs to do, what someone's no longer allowed to do, what the new campaign is, what the new project is. They focus on details and step-by-step instructions and ensure everyone understands what to do and when they need to do it.

But you are becoming the master of the why and you are learning the power of the why. So perhaps you can lend your new skills to comms, not because you're so much smarter than they are, but because you can support their goals. If more people know why they should refer applicants, they will. If more people know why the company exists and why it's made strategic decisions, people will absorb those messages more readily (and then communicate them out for you). If people feel like everyone around them is working for the same why, they will feel better connected to the business.

So help comms communicate the why. Not only will you help them, you'll also be helping yourself.

What Can Leadership Do?
Large swaths of staff will take their cues from leadership. What the executive team talks about is what other people begin to care about. For example, if you want to increase the number of referrals, a bonus helps. But the real spur to change that part of the culture is to have someone from the executive team talk about who drove the most referrals that quarter at the all-staff meeting. Bonus points if that message comes not from the CHRO (who people will assume is invested in supporting the idea), but from the COO or CEO (reinforcing the idea that referrals support the business, not just recruiting).

Executive communications should mention the EVP, brand promise, and/or tagline. They should be seen holding bottles with your tagline or sticker. They should be the first to put your posters on their doors. They should be referring people and be willing to complete employee profiles (and not just letting their executive assistants do it).

Leadership is staff, albeit with more visibility, so ask them to play a role in communicating the message.

What Can the New Hire Do?
New hires do not walk in the door ready to become advocates for your brand. Sure, they are likely excited and engaged with the

opportunity this new role brings, but they will likely take on the bearing and demeanor of the rest of the staff very quickly. If morale is low, new staff will quickly be taught to lower their morale to match it.

That is, unless you intervene. New hires are your chance to establish expectations moving forward, and they can be the seeds that begin to shift how all staff see themselves. It's a lot easier to get someone who doesn't have years of existing emotional scar tissue to engage the brand to tell more stories

Don't let the fact that new hires don't know a lot about the company yet dissuade you. Remember that a culture is "people like us do things like this," so explain to these new hires, "people who work at this company do things like review us on review sites, share social posts, tell stories, refer other people, and talk about their why." Injecting new ideas into the culture is an effective means of turning culture around.

Everything in the Right Place
Go ask your training team: If you teach someone a skill but don't make them immediately practice that skill, they won't have learned a thing. A well-launched referral program will be forgotten by 98% of all staff by the time they get back to their desks.

While I'm asking, when you launched that program, did you ask people to refer for a specific role? Or did you just ask them to refer people in general? Because if I ask you to refer "someone" for "something" and I'm not specific, what am I asking for? A vague request is more easily forgotten than recent John Cusack movie titles. There's no hook for them to engage with, and it just falls out of their heads.

A successful program starts at the moment of need. That is, the moment a requisition goes live, the recruiter should ask their team to submit a referral for that specific role. Why? Well, for one, data scientists know other data scientists and nurses know other nurses. If you want a new content marketer, ask your existing content marketers. Ask them to refer someone for that particular role, because it is specific. The team can read the role and envision someone for it, leading to the connection. That ask should also remind the team how to refer and why they should refer.

INTERVIEW:
LANE SUTTON

Lane is a natural-born employer brander, seemingly materializing as a seasoned pro from out of nowhere, landing gigs at some very well-known companies and becoming one of the clearest voices of what younger talent wants today. You know that saying about how one generation learned the internet and the next was born into it? Lane is of the generation that was born into modern employer branding. It's as if he didn't have to learn it, he just natively understood it. So yeah, I'm absolutely jealous.

How do you define "employer brand?"

Employer brand is what people say, think, feel, or do when it comes to your brand as an employer. It's what people say when you're not in the room. Do they tell family or friends about working for you? Do they think you're a "best" place to work? Do they feel your brand, resonate with it, and see themselves there? Do they apply or want to apply?

What do most people get wrong about employer branding?

Missing the story. Often, our employer value propositions feel and sound the same. Differentiate yourself from the competition. What's unique about your culture or company? Don't just say it, let your employees say and share it. They're your best ambassadors and storytellers. Candidates want to hear from people like them. Ask: Can I see myself here?

What advice would you give?

Don't go it alone. Most of us have come from HR or marketing backgrounds, and there's plenty of resources or people who have solved similar problems. We're willing to help.

Ask for help, leverage your resources, and build partnerships. Employer brand teams all start small. Make friends with Marketing, as they may already have what you need or they can help. They might be willing to help design for you, write, or offer help.

Don't assume you know your talent. Do the research. Before running a campaign, research your audience, develop a candidate persona, and craft a message that resonates with them.

What is one surprising thing you've seen or done that worked?

iPhone videos from your employees. Don't over-engineer, overthink, or overproduce your content. Sometimes, the unedited iPhone video from an employee does the job and it feels real. This could be done in the form of Q&A or video job descriptions from the hiring manager.

What is employer branding's biggest challenge?

Being true and authentic to your brand and what it's really like vs. overly aspirational. There's a balance between saying who you are and who you're not. There's a lot to be said about painting an accurate picture of what it's like to work for your company to attract the right people and let them opt-in.

Data. There is lots to measure. Find the metrics that work for you and the metrics important to leadership. What do they want to see? How do they determine value? Now, find the system and tools to measure it and tell the story of your work. A lot of it is influence and hard to attribute, but recruitment marketing, campaigns, or platforms will provide a lot of the metrics. Good employer brand people are storytellers, but we often struggle telling the story of data or our own work.

James Ellis

CHAPTER NINE:
INTO THE UNKNOWN

Employer brand professionals are a strange lot, in that we are often people without a country. If we're based inside the recruiting team, we aren't recruiters. If we live in marketing, we're a very different breed of marketer. The market itself is still emerging to define what it is we do. Commonly, we're only noticed when something goes wrong.

So this is our rallying cry, a flag all employer brand professionals can point to and say, "yeah, this is why we're amazing (and different by design)" that can be understood by recruiters, HR, business leaders, and marketers/comms (our big four internal partners).

This is the manifesto that declares, "We're not your swag mavens, your job post writers, or tool buyers. We are the orchestra conductors seeing the big picture, understanding and communicating the brand to the world so the business grows."

THE THREE EMPLOYER BRANDING HATS

With apologies to thinking and cognition expert Edward de Bono, whose Six Thinking Hats is an absolutely classic of how to solve problems creatively, employer brand pros eventually find themselves solving their own challenges while swapping between their own three hats: tactical, strategic, and political.

Tactical Hat

This isn't some idle notion. When most of us start in employer brand, we're tasked with thinking tactically: go respond to reviews, go write job posts, go run that event, etc. We often create the job by simply specializing in some form of content creation arcana that recruiters don't want to touch. Once established, we learn to properly manage the tactics necessary to manage a brand mostly by bolting on new skills, learning new tools, and adding new weapons to our own personal arsenals. So it stands to reason that growth is more of the same. But each additional add-on has fundamentally less value than the previous ones, because the value isn't in knowing how to complete a task, but in having the awareness of knowing when to decide to complete the task.

Strategic Hat

It's a classic case of what got you here won't get you there. Being a walking encyclopedia of skills and settings makes you indispensable to the team, but it won't get you promoted. To raise your apparent value to the organization, you need to focus less on being "the one who does things" and more on being "the one who makes smart decisions."

This is the strategic hat, the higher-level thinking that decides what tool to apply and when or how to apply it. Anyone can make a video, but only the strategic hat knows the best time (and subject and point of view, etc.) to make more video content.

The strategic hat and the tactical hats are often in conflict, because they want different things. The tactical hat tends to make you feel good when you complete a task, when you know how to solve that problem and then solve it. The strategic hat feels good when it has created outsized value relative to the work put into it. The strategic hat knows there are times when small, almost noticeable changes in a process can make huge impacts and feels good that it made the impact with little effort; whereas, the tactical hat frets that no one noticed that it solved the problem.

Additionally, what it takes to get better with each hat is very different. Adding a new skill to the tactical hat might be as simple as watching a how-to video online. Adding new levels of competency as a strategy can't be learned nearly as easily. You get better as a strategist by reading better books and spending that hour in the car, thinking of all the permutations and outcomes for various actions taken. Strategists see paths forward, which is a skill you can't learn in school.

Political Hat
But the third hat makes things even more complicated. As you become a strong strategist, you may start to realize there are levers and buttons of power within the company that you never seem to have access to. You feel a level or two removed from the people who seem to know how to get things done. It isn't title and level, strictly, but that some people can always get into the meeting, are always on the periphery of an announcement, and just know how to nudge something across the finish line.

This is the political hat, and it is both powerful and strange. This isn't to say that you should go out and buy all the Robert Greene books and commit them to memory (though, that's not exactly a waste of time). The political hat is the ability to see individual's motivations and drivers. It knows what your opponent or team-member wants, and it can move pieces and resources around in seemingly random ways until you deliver what they want, and they, in turn, give you what you want. The first season of House of Cards is probably the best example of how a political player can turn scraps of something into pressure and change.

The Hats in Action

These three concepts are very vague. I mean, hats? But here's an example that illustrates how each of these hats have their own merits, especially when the employer brand manager knows when to switch between them adroitly.

Maybe you decide unilaterally to build some recruiting-focused social media content for your LinkedIn channel, because you know that your audience goes there for insight into what it might be like to work there. You end up building a bunch of posts with photos that you know will engage and attract more prospects and still align fairly well with the consumer brand. You aren't expecting a parade, but you assume that eventually the marketing and comms teams will realize the gift you've sent them and send their thanks.

But marketing and comms, who claim exclusive ownership of the LinkedIn channel, reject your posts and say the channel should be consumer-facing only, despite a lack of evidence that consumers engage there.

Despite feeling frustrated, you decide to build a separate recruiting-focused Instagram channel to show off the staff doing various employer branding-type stuff and also various recruiting events. And in the zeitgeist of the channel, you also throw in some inspirational quotes that align to your EVP (even if people don't really realize it). You also start using a hashtag of your own design, because that's just what you do.

The best way to get people to use a hashtag is to make sure they see it, which means asking the comms and marketing teams to occasionally add your hashtag to their work as appropriate. It's not a big ask, but it will extend your audience and lend some legitimacy to your own channel, which you need early on. In return, you tell the marketing and comms teams that you'll reshare some of their content on your own channel to extend their reach.

Then you chat with the events team and convince them that your hashtag is "official" and that they should use it, too. In return, you make sure pictures of them at events will be seen by more people internally and externally (because everyone wants to be seen doing a good job).

The end result of your ally-building and regular content cadence is that you begin to amass a nice little audience.

The next step is to get more of the staff to use the hashtag organically when they share pictures and tweets from and about work. But no one uses it, no matter how many posters you put up in the kitchen or email reminders you send. This time, you work with business team leaders who have some pretty serious talent needs coming up in the near future and ask them to talk up the hashtag to their teams, encouraging at least one post a week about office events, team celebrations, and wins. You mention that the more content that you receive from their teams, the easier it is to promote their open roles, which catches their attention and cements their commitment to post.

Finally, you go to some other business team leaders and show them that their peers are using the hashtag. In passing, you remind them that you sent your own metrics to the comms team on social and hashtag use, which gets reported up the chain. Suddenly, these business leaders are happy to help.

It takes eight months, but your recruiting-focused Instagram channel is working, drawing attention from candidates and recruiters, and getting the content from staff shared all over the organization. Which means it's time for the final phase of your plan.

You book a short 15-minute meeting with the marketing and comms teams to show off (nicely!) how your audience has grown into a real tribe of engaged users. You show them how your new audience (mostly the prospects and candidates they weren't reaching) should be seeing their LinkedIn content and how their consumer-facing audience should be seeing your employer brand content. After a friendly conversation, you all agree that you can have one employer brand post per week on their LinkedIn channel.

Everyone wins. Especially you.

Did you see how many times you could have gotten "trapped" in a roadblock or obstacle out of your control if you had seen the initial problem purely as a tactical one? You would have focused on trying to build better content for the comms team to reject, because you didn't see that they needed a political touch. You leveraged your ability to build content (tactical hat) fuel your ability to move the game away from comms oversight (strategic hat) until you had enough successes to meet them strength for strength (political hat).

Don't be fooled into thinking that the political hat is the best hat. The political hat is supported by the ability to think strategically and the skill to execute tactically. Cherish the tactical skills you started with, but know that it is the addition of new hats that gives you the ability to make real impact.

If you look back on this book, you'll see that at any given time, what we're discussing assumes that you'll be wearing one of the three hats. That might help you understand why a problem is occurring and potentially how to resolve it.

INTERVIEW: MATT CHARNEY

What, you don't know Matt? I find that hard to believe, as he has been poking logical holes in faulty recruitment thinking since...I can't guess when. Aside from editing all my content on RecruitingDaily for years (he kindly endeavored to make me sound cool), he was literally the first person I ever talked to about recruitment marketing when I was just starting out. Some people see him as the kid in the back row throwing popcorn at the screen, but in reality he's the adult who's just had it with the artifice and double-talk that permeates the industry. Rather than write a white paper rejecting the idea, chances are he's tweeting the shutdown in less time than it takes to click "disposition candidate." He's become a fixture in recruiting, which hasn't dulled his edge in the slightest.

How do you define "employer brand?"

Employer brand is the external perception of employee experience.

What do most people get wrong about employer branding?

That it belongs in talent acquisition to begin with. It's just PR and corporate communications with a different filter, which is to say, it's about creating perception instead of reflecting reality. Companies conflate EB with company culture, the difference being one of them is largely static and managed by the employer and the other is dynamic and driven by employees.

What advice would you give?

Pay above market, and your problems are solved. If you pay more than the competition, then branding becomes irrelevant, because you don't need to differentiate with anything other than total rewards, and anyone who tells you differently is selling professional services.

What is one surprising thing you've seen or done that worked?

We realized that Glassdoor, Indeed, and other review sites get about 90% of their traffic from Google, so we took our spend and focus away from employee review sites or landing page factories like The Muse and shifted it into SEO/SEM. Now a huge share of that traffic is redirected to sites we own, manage, and drive job applies.

What is employer branding's biggest challenge?

Having any supporting evidence that there's a measurable business impact or any tangible outcomes to justify continued spend to anyone who makes P&L decisions. It's impossible for traditional brand marketers, too, but at least they can tie sales and revenue to their activities, since they don't sit in a cost center.

VALUES: WHAT MAKES A GREAT
EMPLOYER BRAND PROFESSIONAL?

My vision is that employer brand is how we will fix a broken recruiting system. It is the lever we use to reinvent how we see, connect with, and engage the people who will make our businesses grow. It provides the "why" to candidates, which attracts the right people to jobs where they will be more satisfied and productive. This shift in perspective leads to better collaboration with all parts of the business to build better systems that give prospective candidates more than they expected, ultimately helping us find the right talent faster.

Add awesome lead-in sentence here to introduce these statements:

We grow businesses. We believe our goal is to grow the business. When people have better fitting roles within a company, they are happier and more productive. Happier, productive people grow businesses.

We approach talent differently. We believe that the various technological and social changes happening around the world give us the chance to completely reinvent how companies think about talent. So we will be the first to ask, "what should it be?"

We collaborate. We believe that employer brand is the place where recruiting, HR, business, and marketing overlap successfully.

We focus. We believe a great employer brand is strong and clear, attracting people whose values and motivations align to those of the company. That isn't the same as having a brand everyone wants to work for.

We revolutionize. We believe this change doesn't happen incrementally. It only happens when you see the big picture and use your employer brand as the glue that connects business to recruiting to marketing and to HR.

THE EMPLOYER BRAND MANIFESTO

The concept of employer branding isn't strictly new. It was invented by Simon Barrow in London in the 1990s, and it has a long history in Europe. But that concept of employer branding predates the internet and a lot of the cultural and structural changes that support this book. I wanted to try and bring the old school and new school models together under a single umbrella, to support a shared sense of community, because employer brand is such a strange job.

If this book has sparked your interest in getting seriously into the employer brand, you're in for a heck of a journey. But others have come before you, and you get to learn some of their lessons. The best and brightest in the industry aren't the best and brightest because they were the best writers or politicians. They brought their entire focus to a strange, often unnamed, problem and tried to solve it in a unique way.

I tried to distill that unique approach and philosophy into a manifesto to provide a little insight into what kind of challenges we face every day, and how they might be solved.

The Future Already Happened
Technology, society, and business changes mean that someone who's talented has more options than ever to make a living (see: war for talent, gig economy, remote work, side hustles, etc.).

It's Not Just the Paycheck
These options are not just about extracting maximum compensation from a company, but about building their own optimal lifestyle, based on a personal and holistic approach to what motivates them.

The Brand Overrules the Role
Having a perfect role to offer is not enough. If the candidate doesn't know or doesn't like the brand, the opportunity may as well not exist in the minds of potential talent.

What Worked Before Won't Work Now
The most sought-after talent doesn't spend time on job boards. They are actively employed in most cases and are being reached out to by headhunters already. This kind of talent knows which employers to talk to when they are ready to make a move. Job boards are only part of the solution.

Earn Awareness Before You Need It
The best way to attract talent is to be on the talent's minds before they start looking for a new position. In other words, shift from hunting and gathering to farming.

Give Talent What They Want
Posting jobs won't get you on the list of someone who isn't looking for a job. But you can spark a connection through sharing something of meaningful value to that person, be it something emotional, informational, or inspirational.

Think Focus, Not Expansion
Employer brand creates faster and more effective matches, helping talent understand what it's really like working for your company while providing ways for recruiting to focus on delivering a personalized candidate experience, one that highlights what truly matters to the candidate.

Your Brand Comes from Within
Your employer brand isn't a veneer or coat of paint. It starts on the inside as a core culture that is reinforced by the people who are hired and stick around. Distilled properly, it can be communicated out, attracting great talent not to apply, but to learn more. As these

new people onboard, they augment the culture, making employer brand a system to be managed, not a button to be pushed.

Your Brand Is Bigger Than You
Employer brand impressions—the raw materials that build employer brand perception—come from staff, former employees, marketing, comms, internal policies, previous candidates, consumer interactions, and more. We must see all the sources as one integrated picture, rather than focusing on those that only fill the top of the funnel.

Influence the Whole System
Despite being responsible for the brand, the employer brand professional doesn't directly control all the internal and external inputs that create the candidate's brand impression. Our job is to influence every part of the business towards aligning to the brand and enhancing the system. Employer branding is a team sport, where the team only wins when it works together.

Mindset, Not Toolset
Employer brand thinking is a philosophy and mindset that permeates the entire business. It is a different perspective that sees, connects, and influences all aspects of the business and all available tools to attract and hire great talent that drive profitable business solutions.

POST

FINAL THOUGHTS

In rereading this book, I was struck by a sudden thought. While I'm pretty sure my passion and love of employer branding comes through, I wonder if my cynicism is showing through as well.

I started this book as a way to champion the idea of employer branding, but, along the way, I wanted to temper it with reality, the honest challenges and frustrations any employer brand professional faces. Building an employer brand, in whatever capacity you choose to do it, is intensely hard work.

Even today, there are a shocking number of business leaders in even the biggest companies who don't understand what employer branding is. Or they read an article somewhere and think they know it.

The trouble is, while you "own" the employer brand, the employer brand is defining and impacted by everyone at work. And they all have a different perspective. Your job is to navigate these waters, listening to opinions and weighing their value, helping people see the big picture without losing touch with their local reality, all while painting a picture that both frontline staff and leadership would see as "accurate."

This is hard work, because it not only asks you to create art, it also asks you to find the artist in yourself.

An artist makes something that wasn't there before. They follow their own path to create value. They see what no one else can see. It isn't about pretty or polished, but about ideation and creation. Employer branding asks you to make art every single day, and it is exhausting and exhilarating at the same time (though not always in equal measures).

Luckily, every great artist steals, cheats, and breaks rules, because rules are the processes designed for "most people." Artists aren't most people. And as an artist, they don't make art by painting by numbers or coloring within the lines. Artists make their own lines. They pick the colors. They decide when the art is "done" and when it is time to move on to the next thing.

That's the life of an employer brand professional: See what already exists and find new ways to turn it into something new or something more. It is a job not of fitting in, but of standing out and differentiating. It is about making stories stick, not safe. It's about relationships inside and outside the organization. It is about putting things together no one thought about before.

Which is why I think it's the best job in the world. Certainly the only I could fall in love with as I have.

So lean in. You now understand the rules enough to know when it makes sense to break them. Stop waiting for permission or thinking you need more information and training. You have everything you need to make that first tentative step forward. And when your world doesn't collapse, do it again. And again.

Go do it. Break some rules. Push some boundaries. Make your art. Because that's what your company needs (even if they forget from time to time).

-James Ellis, Employer Brand Nerd, May 2020

ADDITIONAL READING

None of us knows it all. Just because I write all this down doesn't mean I have all the answers. Listen to the immortal words of William Goldman when he said (rightly), "Nobody knows anything."

So your job is to always be learning. Personally, I don't read any employer brand or recruitment marketing books. I look for inspiration from way outside the industry. Once you understand how an employer brand works, your job is to take those outside ideas and influences and turn them into amazing work. Here's a list of my favorite books and podcasts (and yes, I have read these books multiple times) to get my brain moving.

The Art of Action by Stephen Bungay. This is the book I go to when I need to remind myself that one person can create big strategies, implement them, and see their impact. (Spoiler: it just won't happen fast.) I think I've read it four times.

A Beautiful Constraint by Adam Morgan and Mark Barden. You don't have enough resources. But here's the secret: No one does. So instead of waiting for resources to build your magnificent plan, leverage the constraints in front of you.

The Pirate Inside by Adam Morgan. Easily the best book on employer branding that has no idea what employer branding even is. But it's a textbook on how to find ways to communicate your company's DNA in order to grow. (Sounds familiar, right?)

Getting Goosebumps by Bryan Adams and David Hazlehurst. Great book on how to tell a story from some people who actually know how to connect it to recruiting.

This Is Marketing by Seth Godin. If you're a recruiter getting into employer brand, this is the first and only book you need to read to understand marketing well enough to do great work.

How Buildings Learn by Stewart Brand. I'm a systems guy. If you think of your brand as a house, this book will blow your mind.

Pattern Recognition by William Gibson. Yes, it is fiction, but it provides a truly amazing way to think about what marketing ultimately is. I loved this book so much, I named my daughter after the main character.

The Business of Expertise by David C. Baker. My favorite book on positioning as a concept, even if it is applied to creative agencies.

Tribes by Seth Godin. Your company is a tribe. Once you see that, this book makes a lot of sense.

The War of Art by Steven Pressfield. I told you, you're an artist. And as an artist, you will face the same pressures a writer, painter, or poet does. Here's the rulebook on how to get past it and get great work done.

The Art of Possibility by the Zanders. Having read this one at least five times, it is the book that reminds me that we can be and do so much more. It's humbling and uplifting all at once.

Small Pieces Loosely Joined by David Weinberger and *Emergence* by Steven Johnson. As the owner of the brand, you have no real power. Only influence. Together, these books will help you see how that little bit of influence, properly applied, can move mountains.

The Fifth Discipline by Peter Senge. This is the systems thinking textbook. Do yourself a favor and read through "The Beer Problem," and you'll see your company brand challenges in a whole new light.

Moneyball by Michael Lewis. I really don't care about baseball. But I love, love, love the story of a guy trying to figure out how to win a rigged game. None of us have the resources we want. We don't have the authority and power of the CEOs to make deep changes to our brand. We have little real power. That said, you don't win by doing what everyone else does. You do it by going back to basics, to questioning everything, to being brave in the face of unrelenting doubt. Everyone thinks about Moneyball as a book about metrics. It's really a book about what it takes to do something impossible.

Viral Change by Leandro Herrero. It boggles my mind that this isn't a more famous book. But here's a much better way to look at an organization in which you seek to make meaningful change.

Good Strategy, Bad Strategy by Richard Rumelt. I love strategy books. This is the one I would want everyone to read to get up to speed in a hurry.

Employee Advocacy by Jörgen Sundberg and Ben Donkor. There's a lot of discussion about using staff to market your products, but it's an easy leap to employer brand advocacy. This book has all the nuts and bolts you might need.

"16 Core Competencies of an Employer Brand Professional" by me and the Talent Brand Alliance (on RecruitingDaily). What are the skills you will need to make the Employer Brand manifesto real? Here they are.

And while I recommend you listen to the Employer Branding Podcast with Jorgen Sundberg to hear how other professionals are doing their jobs, don't limit yourself to employer branding podcasts. Some of the best employer brand thinking is actually happening in places that don't talk about employer brand. For example, Unseen/Unknown with Jasmine Bina, 2Bobs with David C. Baker and Blair Enns, The Knowledge Project with Shane Parrish, How to Make Brands Real Famous, and Everyone Hates Marketers are amazing sources of thinking and inspiration.

James Ellis

ABOUT JAMES ELLIS

Before falling in love with the art and craft of employer branding, James Ellis was a digital marketer with 15 years' experience in how audiences think and behave online. Since then, he has taken those skills to become one of employer branding's leading voices and practitioners.

In his career, James has worked with dozens of brands from companies of every size and shape like Amazon, Coca-Cola, Veterans Administration, Target, Tradeshift, CNH Industrial, Enova, QuEST Global, and many others. As an in-house practitioner, he transformed Groupon's employer brand, reaching Hired's list of strongest employer brands in Chicago, after spending a stunningly small amount of the budget. He is the Director of Employer Brand at Universum Communications, helping some of the biggest companies understand their own brands and how talent engages with them.

James' mission is to evolve the conversation around recruiting and hiring. In order to serve that mission to the widest possible audience and make that evolution accessible to any recruiter or marketer, he has hosted The Talent Cast podcast for more than three years, hosted the Employer Brand Headlines newsletter, and written for a number of industry publications like RecruitingDaily, ERE, Indeed Blog, Recruitment Marketing Magazine, Talent Economy, The Chad & Cheese Podcast, Marketing People Podcast, Strong Suit podcast, and the Recruiting Future podcast. He has spoken at SHRM, MRA, Hired's Roadshow, HIREConf, the Social Recruiting Strategies Conference, RecruitCon, and to multiple private clients. He was also an inaugural member of the Talent Brand Alliance Board.

James lives in Chicago with his wife and daughter. You can find him on Twitter @TheWarForTalent. You can also reach him via EmployerBrand.News, TheTalentCast.com, or just LinkedIn (duh). And yes, he would love another cup of coffee, thank you.

Talent Chooses You

James Ellis

Printed in Great Britain
by Amazon